Making a Living Without a Job

Making a Living Without a Job

Winning Ways for Creating Work That You Love

BARBARA J. WINTER

BANTAM BOOKS
NEW YORK · TORONTO · LONDON
SYDNEY · AUCKLAND

MAKING A LIVING WITHOUT A JOB
A Bantam Book / August 1993

Grateful acknowledgment is made for permission to reprint "Faith" by Patrick Overton
from *The Learning Tree* by Patrick Overton. Copyright © 1975. Also from *Rebuilding
the Front Porch of America* by Patrick Overton. Copyright © 1996. Reprinted by
permission of the author.

Contact: The Front Porch Institute
964 17th Street
Astoria, Oregon 97103
Tel: 503-338-6218
Website: patrickoverton.com

Library of Congress Cataloging-in-Publication Data
Winter, Barbara (Barbara Joanne)
    Making a living without a job : winning ways for creating work
that you love / Barbara Winter.
        p. cm.
    Includes bibliographical references.
    ISBN 0-553-37165-7
    1. New business enterprises—Management.   2. Small business—
Management.   3. Self-employed.   4. Career change.   5. Career
development.   I. Title.
HD62.5.W495   1993
658'.041—dc20   93-9450
                                                                    CIP

Published simultaneously in the United States and Canada

Bantam Books are published by Bantam Books, a division of Random House, Inc. Its
trademark, consisting of the words "Bantam Books" and the portrayal of a rooster, is
Registered in U.S. Patent and Trademark Office and in other countries. Marca Regis-
trada. Bantam Books, 1540 Broadway, New York, New York 10036.

PRINTED IN THE UNITED STATES OF AMERICA
QWV 15 14 13

For Jennifer,
the proof of the pudding

and Margaret,
the personification of sisterhood

Contents

Acknowledgments

Many people kept my spirits high during the writing of this book. My love and gratitude to:

Georgia Pergakis, John Schroeder, and Margaret Winter, keepers of the faith

Jan Dean, Ruth Reneer, and Chris Utterback, unfailing sources of long distance laughter

Jill Bauman, who makes friendship an art form

Minnesota Public Radio and Eric Clapton, who kept the music flowing

Leslie Meredith, an editor with vision

Brian Tart, hand-holder and nerve-soother extraordinaire

My students, subscribers, and strangers on airplanes, who were kind enough to say, "I can't wait to read your book"

Introduction

For the first couple of years that I taught a seminar called "Making A Living Without A Job," I kept meeting people who would say, "Oh, you're that woman who teaches the class about not working, aren't you?" As politely as possible, I would respond, "No, I teach a class about not working for somebody else." I do, however, understand the confusion.

I was motivated to write this book by a simple vision: I want to live in a world where we all get out of bed excited and happy about how we're going to spend the day. Some people can achieve this happiness through a job and working for someone else, but I couldn't. I realized that I didn't fit into the world as a jobholder when I once paged through an awesomely big book called *The Dictionary of Occupational Titles*. This tome outlines thousands of jobs—and not one of them fit me. Some time later, I got the idea of creating my own job description and work.

Oliver Wendell Holmes observed, "A person's mind stretched to a new idea can never return to its original dimensions." I had to turn myself into an entrepreneur because I was curious about what I could become. This curiosity was not shared by any of my employers. Nearly twenty years ago I converted that curiosity about what I could do into the courage and determination to search until I found out. Today, my life is richer, happier, and more adventurous than I could possibly have foreseen at the beginning. My entire life has been altered by that single idea.

If you are ready to stretch your mind to the idea of making a living without a job, you'll find plenty of encouragement and practical information here. Designing a lifestyle for yourself that nurtures and supports who you are and what you value won't happen instantaneously, but this book will certainly make the process simpler and easier for you. Becoming joyfully jobless begins with a commitment to self-discovery, a curiosity about your potential, and a willingness to acquire the information and skills that will enhance your work. Your way will be unlike anyone else's, although you will share a deep camaraderie with others on this path. Being your own boss is both heady and humbling, but it's seldom boring.

The joyfully jobless who make a living without a job defy easy descriptions and pigeonholing. Ours is a lifestyle that's full of paradoxes. We have gone beyond being employees, but we're not conventional entrepreneurs. Our bottom line is measured by our character as much as by our profits. The joyfully jobless often pursue lines of work that make a difference to the rest of the world, that are more than just a way to earn food to eat and a roof over our heads. We see our business as a natural extension of who we are and what we love to do. We have spent time and energy exploring and understanding ourselves, so that we could find ways to earn a living by being ourselves. Some of us think of ourselves as working artists of life, although our work may not fit traditional concepts of artistic endeavor.

Because we are joyfully jobless, we get out of bed excited and happy, pulled ahead by a vision, but strive constantly to act in the present moment. Most of all, making a living without a job is a personal journey that is a continuing adventure.

You're going to meet some wonderful people on these pages. Keep in mind that wherever you are in your journey, these folks have already been. They've made it over the wall and they're eager to have you get over, too. There's a party going on on this side, and you're invited!

No matter why you've decided to consider making a living without a job, you'll find enthusiastic support in the pages ahead. I'd like to suggest that you read this book with pencil or highlighter in hand. (You do own this copy, don't you?) Jot down ideas as you go. Notice, too, that you'll find exercises at the end of each chapter that you can work on when you get to them or come back to after you've finished the book.

I'm delighted to have you along.

PART I

Getting to Know Your New Boss

Our individuality is all, all that we have. There are those who would barter it for security, but blessed in the twinkle of the morning star is the one who nurtures and rides it, in grace and love and wit.

Tom Robbins

CHAPTER 1

Becoming Joyfully Jobless

If a man will begin with certainties, he shall end in doubts; but if
he will be content to begin with doubts he shall end in certainties.

Francis Bacon

Think of someone you know who is joyfully jobless.

You say you don't know a soul who qualifies? Of course you do. Many jobless earners are highly visible. If you don't personally know someone, consider those whom you've read or heard about. Look at any issue of *Architectural Digest* or *House and Garden*. Their pages are filled with splendid homes belonging to the self-employed.

Or turn on your television. Five days a week you can observe success in action by tuning in to *The Oprah Winfrey Show*. This program, the highest-rated talk show in television history, earned an estimated $39 million for its spunky host in 1991. Besides owning the production company which produces this show, Winfrey's Harpo Productions also owns the studio where the show is taped. In addition, Winfrey has diversified her business by purchasing a restaurant, producing an off-Broadway play, and making films and other television programs.

Not yet forty, Oprah Winfrey came to her success with several characteristics that seem to be obvious obstacles in our culture: she's female, black, and overweight. She frequently shares her experiences in the course of her program and tells viewers about her own personal growth and setbacks. Yet Winfrey credits her personal philosophy with generating all this success, reminding her audience that inner beliefs and attitudes are as important as hard work. "The Bible has taught us, metaphysics has taught us, myth has taught us," she points out, "that if you get into the flow, if you do what you're supposed to do, you'll be rewarded with riches you've never even imagined. And so what I have received is the natural order of things. You always, always, always reap what you sow."

What Winfrey demonstrates—along with countless others who have made the same discovery—is that our work can and should be more than just a means of paying the bills. It's an idea that is gathering momentum as more of us question the choices and assumptions we have made about the role that work plays in our lives.

Yet few of us are in a position to do what one wealthy man did. Returning to his office in his chauffeured Rolls-Royce, this millionaire had a sudden urge to chuck it all and board his sailboat for a slow trip around the world. His story produced headlines which declared, "Wealthy Businessman Trades In Fortune for Happiness." Perhaps. For most of us, making a dramatic lifestyle change requires more than a split-second decision. We need to plan, lay the groundwork, consider which parts of our life to keep and which to throw away. Walking away from a less than satisfying career or relationship takes time—and courage.

An adage says, "There are three kinds of people in the world: those who make things happen; those who watch things happen; and those who don't even know anything is happening." Well, something is happening in the world of work. People are bravely demanding more. After examining the alternatives, many see that becoming joyfully jobless provides the greatest opportunities for financial, emotional, and even spiritual well-being in their workplace. These hardy pioneers are making things happen, often with spectacular results. Should you decide to join them, be prepared for some unexpected rewards and riches. Not only will you amaze yourself with a new enthusiasm and energy for your work, you'll discover that you're part of a growing trend, one that is more far-reaching than you may realize. You're even going to have fun!

The Quiet Revolution

Business and government leaders used to say, "What's good for General Motors is good for the country." But GM is no longer the paragon of American business. And other big businesses have also lost their cachet, as well as the belief that they were the foundation of our society's economic health. Big business is no longer the place where the action is.

A quiet revolution is taking place. Unlike the sexual revolution, which was scrutinized and dissected in minute detail, the workplace revolution seldom shows up on the nightly news or attracts much media attention.

Nevertheless, this change is making itself felt in the lives of millions of people who are thoughtfully questioning how they will earn their living. A recent study by the U.S. government reported that an estimated 31 million of us now work at home. The study also noted that these statistics are difficult to verify. Although these workplace revolutionaries have been making changes individually—and welcoming others to the movement—their very independence and unorthodox methods have given them a low profile. They quietly go about their business while staying out of the spotlight.

According to Link Resources, a New York–based research firm, approximately 39 million Americans do part or all of their work at home, a 56.6 percent increase over the past five years. Whatever the correct number, it's clear that we no longer agree that a commercial setting is the only proper place to work.

This workplace movement has its proponents reporting changes beyond just a shift in office space. In a recent survey of the readership of *Home Office Computing* magazine, respondents pointed out additional advantages of leaving the nine-to-five world behind. The survey reported that 85 percent feel more relaxed working from home, 40 percent enjoy a healthier diet, 39 percent take more time off, 38 percent exercise more often, 32 percent feel they have a better marriage or sex life, 98 percent are happier in general, 96 percent would recommend working from home to other people, and 88 percent say they would never return to the corporate world again.

What this study suggests is that the rewards of making a living without a job go far beyond eliminating the hassles of commuting or dealing with incompatible coworkers. Whatever the reason for trying to work on our own, most of us have been pleasantly surprised that being joyfully jobless led us to being joyful in other ways as well.

It's important to realize, however, that you have to be working at something you love in order to receive the other benefits. Deb Leopold is a bubbly, enthusiastic self-bosser who started First Class, an adult learning center, in Washington, D.C., eight years ago. Leopold had worked for a similar program for several years and is still a confessed "seminar junkie" who says she could happily attend a class every day of the year. Coupling her passion for adult education with a desire to own her own business was her motivation for opening First Class. During the time she's been running her business, half a dozen other independent programs have come and gone. Why has she outlasted the competition? "Probably because I love what I'm doing so much," she surmises. "I know that at least a couple of the other programs were started by people thinking they would make a financial killing in this business. Even though I have part-time help, this is a very hands-on business for me. I plan the catalog, schedule the teachers, and take registrations over the phone. I want to bring good classes—and unique ones—to the community. I want other people to have as much fun learning as I do."

Deb Leopold's attitude about her venture is echoed by successful self-bossers everywhere. Our work *can* be far more than simply a way to earn money; it can be a vehicle for making a unique contribution to our community and our world. This attitude pervades any discussion with the joyfully jobless. It's a stunning contrast to the disgruntled complaints we often hear from the employed.

Despite the fact that we who are making a living without a job are almost universally enthusiastic about this lifestyle, we inevitably face questions from the astonished and skeptical. When people discover that I'm jobless, they bombard me with questions. Don't you get nervous not having a regular paycheck? Have you taken a vow of poverty? Do you live on rice and beans? Have a trust fund? Do something illegal? Do you have health insurance? (The answers, by the way, are no, no, no, no, no, and yes.)

Updating an Old Tradition

Should you decide to make a living without a job, you'll be part of an old tradition—and on the leading edge of a new working movement. What seems to be a revolutionary lifestyle is really as old as the American Revolution.

Our wise forefathers envisioned a land where free enterprise would be a significant key to the growth and development of this fragile new nation. So important did they believe this system that John Hancock declared, "The more people who own little businesses of their own, the safer our country will be . . . for the people who have a stake in their country and their community are its best citizens." Not only would self-employment bring financial rewards, it would have a positive impact on the social structure where it was practiced.

For the first century or so of our history, self-employment flourished. At the beginning of the twentieth century, nine out of ten Americans worked for themselves. The economic freedom and civil harmony predicted by those early patriots prevailed.

Then around 1900, the tide began to turn. The Industrial Revolution needed workers, and people flocked to jobs in plants and factories. With each passing decade, fewer and fewer of us exercised the option to build something of our own. The effect of this was stunning. Before long, few of us believed that it was possible to work independently. We became dependent on others, looking outside ourselves for support and validation. An employer or union or, surely, the government would take care of us.

We are now living with the consequences of that thinking. Economic hardship and civil unrest have become the top stories on the nightly news. Today, nine out of ten of us who work labor in someone else's fields. While there's a general consensus that change is needed, widespread solutions are in short supply.

There is an option that can make a difference—and a profound difference at that. It's not dependent on any political backing, nor does it require that society fix itself at once. It's an option that's available whether the economy improves or it doesn't. You can exercise this option without enormous amounts of capital, although it will require heavy doses of action and imagination.

You may have to change your thinking and challenge your self-imposed limitations. I promise you, however, that you do have the equipment you need for becoming joyfully jobless. The only question remaining is this: do you have the desire?

Taking Another Look at Work

Most of us have gotten precious little guidance in selecting our life's work. While we giggle at the famous scene in the movie *The Graduate* where Dustin Hoffman is counseled to make his future in plastics, many of us came to our careers because of equally foolish advice. Entering a profession because it looks promising or secure is the ultimate crapshoot. My classes are filled with folks who spend their days miserably sitting at computers because they were urged to get into that growing field. Their personal skills and passions were ignored or devalued.

Even more damaging to our vocational development is the belief that work is nothing more than a way to earn money. Why should we commit a third—or more—of our time to doing something that we don't care about? Why can't we get paid for being happy?

My friend Ruth attended a jazz concert at the Metropolitan Museum of Art in New York not long ago. After several pieces had been played, pianist Billy Taylor announced that they would take a break and entertain questions from the audience. Several people asked technical questions of the musicians, and then Ruth raised her hand and asked, "I know how I feel listening to your music, but what I want to know is how *you* feel when you're playing. What do you feel when you finish an evening like this?" At first, the musicians were a bit uncomfortable with the rather intimate question, but once they began talking about their feelings, their passion for making music, they shared their immense joy about their chosen profession. When the evening ended, they individually sought Ruth out and thanked her for asking the question. One of them admitted feeling somewhat embarrassed talking about his pleasure when he knew that most of his audience worked at things that brought them no joy whatsoever.

How could we have gotten it so wrong all this time, thinking that money was adequate compensation for doing work that we loathed—or, at least, cared little about? What if we began to expect from our work high levels of satisfaction? What if we refused to have less than that? And what if we believed that our work was one part of a grander goal?

In 1966, Rohn and Jeri Engh settled on a 100-acre farm in Osceola, Wisconsin. Their goal was "to make a life, not just a living." They have managed to do both, and today their barn serves as the headquarters for their growing international business.

At first the Enghs freelanced articles and photographs for national magazines and textbook companies. Then Rohn got the idea that was the beginning of PhotoSource International. He started a newsletter that served as a clearinghouse between editors and photographers. With time and technology, that newsletter has grown into several newsletters, including an electronic one. In addition, Rohn conducts seminars for photographers, both in Wisconsin and around the country.

Talking to him, you get the impression that he's as proud of his unique lifestyle as he is of his business. "I've never considered what I do work and I don't relate to city people who are fond of muttering 'TGIF.' Often I don't know if it's Wednesday, Friday, or Monday. I don't even own a watch. We get up whenever we want to—usually at dawn. We never keep track of time. I don't even know how old I am."

What strikes me about Rohn Engh's philosophy is a desire he shares with other self-bossers to make a life, not just a living. Paul Hawken, the author of *Growing a Business*, reaffirms this notion when he says, "Being in business is not about making money. It is a way to become who you are." It's this grander concept of the purpose of work in our lives that's leading so many to seek alternatives.

Have I become the person that I want to be? we wonder, and if not, is it too late? We begin questioning our choices and asking new questions of ourselves. Have I followed my dreams? Lived as I wanted? Exercised my creative spirit? Lived my values? Built something of my own? Made my children proud? Thought my own thoughts? Acted with courage and magnificence?

Questions like these (and my uncomfortable answers) forced

me to shift gears and take another look at my life and my work. Let me tell you how I got here. It's a tale of trial and error.

Getting Off the Beaten Path

The small town in southern Minnesota where I grew up is the sort of place that is charming when Garrison Keillor talks about it, but stifling when you live there. Even as a kid, I knew that the people around me were leading humdrum lives. I vowed not to follow in their footsteps.

Thanks to my love of reading, I had discovered that another world existed that was far more exciting than the one I saw around me. I spent hours daydreaming about glamorous careers, exotic travel, and sophisticated friends. By the time I reached high school, my mother would regularly ask, "What are you going to be this week?" I always had a fresh answer.

My dreams faded quickly when I followed my peers off to college and was advised to make sensible plans. I entered college not knowing what I wanted to do, and when I graduated I wasn't much clearer. However, I now had a diploma that authorized me to teach high school English and speech. Off I went to do just that in another tiny community near my hometown.

My teaching career began with great enthusiasm. Having had a lifelong love affair with all things British, I was certain I could share my passion for English literature with adolescents who didn't know what they were missing. The first two years turned out to be enormous fun as I grew confident in my ability to motivate and inspire unruly teenagers. By my third year, things began to change and I found myself saying, "The nice thing about teaching is that you get a lot of time off." I was also bumping heads too frequently with an administration who wished I'd just stick to the syllabus and not spice things up.

In my fourth year came what I now think of as My Horrible Moment of Truth, when I realized that I could predict with absolute certainty where I was going to be and what I was going to be doing every hour of every day of the year. I was doomed to go through life saying, "If this is March, it must be *Macbeth*." It was a terrifying prospect.

It took another year for me to summon my courage and resign.

When I did, I received zero support from the people around me, who greeted my decision with dismay. They added to my own uncertainty about leaving a secure position because of something as common as boredom.

I decided I'd better hurry up and find another job, but had no idea how to begin. I remembered hearing about the State Employment Service and went in for an interview. To my astonishment, they invited me to come to work for them as a job counselor. I gratefully accepted, but the absurdity of this dawned on me as soon as I began. I had no idea what I wanted to do, but now I was being paid to counsel others on their careers. Before long I knew that I would not become a model civil servant, but I was too embarrassed to leave my second career so soon.

My daughter, Jennifer, came to my rescue and gave me a perfect excuse for resigning. My husband and I had wanted to start a family, and when I discovered I was pregnant my joy was multiplied by the fact that I now had an acceptable reason for leaving the Employment Service behind. I knew that my "retirement" would be temporary, but I was determined to use those early years of motherhood to find work that I could love. I didn't know it at the time, but I had to find myself first. The real adventure had begun!

When my daughter was only a few months old, I met a group of people involved in personal development training. This was a new world for me, but one in which I felt immediately at home. I started attending motivational seminars, studying books on self-esteem and every other self-help tome I could find. I devoured *The Power of Positive Thinking*, *The Magic of Believing*, and *Think and Grow Rich*. Where had these ideas been hiding? I began to believe in myself. It took some time before I understood what Sydney Harris meant when he wrote, "Young people searching for their 'real self' must learn that the real self is not something one finds as much as it is something one makes; and it is one's daily actions that shape the inner personality far more permanently than any amount of introspection or intellection." The form that my next step would take was still fuzzy, but I sensed that I was getting closer.

The push I needed came in the most unexpected way. One evening I picked up the newspaper and read a story about two women in New York named Claudia Jessup and Genie Chipps. Friends since their school days, they had moved to New York in hope of becoming actresses. While waiting to be discovered, they supported themselves the way many out-of-work actors do, with a variety of available jobs.

At dinner with friends one night, Chipps said, "We ought to stop trying to figure out where we might fit in. Let's do something on our own. Let's start a business!" One guest had the nerve to ask just what this business was going to sell. "Ourselves, of course," they improvised. "We'll sell our time and energy to people and do whatever comes along."

And so the seeds of their business, Supergirls, Ltd., were sown. Setting up shop in Jessup's apartment, they purchased a few supplies, including a record called "Sounds of the Office," which they played whenever the phone rang, giving the impression that Supergirls had a large staff busily working to meet any and all requests. From such humble beginnings, they went on to create a large and sophisticated public relations company.

I was dazzled! What Jessup and Chipps had done was a new idea for me. If I had ever thought about starting a business as an option, I would have assumed it meant gathering capital and opening a store. The Supergirls were telling me that there was another way to work for myself. I wanted to know more. I got my copy of the book about their experiences, *Supergirls: The Autobiography of an Outrageous Business*, the very next day and read it cover to cover. At the end of the book Jessup wrote, "Genie and I didn't lead our class at Harvard Business School. We didn't even go to business school. But we started a business, and we found out that we knew enough about most of the things we needed to know about to get along. We weren't and aren't extraordinary people. The point is, Genie and I didn't start out being super. We just wanted to be."

If "wanting to be" was what it took, I was highly qualified. I mulled and dreamed and planned and fretted and finally took a deep breath and launched my first little venture. *Supergirls* became my handbook and constant companion. It was the only resource I could find to guide me in creating an unconventional business.

The Successful Woman, which I started in September of 1974, brought together my passions for personal development and the women's movement. At that time, no one had designed a program on goal-setting and self-esteem aimed at women. I organized a seminar, added the idea of publishing a newsletter, and began letting people know about my business. It was both exhilarating and scary. After I publicized the business, I was interviewed by magazines, on television and radio, and in the newspaper. Speaking invitations began to come in from women's groups, churches, colleges, and businesses. I accepted every one. My seminars got smoother and fuller; newsletter subscribers came from around the country. I was on my way.

As time went on, other opportunities and ideas presented themselves. With my confidence growing from my early triumph with The Successful Woman, I eagerly tried other ventures. I started a mail-order business, which was enormously successful, and branched out into special-event planning and creative marketing seminars. Eventually, I stopped working exclusively with women and broadened the scope of my training.

More important, I began to see that I had inadvertently stumbled onto the most effective personal development program invented. Running a business taught me about myself and other people. It challenged me to expand in every possible way. When I had been a jobholder, I had given little thought to building character or clarifying my values or serving others. All of these things became momentous aspects of self-employment.

It became easy and natural for me to share these discoveries with other people and urge them to consider making a living without a job, too. These days, most of my time is spent coaching others who want to live their own jobless lives. Their success is every bit as exciting to me as my own success continues to be. They inspire me and make the way for being joyfully jobless a bit straighter for others. And, not surprisingly, these newly liberated self-bossers say, "I can't imagine why I waited so long."

Why Are You Here?

Before my "Making a Living Without a Job" seminars grew from twenty people to more than several hundred, I would begin with an exercise I call Three Questions. Each person would answer these simple queries: Who are you? What do you do? Why are you here?

Although my students invariably came from disparate backgrounds and occupations, a mix of blue- and white-collar jobs, they weren't coming to the seminar merely because they were curious. They weren't even coming because they had lost their jobs, but, usually, their current careers weren't delivering the satisfaction or security they had expected. My students all gave thoughtful—even poignant—explanations for wanting to become independent. "I want to see my kids grow up," was a common response, along with "My workplace has become so stressful that I get stomach pains when I start to drive to work," or "It's time for me to devote full time to an idea I've had for years." Almost all of them said they had glimpsed the future and it looked like more of the same—unless they made changes now. Let's eavesdrop for a moment and see whether your personal motivation reflects any of the answers I've heard.

• *I want more control over my own time and life.* Writer Peter Mayle sums it up nicely when he says, "I'd rather live precariously in my own office than comfortably in somebody else's." Many workers and professionals are increasingly frustrated over having so little to say about when they work and when they have time off. Men and women want to spend more time doing the things they enjoy and being with their families. Working for someone else often creates an unpleasant dichotomy in our lives. As we mature and clarify our values, we may find it difficult to spend time in ways that do not reflect what we believe and care about. Breaking free seems the best option for changing that.

• *My work is no longer challenging. It's time to do something creative.* More and more restless souls are questioning the assumption that once they've been trained for an occupation or have acquired years of experience in it, they must do it for the rest of their days. Several years ago, a group of California environmentalists adopted as their slogan, "Just Because You Can, Doesn't Mean You Should." It's an attitude that many are now taking about their work. Why, we wonder, should our lives be limited to a single occupation?

Dr. Cleve Francis would understand this questioning completely. After running one of the largest cardiology practices in Virginia, he's now on his way to a second career as a country music singer. "When I started out in cardiology, I couldn't wait to see the next patient," he says. "Now there's not that much excitement in cardiology. But I think that my music can bring just as much joy into people's lives as pills and medicine." It's important to have the courage to act on your ambitions.

• *I've spent the past ten years helping other people achieve their goals. Now I want to go after my own dreams.* Barbara T. Roessner, writing about career changing in *The Hartford Courant*, has this to say: "There is a feeling that life outside the office has suffered, that what we have given up—time for our children, our spouse, ourselves—has not been worth the payback. If we have worked this hard for this long, should we not have more to show for it, at least in a nonmaterial way?" Knowing that you've helped someone else succeed in business is rewarding only when you have benefited as well.

Few jobs make it possible for us to pursue other, personal goals. The best interests of the company are frequently not in sync with your own, business *or* personal, and often can sabotage the furthering of your personal goals. "If only I had more time," we sigh wistfully. Besides identifying your goals, you need time, the wherewithal, and the commitment to making them happen. No one else can do it for you.

• *I'm tired of working with negative people.* Discontented coworkers can be toxic to your aspirations and your soul, and too many organizations are loaded with unhappy people who can ruin the finest career. A self-bossing friend of mine recently wrote about a visit she made to a teachers' meeting where the teachers did nothing but complain about their jobs—and this was before school had opened for the year. An atmosphere of negativity can sap your energy and destroy your attitude and self-esteem. As a self-bosser you will find a new desire to surround yourself with healthy people who energize and encourage your efforts. Becoming self-employed connects you with a new cast of characters, people who are in your life by choice, not chance.

• *My job pays me a good salary, but I'm miserable doing it. There's got to be more.* These days if you mention dissatisfaction with your job, you're bound to be reminded that you're lucky to *have* a job. That only adds, of course, to the frustration of working at something you hate. Simply suspecting that life can be richer and happier than it has been can be a crucial starting point for exploring other options. In fact, dissatisfaction can be downright healthy if it leads you to positive action. Trust that your suspicions are correct and let your discontent be a catalyst for moving you in a new direction.

When I was a freshman in college, I took the requisite speech class my first quarter. Although I didn't deliver any memorable talks, I enjoyed the class so much that I decided to make speech my second major. Shortly after I'd made this choice, I met my speech professor in the hall. Thinking he'd be flattered that his class had inspired me, I told him about my plan to get a speech degree. He smiled patronizingly at me and said, "You won't like it." I knew that he really meant, "You won't be any good at it." In that moment, my motivation shifted and I became more determined than ever. I was going to prove him wrong! That wasn't, of course, the most mature reason to go ahead with my decision, but it's been oddly satisfying. I approach every speech, every seminar thinking, "This one's for you, Dr. Meisel." His unkind words may have been wiser than I knew at the time.

Whether your motivation is to spend more time with your kids or to see the world or to become the eccentric neighborhood inventor puttering around in your garage, becoming joyfully jobless can help you realize those dreams—and more. The time you spend now giving thoughtful consideration to your goals, your motivations, your priorities, will be valuable preliminaries to making specific plans. The best way to begin is by getting to know your new boss.

Winning Ways for Becoming Joyfully Jobless

• What do you think is your primary motivation for wanting to be joyfully jobless? This question can be difficult to answer and, in fact, may generate different responses at different times in your life. Knowing what motivates you, however, can be helpful in making better choices for yourself. For instance, a woman I know would say she's motivated by a desire to help those who are less fortunate. Observing her behavior shows that another factor is at work. When she is in a group, she has a strong desire to be the center of attention. Perhaps her true motivation is to receive recognition—albeit through helping others.

Look over the following list of possible motivating desires and check those which are true for you.

____ More time with family and friends
____ Less structured lifestyle
____ More independence of thought
____ Opportunity to try own ideas
____ Recognition
____ Wealth
____ Less stress from demands of others
____ Satisfaction of curiosity about self
____ More variety of work
____ Time to think about personal philosophy
____ More nurturing relationships
____ Exploration of the unknown
____ More creativity
____ More satisfaction from work
____ Sense of being responsible and in control
____ Escape from frustration of carrying out someone else's plan
____ Better use of talents
____ More time for travel, personal pursuits
____ Part-time work
____ Bigger contribution to society
____ Other (specify)

• Abraham Maslow, the psychologist who studied self-actualization, noted that all people who reached their fullest potential had a model in their life who inspired them. The idea of making a living without a job will seem less unusual if you raise your own awareness of others who have done it or are doing it. Pay closer attention to stories about self-bossers in magazines, in your local newspaper, and on television. These people can serve to inspire and educate you by their example.

Go even further and select a person, living or dead, whom you admire. Become an expert on that person's life. Besides learning the facts of his or her personal history, scout for the underlying philosophy. What motivated this person? How did he or she view his or her contribution to the world? What sacrifices did your model make? What obstacles did he or she overcome? Why was this person special? Why are you inspired by him or her? My current study includes two very different women: Coco Chanel, the French designer, and Barbara Pym, the English novelist. Outwardly, they have nothing in common, but their lives had several fascinating parallels. Both enjoyed early success, followed by a period of failure, followed by a stunning comeback. No, you are not too old to have heroes!

• Think about the idea of "making a life, not just a living." What does that mean to you? Answer the following questions, keeping that idea in mind.

What would a balanced lifestyle include?

Where would you live?

How much time would you devote to working?

What non-working activities are important to you?

What people would you spend time with?

What personal goals have you neglected that would become a priority again?

How would you express your values through your work?

Where would you volunteer time and resources?

How would you be involved with a cause or community?

How would your family or other significant people be included?

How would your daily life become richer?

What about your current life would you eliminate immediately?

What rewards other than money would you expect to receive from your work?

What skills do you most enjoy using?

How can you incorporate more positive experiences into your life?

What material things would you acquire? Give up?

• Start your own Living Without a Job notebook. A three-ring binder is perfect. Use it to trap ideas, store articles about interesting people and businesses, jot down quotes, etc. Fill your notebook with plenty of blank paper, too, so that you can quickly add thoughts and inspirations as they come. Having a central location for idea-starters adds order and ease.

• A useful technique to employ in achieving any goal is that of creative visualization. You can use visualization daily to strengthen your determination, clarify your goals, and accelerate your progress.

Begin by setting aside a regular time every day to quietly create a mental picture of what you want to accomplish. Close your eyes, take several deep breaths, and picture a specific goal you want to achieve. You might, for example, have decided you want to put your love of gardening to work as a vocation, not just a hobby. In your daily visualization period, see yourself working out of doors, bringing beauty to different environments. Mentally, run through an ideal day—rising early, donning jeans and a T-shirt, jumping in your new Toyota pickup truck with your business's name painted on the side. Visualize your clients exclaiming over your glorious landscapes. See them referring their friends to you, bringing you more opportunities to do the work you love so much. Include any ideas that appeal to you and run this mental movie over again and again. Keep adding details, color, smells, and sensory images.

Even if you aren't yet clear about the specific ways in which you could be joyfully jobless, you can use visualization to create a clear picture of a happier, freer lifestyle. Use the thoughts you had in the earlier exercise about making a life, not just a living, as the basis for your visualization session. Taking time to do this regularly will bring great rewards in clarity and achievement.

After all, visualization is nothing more than consciously creating a preview of coming attractions. It's the way to manifest the adage, "What the mind can conceive and believe, it can achieve." Quite simply, creative visualization makes good things happen.

CHAPTER 2

Doing First Things First

Being yourself is not remaining where you are, or being satisfied
with what you are. It is the point of departure.

Sydney J. Harris

During the mid-seventies, I moved to California, eager to
investigate the Human Potential Movement, which was going
strong at the time. I had heard rumors that there was a different
seminar on every corner. It sounded like Nirvana for the self-
help junkie I had become.

Once there, I was not disappointed. There was a dazzling array
of personal development training to choose from. Besides the
well-known est, Lifespring, and Dianetics, you could engage in
Rolfing, Rebirthing, Primal Scream Therapy, Transactional
Analysis, Silva Mind Control, dozens of meditation techniques,
and various wild and wonderful therapies, many with clothing
optional. Any respectable Californian could have her weekends
booked for years. Everyone I met had indulged in at least one,
and usually several, of these programs. Not only did I become an
avid participant, I also attended many seminars as an observer.
As a publisher, I received numerous invitations to come as a
journalist in return for publicity in my newsletter.

Before long, I noticed a strong tendency in my fellow students.
No matter what program they studied, once people had raised
their self-esteem, they desired to be self-employed. Over and

over again, in questionnaires filled out in class, in discussions during seminar breaks, or in letters to my newsletter, these students and seekers listed doing something on their own as a primary goal.

Psychologist Nathaniel Branden, a leading authority on self-esteem, made the same observation. "Productive achievement is a consequence and an expression of healthy self-esteem, *not* its cause," he says. The link between self-esteem and successful self-bossing is so strong that it deserves to be a top priority for anyone who aspires to be joyfully jobless.

What Does It Look Like?

Until recently, nobody paid much attention to the importance of self-esteem. Our parents, for the most part, had no idea what it was or that it mattered. Unless they were rare creatures whose own self-esteem was in good repair, they did little actively to foster it in their children. I grew up in a home where criticism and sarcasm were considered appropriate parenting techniques—and that was not unique to my family. Sadly, that legacy continues for many adults today. When I complimented my daughter in front of relatives not long ago, I was warned to be careful or she might get a big head! A much-quoted German proverb in our family carried a strong admonition: "Self-praise stinks!" With these repeated messages of self-denial as our guidelines, it's little wonder that we wrestle with our self-esteem as adults.

Even now, with "self-esteem" used liberally in our vocabulary, many people still misunderstand what it means. I saw an interview with a celebrated author on *60 Minutes* that brought that into focus for me. The woman displayed many signs of low self-esteem throughout the interview: her eye contact was poor; she sounded angry and showed little warmth or empathy with the interviewer. Even more telling were the scenes showing her speaking to a large audience. Every third or fourth sentence of her talk ended with "Okay?", as if she were seeking instant validation from her listeners. She sounded unsure one minute and defensive the next. The most revealing moment came at the end of the interview when she snapped, "*I* have no self-esteem problems!" I thought, "She doth protest too much." Being brassy and brazen is not a characteristic of sound self-esteem; neither is the need to announce it.

So what is self-esteem anyway? It is *not* self-confidence, with which it is often confused. The difference between the two, it seems to me, is this: you can't fake self-esteem, for it is, quite simply, the high regard that you have for yourself. It begins to grow the moment that you give up wanting to be someone else and respect your own talents and temperament.

While it may be intangible, self-esteem is not invisible. It's easy to spot people who have high self-esteem by their behavior. Chances are that the people you most like being with possess it in abundance. These people are frequently described as "gracious" and "thoughtful," which makes them desirable as friends. They love and care for themselves, but they are not arrogant. They have compassion for others, which rises out of their compassion for themselves. Since few of us arrive at a place of healthy self-esteem by accident or birth, these folks may be constantly aware of their own struggle to achieve it—and their ongoing effort to nurture it. Their curiosity and interest in others lead them to be excellent listeners, another magnetic quality. In addition, they have an elevated sense of personal responsibility; they rarely blame others for their problems or misfortunes. They may have a passionate desire to contribute to society. Whether they speak of it or not, they frequently have a sense of mission in their lives that others lack. Knowing their own worth gives them a profound sense that they are here for some purpose, which, in turn, shows itself in a reverence for life. Forward-thinking, they are aware that all past experiences in their lives have helped to mold their character. Even when their lives have seemed difficult, you'll hear them say, "I wouldn't change a thing." They have a strong aura of integrity and truthfulness about them, but they are truly sensitive to the feelings of others. People with high self-esteem don't have the need to say everything that's on their minds! The bonus you receive for hanging out with these folks is that in their presence you feel safe and accepted just as you are. In fact, when you leave them you may find that you like yourself a bit more.

A few years ago, a friend of mine underwent a startling transformation. Suddenly angry with his life, he became critical of others and negative in his attitude. Phone calls from him turned into scathing monologues about other people's stupidity. Being with him was no pleasure and I came to dread our dates, which were certain to include personal criticisms of me. When I confronted him about his attitude, he blamed it on his astrological sign!

While I had genuinely enjoyed his companionship, it became clear that our time together was coming to an end. I was saddened by his growing misery, but puzzled about the cause. There were no obvious crises or upheavals in his life; in fact, I had many friends who were facing truly difficult problems with grace and poise. Why had he become such a jerk?

At last it dawned on me that he was the only person I knew who had scrupulously avoided doing any "personal development work." While all my other friends had actively worked to build their self-esteem and become conscious in their approaches to their life problems, he had done nothing. The difference it made was painfully obvious. Had my unhappy friend been willing to put some time and energy into self-discovery, he might have avoided—or effectively handled—whatever had contributed to his negative situation.

Television producer Norman Lear once said, "We all deliver personal peace to ourselves. No maid or money does it. We do it, reaching toward excellence." Self-esteem is an inside job and no matter how high or low yours is, you can raise it by keeping two things in mind: (1) self-esteem is important and deserves your attention and (2) there are numerous commonsense techniques and tools available for enhancing it.

Repairing the Damage

In a perfect world, our self-esteem would have been nurtured from the moment of our birth. Few of us have been so blessed. Mostly, we validate Buckminster Fuller's observation that some of us manage to grow up less damaged than others. Like love, self-esteem is hard to give if you don't have it yourself. Since we are surrounded by folks whose own self-esteem may be less than healthy, we can't realistically expect them to behave in ways that will nurture our self-esteem. "Every day," writes Harvard's Dr. Gordon Allport in *Pattern and Growth in Personality*, "we experience grave threats to our self-esteem: we feel inferior, guilty, insecure, unloved. Not only big things, but little things put us in the wrong: we trip up in an examination, we make a social boner, we dress inappropriately for an occasion. The ego sweats. We suffer discomfort, perhaps anxiety, and we hasten to repair the narcissistic wound."

A large part of the task of achieving healthy self-esteem lies simply in getting to know yourself better—discovering the ideas and things that are important to you and knowing why they are important. Some of the ideas you have about yourself and the world come from your past. Think about some of the influences in your life.

• What was the attitude and tone of the community where you grew up? What was most valued there? What prejudices were in evidence?

• How did you feel about families with more money than yours? With less?

• What did you think about your parents' occupations? How did that influence your own career choices?

• What messages about your value and worth did you get at home, in school?

• What part did religion play in your life? If you grew up in a religion, did it foster or inhibit self-esteem?

• How quickly can you list five good things about yourself?

• How quickly can you list five shortcomings you have?

• How do the thoughts you have about yourself manifest in your relationships with others?

• How much of what you think and do is determined by what others expect of you?

Thoughtfully, painfully, and perhaps even prayerfully answering questions like these will help increase your self-awareness and hence your self-esteem. Building healthy self-esteem is a lot like building a healthy body. If you started to eat more healthful foods and then reverted to a diet of potato chips and ice cream, you wouldn't expect permanent, positive results in your body, would you? Your self-esteem needs to be fed a nurturing diet as well. One of the best "foods" you can feed it is positive affirmations.

An affirmation is a strong, positive statement you can use to enhance feelings about yourself, make changes in your life, or reinforce your self-esteem. Using affirmations is both a discipline and an action that signals your conscious and unconscious mind that you're determined to create a life-enhancing environment for yourself. Affirmations force you to challenge old, self-limiting thoughts and replace them with more desirable words and images. More important, affirmations get you to think about yourself and your life in new ways, ways that expand your power and possibilities.

To put this technique to work, select one or two areas where you'd like to strengthen your attitude about yourself. Perhaps you've discovered that you find the idea of public speaking terrifying. You also realize that conquering the belief that you can't speak well in public would be personally satisfying and professionally enriching. You've probably spent years feeding your mind with *negative* statements about public speaking which go something like, "I'd rather swallow arsenic than speak in front of a group." Doing that repeatedly has had a big impact on your behavior and belief system. In order to change your old idea, you're going to use essentially the same process—only now you will feed your mind with an opposite thought, such as, "I am delighted to share my thoughts and ideas and expertise with eager audiences. I am an exquisite public speaker. I welcome speaking invitations." As you can see, using affirmations can be an uncomfortable experience. It can also be a key to the door of change and growth.

When I first learned about affirmations, I found it very difficult to create them for myself. My own self-esteem was so lousy that I couldn't think of positive things to say. I began by borrowing affirmations from others and gradually learned to write my own. Sondra Ray's book *I Deserve Love* was a favorite source of mine for self-esteem-building affirmations. Among the affirmations that were (and are) most helpful are these:

- I am highly pleasing to myself in the presence of other people.

- As I think more positively, I attract positive-thinking people into my life with whom I have satisfying relationships.
- I deserve to be happy and rejoice in the happiness of others.
- I am lovable and capable.
- I am attractive and lovable and the more I acknowledge that, the more true it becomes.
- I am a self-determined person and I allow others the same right.

You can make affirmations work on your behalf by silently repeating them or by writing them out. Both techniques will contribute to healing low self-esteem and enhancing sound self-esteem. Once you make this a habit, you'll find many ways to use this empowering technique. Affirmations can add confidence to your ability to make a living without a job. Here are several affirmations written by my students:

- I trust my ideas and am willing to follow my intuition.
- My business is fun and interesting and it makes my life more fun.
- My business is an extension of my personality and a manifestation of what I love to do.
- My business is a prosperous, growing expression of my true joy.
- Opportunities are everywhere and I am smart enough to select the best ones for me.
- As I nurture myself, I see my business grow.
- My work is the most creative expression of the best that is in me, everything I have become, am now, am yet to be.

Affirmations are more than just giving yourself a pat on the back. Constructing a positive statement compels you to be crystal clear about your objectives, your goals, and your desires. You could think of them as vitamins for your mind!

Practice writing your own affirmations in the space provided.

I am _____.

I am _____.

I am _____ .

I can _____ .

I can _____ .

I can _____ .

I will _____ .

I will _____ .

I will _____ .

A Portrait of Yourself

If we were to diagram the process of becoming joyfully jobless, it would look like this:

SELF-DISCOVERY

leads to

SELF-ESTEEM

leads to

SELF-EMPLOYMENT

leads to

SELF-DISCOVERY

leads to

SELF-ESTEEM

Self-employment is the child of self-discovery and self-esteem. Complete the following statements and see what discoveries you make for yourself.

I feel terrific when _____ .

I feel terrific when I spend time with _____ .

To me, the future looks _____ .

The best thing I ever did was _____ .

I wish I could lose my fear of _____ .

I know I have the talent to _____ .

I enjoy people who _____.

I admire _____.

I feel most productive when _____.

I am motivated by _____.

I almost never _____.

I laugh at _____.

My idea of fun is _____.

Work is exciting when _____.

The best advice I ever got was _____.

The thing I value most is _____.

If money were no object, I would _____.

It's easy for me to focus on _____.

My imagination is _____.

When I talk about myself, I _____.

My idea of a perfect life is _____.

My best days are _____.

My dream is _____.

I always wanted to _____.

I look forward to _____.

I spend too much time _____.

When I try to change something _____.

The thing my friends like about me is _____.

I would have more fun if _____.

In a group I like to _____.

If I ever win a prize it will be for _____.

All of these bits of self-knowledge will help you come to wiser choices about how you can make your living without a job. As I learned, all too painfully, if you don't continue to build your self-esteem, it can all slip away—taking your business with it. Despite all the work I had done to nurture my own self-esteem, I found that ignoring what I had learned was the costliest error I ever made.

To the Bottom and Back Again

There's a reason that I'm willing to risk appearing to be a nag on this subject. Remember Sophie Tucker's saying, "I have been rich and I have been poor. Rich is better."? Well, my self-esteem has been up and it's been down. Up *is* better.

In 1986, I ended a five-year stint in Colorado. Both my bank account and my self-esteem were a shambles. Moving to Boulder had been a dreadful mistake, a move that had not been well planned. After getting divorced in 1981, I wanted badly to leave California and start over. I had chosen Boulder basically because it wasn't in California and it had a reputation as an entrepreneurial hotbed.

Once there, I felt alienated and out of place. This lovely little city wasn't what I was looking for after all, but I was so confused and miserable that staying seemed the only choice. I was full of self-doubt, which was followed by self-pity. I started to berate myself. "How could you have been so stupid?" Even more damaging was the effect this had on my creative spirit. I was too exhausted to pick myself up and get going again.

Within the first year, my tiny nest egg was used up. I did temporary work and gradually started a couple of small projects of my own. By the third year, I was feeling better about myself and began to organize a few seminars and do some writing. It was all a gigantic struggle, however.

The turning point came when I received a call from a woman named Chris Utterback. I had contacted an association of home-based business people in Denver about doing a program for their group. Chris was their new president and called to set up a date. We talked for two hours and I hung up the phone knowing I had met a kindred spirit. Our friendship grew and became an important and positive force in my life. Finally I had someone to share ideas with. I began to see an immediate upswing in both my attitude and my business, but I still had a long way to go.

One day Chris called to tell me that her engineer husband was being transferred to Connecticut. I was despondent at the prospect of losing my friend so soon. It turned out to be a catalyst for my own move, however. I had been thinking about moving to Minneapolis for some time. This was not as frivolous a move as the one to Boulder. I had made a list of the things I wanted from my perfect town, researched several possibilities, and found that Minneapolis fit the bill on every count. With Chris leaving, I decided to reconsider moving once more.

Money was still an obstacle. I calculated the amount I would need to move and support my daughter and myself through a transition. With careful planning and frugality, I decided, we could manage on $5,000. Another telephone call answered my prayers. This one came from a seminar company in New Jersey called the Business Women's Forum. They had heard about me (I never knew how) and told me they were looking for trainers. Would I be interested in doing a stress management program? I assured them I'd welcome the opportunity. Would I be willing to do several cities in the Midwest beginning in six months? Again I agreed. In addition to setting up the programs and covering all expenses, they offered me $5,000 to conduct ten programs. I was on my way back up!

My daughter and I arrived in Minneapolis in late August 1986. I had a few weeks until the stress management seminars began, and I used the time to rethink my goals and plan my new life. My first priority and major goal for my first year in Minnesota was to focus on rebuilding my confidence and self-esteem. Even though I was feeling much better about myself, I could see that taking care of my inner needs would have to come first. As it turned out, my previous exposure to personal development work had not been in vain, and regaining my self-esteem and self-bossing equilibrium was more like getting over a cold than curing a serious disease.

One of my most healing experiences was also one of the most unexpected. When my daughter and I went to a film festival at the Walker Art Center, I stopped by the gift shop at the adjacent

Guthrie Theater, a place I had always loved. When I noticed the shopkeeper wearing a button that said, "Volunteer," I casually inquired about her involvement with the theater. Two days later, I called the community outreach director and volunteered as a backstage tour guide. With my flexible schedule, I soon found myself conducting more tours than the other guides. I approached each one with great gusto. Telling visitors about the history, the costumes, the behind-the-scene stories was always a thrill, but I was receiving a lot more than I was giving. By sharing my passion for the Guthrie, I was getting myself back. It was an excellent trade-off.

Stewart Emery once said, "Nothing in the Universe is neutral; it either costs or it contributes." During this first year, I kept actively looking for ways to add to my own personal growth. I began by making a list of everything I could think of that might make a positive contribution. That list included:

- Being gentle and noncritical with myself. Stopping myself when I note a temptation to berate myself.
- Giving myself credit for the things I do get done—being patient about the things I haven't yet accomplished.
- Giving myself experiences that are pleasurable, such as dining out, going to the theater, visiting museums, attending concerts.
- Spending time with people who are healthy and treat me well.
- Slowing down and living each day as well as I can. Not trying to solve all my problems at once.
- Being willing to accept compliments and gifts from others.
- Reading books and listening to tapes that feed positive self-thoughts.
- Laughing as often as possible.
- Spending time with my daughter exploring new places.
- Doing daily affirmations to enhance my self-image.

As you can see, the list was action-oriented. I posted it on my bathroom mirror and kept looking for ways to incorporate these ideas.

Along with recovering my self-esteem, spending time with my

daughter was a high priority. Since I knew this was our final year of living together, Jennifer's last year in high school, we shared many experiences. Over and over again, one of us would spontaneously declare, "I love our new life!" It had been a long time since I felt as happy as I did that first year.

So what about money? It seemed I had thought about nothing else while I was in Colorado—but it hadn't brought me a smidgen of financial success. Obviously, I needed to take a different approach. Again, it started with a list, which included:

- The amount of money I need to cover basic expenses
- A list of current income sources
- A list of new projects
- A daily and weekly plan for accomplishing my financial goals

The Business Women's Forum seminars were a major income source, as was my newsletter, which I had begun promoting vigorously. An old friend learned that I had moved to Minnesota and offered me the opportunity to work as an editor and consultant for a personal development program he had created. When I came across a catalog for Open U, an independent adult education company, I submitted several course ideas. One was for a seminar about making a living without a job. I never dreamed it would be one of the best ideas I'd ever had.

Long before my first year in Minnesota was up, I had begun earning more money than ever before in my life. Would it have happened if self-esteem had not been a priority? I doubt it very much. I know, too, that it needs to remain a top priority for the rest of my life.

A Program of Your Own

Building self-esteem is an ongoing process. Like a strong body, self-esteem requires tending and feeding if we are going to keep it healthy so that we can live happily and successfully in an often threatening world, as I learned from my years in Boulder.

Have you ever met anyone with *too much* self-esteem? Neither have I. None of the people I know who exhibit healthy self-esteem leave their self-image to chance. Formally or casually, behind high self-esteem is a program that enriches and expands this valuable commodity.

Your own self-esteem program can be tailored to your needs and goals. The people, activities, and things that nurture you will be different from the things that support me. In many ways, this is the ultimate do-it-yourself project. You can only begin from where you are right now and go on from there.

When I look back over the process I went through to regain what I had lost, I can see I took definite steps. These are the same steps I repeat in order to expand further. There are only four parts to my program, but each is equally important to a successful outcome. Here they are:

Create a new picture. Formulate in as much detail as possible what you want your life and yourself to exhibit. Begin with a broad idea and move in from there. I regularly review and answer these questions:

- What kind of community do I want to live in? What kind of community will nurture me? What must this place include? A theater? Good educational facilities? A strong work ethic? An airport? Good weather? A low crime rate? Shopping malls? Bookstores and libraries? Sports? For instance, I had always wanted to travel personally and professionally and yet had never lived near a major airport. That became important in selecting a community.
- How do I see myself living within this place? Am I a community activist? Resident? Church member? Local politician? Artist?
- What kind of people do I want to associate with? Are they likely to be found in a small town or large city, or does that even matter? How will I relate to these people?
- What activities do I want to share with others? Where would I go to do that? Do I want to participate in a book discussion group? An entrepreneurs' club? Do I want to go camping? Swimming? Attend the symphony?
- What kind of home will I live in? What things do I want in that home? Will I work in the place where I live? Will I be close to schools, shopping, theaters? Would I enjoy living in a rural setting and driving a lot?

- What kind of work will I do? Will it be alone, with a regular team of people, or with different groups? Will I work all year or part of it? And what am I wearing when I do this work? (This question is more significant than you may think!)
- How do I see myself in one year? Five years? Can I grow through my new plans? Will I be making changes?

Answering these questions helped me formulate a mental picture that was quite unlike my actual life in Colorado. I saw, for instance, that the things I wanted from my town and neighborhood were not available where I was. My list included living in a place that had a sense of community; a cultural center with theaters, symphonies, and museums; a major airport, and a low crime rate. I also envisioned myself smiling a lot and interacting with positive people. Whenever I would call up this mental picture, I noticed myself saying, "Yes! *Yes!*" All along I had known what would nurture me; I had just forgotten to listen.

A geographic relocation may, of course, not be part of your plan. Even so, if you make the change to self-bossing, your place in your community will be different. Your mental picture can include the same backdrop, but with new activities.

Implement proven techniques for building self-esteem. Again, I knew very well what these tools were and how they could make a difference. When you're looking for teachers who can help you save your life, I reminded myself, pick the best ones you can find. Reading, always a source of help for me, became a daily ritual. I reread my favorite self-help books and found several new ones that inspired me. Spending time with inspirational authors remains important to my wellness.

Although I did not enroll in any classes, learning in a formal setting had been valuable in my earlier search for self-esteem. You can find these classes almost everywhere. Even small towns offer basic self-esteem training in places such as the YMCA, adult education centers, and churches. Participation in such a program can not only give you valuable life skills, it will put you in touch with others who share your quest.

Many people report that aligning themselves with a twelve-step program has helped their self-esteem. Widely available and enormously effective, these leaderless support groups are empowering in a practical way. You can also reinforce your classroom learning with books and audiotapes for use on your own. Nathaniel Branden, John Bradshaw, and Earnie Larsen are among the finest authors on the subject. Get to know them, too.

Another easy thing I did was to start a new journal whose purpose was to record all the good things that were happening, new pleasures I had found, and inspiring quotes. Some of these journal entries included:

- *I found a wonderful quote from Logan Pearsall Smith: "Never lose a sense of the whimsical and perilous charm of daily life, with its meetings and words and accidents."*
- *Think of this: Paul McCartney can't read music.*
- *There have been some truly magical moments, such as Thursday when I got great seats for opening night of* Frankenstein, *heard Mozart's Sonata in A, found a blue salvia for my garden, got a wonderful card from Linda, listened to John read the beginning of a superb story he's writing.*
- *My project for this year is to find all the ways to put raspberry and chocolate together (and taste each), and see all the Monets I can see with my own two eyes.*
- *I am transforming my plain balcony into a luscious garden.*
- *Guthrie Artistic Director Garland Wright said, "We must find ideas big enough to be afraid of again." Remember that.*

The more I noticed and appreciated these small pleasures, the more I seemed to have to write about. I was seeing proof that whatever you focus on will expand. Earlier I had focused on my problems and unhappiness, which had grown by leaps and bounds. Reversing the focus in a disciplined activity produced happier results.

Just as you don't need a degree from a business school in order to make a living without a job, you don't need a degree in psychology to have healthy self-esteem. Listen to your heart and feed it lovingly and frequently with nurturing words.

Hang out with good people. Author Jess Lair once said that we all need four or five people in our lives whose faces light up when we walk into the room. I love that notion. No matter how many ignore or reject you, if you are connected to a few kindred spirits, you can keep your soul in flight.

This can be, surprisingly, the most difficult step of any self-esteem-building program. We all have to deal with annoying folks sometimes, but need to balance this with wonderful relationships. My simple test for a relationship is shared laughter. Looking back on the failed relationships in my life, I notice that there is always a warning signal that things were going awry: the laughter stopped. Whether you use laughter as a touchstone or have another criterion, at some level you know which people contribute to your good feelings about yourself and which ones rob you of them. I once had a friend who began saying cruel things to me, but they were always cloaked in a semicompliment. She'd say things like, "You should always wear blue. It looks much better on you than the green that you usually wear." After a series of personal attacks on my eating habits, clothes, and friends, it finally hit me that I was spending time with a thief— one who was slowly taking away my hard-won serenity. It's a price I don't have to pay, nor do you.

"I refuse to spend time with people who don't recognize my magnificence," I once heard a man say. It sounded a trifle arrogant at the time, but now I see that it's a practical idea. Do a quick inventory of the people in your life right now:

- How many of them light up when you walk into the room?
- How many invalidate you? Help you to feel like Lowly Worm?
- How many encourage your dreams?
- How many make you feel wonderful just as you are?
- How many have your self-improvement as a hobby?
- How many can you feel open with?

When your personal self-esteem account is filled to overflowing, perhaps you can afford to spend time with diminishers. Until then, exercise caution. Let those who interfere with your self-esteem know that you are serious about your own growth and that you may not be seeing them for a while. If this is uncomfortable, you might say something like, "I'm making a number of changes in my life and need some time alone, so I won't be available to get together as I have in the past." Try not to be defensive—or blaming—about avoiding them, but be as firm as necessary about your decision.

Know what's fun for you and indulge constantly. Somewhere we've gotten to thinking that "fun" and "irresponsible" are synonymous. Not so! Enjoying your life is the most responsible thing you can do. I learned about this from Harry Browne in his book *How I Found Freedom in an Unfree World*. He pointed out that knowing what brings you joy—and spending time in joyful ways—is the path to freedom. You lose your dependence on the opinions of others and act in accordance with your heart.

What's fun for you? Giving tours at the Guthrie, sipping afternoon tea in a hotel, and scouting in thrift shops are high on my list, but might be agony for you. What would your list include? Here are some things to consider:

- What activities give you the most pleasure?

- How often do you spend time doing those things?

- When was the last time you tried something new?

- Do you limit the amount of fun you permit yourself?

- How many things that you think of as fun do you like to do alone? With others? With a special partner?

- Why is having fun good for you?

- Are you a Fun Miser or Philanthropist?

- Do you think fun is only for the weekends?

Discover your own sources of delight and keep expanding your list. A fascinating book that I once read was *The Pleasure Book* by Julius Fast, who wrote that he realized that his friends all enjoyed activities he'd never tried for himself, so he decided to sample new pleasures. He discovered dozens of new kinds of fun, including needlework, golf, ballooning, and creating new traditions.

Don't give yourself a quota for fun. This is an area where less is *not* more.

The link between self-esteem and successful self-bossing is so undeniable that it must not be overlooked. With this important emotional backing, you can become joyful as well as jobless. While it is possible to make a living without self-esteem, what's the point?

Shakespeare wrote many beautiful lines, but none more profound than this one from *Henry V:* "Self-love, my liege, is not so vile a sin as self-neglecting." It's a reminder that nothing less than your life is on the line.

Winning Ways for Doing First Things First

Self-esteem isn't something that manifests when you win the Nobel prize. It determines your behavior in daily life. Read the following statements and circle the number that represents how true each is for you. Use the following key: 1 = rarely, 2 = sometimes, 3 = often, 4 = always.

I am an attentive listener. 1 2 3 4

It's easy for me to accept compliments. 1 2 3 4

I would describe my attitude as positive. 1 2 3 4

When others share their plans and ideas, I give them encouragement. 1 2 3 4

I find a lot in life to laugh about. 1 2 3 4

I take an active approach to building my self-esteem. 1 2 3 4

I am sensitive to the feelings of others. 1 2 3 4

I believe it's okay to make mistakes. 1 2 3 4

I am not unduly bothered by the opinions of others. 1 2 3 4

I know I have a lot to offer. 1 2 3 4

It's easy for me to make a commitment to things I believe in. 1 2 3 4

Personal growth is important to me. 1 2 3 4

I believe that my life can make a difference. 1 2 3 4

I care for my body by eating healthy food and exercising regularly. 1 2 3 4

I like to try new ideas. 1 2 3 4

I welcome positive change. 1 2 3 4

My friends have healthy self-esteem. 1 2 3 4

I think work should be fun and satisfying. 1 2 3 4

I trust my ability to solve problems. 1 2 3 4

I enjoy my own company. 1 2 3 4

While this quiz has no right or wrong answers, you can spot areas that you have achieved mastery in and those you need to work on, since 4s indicate high self-esteem and 1s low self-esteem.

How can you add activities to your daily schedule that will heighten your self-esteem? List a few ideas in each of the following areas.

Create a new picture

_____

_____

_____

Implement proven self-esteem techniques

_____

_____

_____

Hang out with good people

_____

_____

_____

Have more fun

_____

_____

_____

CHAPTER 3

Finding Your Lost Passion

There is at bottom only one problem in the world and this is its name: how does one break through? How does one get into the open? How does one burst the cocoon and become a butterfly?

Thomas Mann

Many of us have delighted in tales about our immigrant grandparents, who risked the familiar for the unknown. Our family histories are peppered with stories about the ups and downs our ancestors faced in building new lives, stories that make a startling contrast to our own routine lives. We long for experiences that we can use to inspire our own grandchildren. Yet, together with the brave stories, much of the advice we've been given has to do with playing it safe.

Following our parents' advice, we may have made them proud. Maybe we finished high school and even pursued more education. We may have mortgages and car payments. Why, then, we may silently wonder, do we feel less than fulfilled? Having done all that we were told to do in order to live the good life, how can we feel so shortchanged?

For one thing, our parents and guidance counselors seem to have left out one important detail in offering their advice. "We act as though comfort and luxury were the chief requirements of life," Victorian novelist Charles Kingsley says. "When all that we need to make us really happy is something to be enthusiastic about." For too many of us, enthusiasm for our work is a feeling that disappeared long ago—if it was present in the first place. While you may have been advised to take up an occupation that you liked, loving your work isn't something that's expected of you. Doing work that you are passionate about is more than just a matter of luck. For the few who are passionate in their work, that passion is basic to their emotional well-being—and to their financial success.

A Psychologist Studies Success

A revealing study conducted by psychologist Srully Blotnick strongly supports the idea that passion is essential to personal achievement.

In 1960, Blotnick began following the lives of 1,500 people. Periodically, he'd send them a questionnaire to keep tabs on their progress. Twenty years later, 1,067 remained in the study; of those still being surveyed, 83 had become millionaires. Blotnick's findings were compiled in a compelling book called *Getting Rich Your Own Way*.

The attitudes of those who became rich and those who didn't were consistent, no matter what field of endeavor the participant was in. For instance, those who had not realized financial success frequently mentioned their plans to do so, which included saving their money so that they could do what they *really* wanted to do. Many said they hoped to make the right stock investment or even win the lottery in order to find wealth. This sort of thinking, however, was not present in the plans of those who ultimately succeeded. Without exception, the millionaires cited "persistence" as their greatest asset; a closer look suggests that their real secret was their passion.

In fact, Blotnick says one of the clearest discoveries of the study was also the most unexpected. "If you don't like your job," he found, "you are losing money. Lots of it. Because, as it turns out, your work is more likely to make you wealthy than any bet or investment you will ever make. A missing ingredient had to be present if someone was ever to become rich: they had to find their work absorbing. Involving. Enthralling."

Sounds like passion to me. Contrary to the popular notion that passion is an unrealistic expectation, Blotnick's study demonstrates that it's an utterly practical idea. Loving what we do is essential to doing it well. It's a message that I never received. My own German-Lutheran background strongly suggested just the opposite. "If it feels good," was the implication, "you shouldn't take money for it." Another myth we need to abolish!

Working with Passion

Comedian George Burns once said, "I would rather be a failure doing something I love than be a success doing something I hate." That statement captures the essence of what it means to work with passion. The *doing* is so pleasurable that it becomes more important than the results. We can't, in fact, imagine life without it.

When we are engaged in work that comes from our passion, it feels natural and right. We feel alive, magnificent, and capable of extraordinary things. Our imagination opens up and we find a steady stream of new ideas, better ways of feeding the work. We can't wait to share it with others. We may have no sense, when we are doing it, of time passing. Hours feel like minutes. (Until I wrote that sentence, I hadn't realized that my office is the only room in my home without a clock!) When we finish a project we are keen on we feel exhilarated rather than exhausted. When we love what we do, we feel as Gloria Steinem did when she described her writing as "the only thing that when I'm doing it I don't think I should be doing something else."

It's not difficult to recognize someone who has found his passion and made it his work. Seeing such people in action can be a breathtaking experience. Last winter, after standing in line in the cold for two hours, I managed to get a returned ticket for the Eric Clapton concert at Royal Albert Hall in London. Besides being astonished at my good fortune, I was dazzled by this extraordinary musician's performance. I kept thinking, "I am in the presence of greatness and this is what it looks like." And it's not only artists and musicians who exhibit greatness in their work.

Where's Your Passion?

Since passion is so critical to making a living without a job, identifying where yours lies is necessary before you can begin making concrete plans. If you haven't yet identified your personal fervor, you are not alone. Despite all of our sophisticated tools for psychological analysis, career counseling paraphernalia, and advanced occupational testing, we have failed to create an environment that allows and encourages people to discover—and follow—their unique path and get paid for it. Self-bossers have to make that discovery for themselves.

It may take time to connect with those activities and situations that you find blissful. So what? Can you think of a worthier project?

You aren't likely to uncover your passion sitting in your living room trying to figure it out, however. This piece of the puzzle will reveal itself in the midst of activity. You can do several easy things to reawaken and remember your particular sources of delight, and I'll tell you what they are. But be patient with yourself as you work through the processes I'm suggesting here. You may even find yourself having a "Eureka!" experience. Believe that you are capable of discovering your passion for yourself—you might even want to create an affirmation about it—and you will do so sooner than you may imagine.

Look Back

Begin your journey with a backward glance. The English poet Wordsworth wrote, "The child is father of the man," and there's your first clue to finding your own passion. If you haven't scouted around in your childhood, go back and take a look. You may be surprised to find forgotten passions waiting to be reignited. Can you recall your childhood dreams? Do you remember what you thought you'd be when you grew up? Chances are that you knew the essence (if not the form) of your perfect work.

Comedian and actor Martin Short told a magazine interviewer, "When I was a kid, I used to fantasize about being an entertainer. When I was eight, I used to do *The Martin Short*

Show in my attic. I'd type things up for the *TV Guide* saying, 'Marty will sing. Marty's guests are . . .' and I'd have an applause record. I'd sing, I'd interview people. Then I'd play the applause record."

Think about it. As children we were all naturally intuitive. We had more dreams and fewer doubts. As time went by, the "guidance" we received may have dimmed the dreams and fueled the doubts. By the time we began thinking about how we would earn our living, we had received considerable advice that may have led us further away from our real desires.

"Everybody said I was nuts when I told them that my dream was to sculpt sand," says ex-architect Todd VanderPluym. A lifelong love affair with building sand castles led him to ignore the negative judgments and turn his childhood hobby into a profitable business. As president of Sand Sculptors International, a firm that crisscrosses the country and the world building elaborate sand works for special events, VanderPluym is now internationally recognized for his unusual occupation. What if he had ignored the promptings of his heart?

What about you? What did you love as a child? Jog your memory and see what you come up with. As you look back, try to recall what made you joyful and happy. What kind of games did you play? What did you pretend? Were you a leader? A creator? The one who made the other kids laugh? A bookworm? It probably wouldn't surprise you to learn that Cher spent her childhood putting on neighborhood shows or that Oprah Winfrey's teachers recall her incessantly asking questions. Similarly, your early fancies could be previews of coming attractions.

Although it's become fashionable to dig around in our childhoods to discover the source of our adult unhappiness, you can use the same process to discover what made you feel truly alive and happy. If you have family photograph albums or scrapbooks, spend an afternoon looking through them. You may find traces of long-forgotten pleasures that can add clarity and vision to your current life.

Whether you left your childhood ten or fifty years ago matters not. Shortly after I moved to Minneapolis in 1986, I was having dinner with an old friend. As I began telling him about my new life, it dawned on me that I had finally created exactly the lifestyle I had envisioned for myself as a teenager. Even though my marriage had been a detour from those dreams, I was living them now. My perfect work seemed to have taken decades to discover, but, in truth, I had had a very accurate sense about it when I was eight or nine years old. I just had to reclaim what that little Barbara kid knew all along.

The child you once were had wisdom. Answer the following questions and see what memories you awaken. You can enhance your remembering even more by writing the answers with your nondominant hand. This technique is used by therapists to help their clients reconnect with the inner child. Listen to that kid again and see what guidance you'll be offered.

- Who was your favorite adult when you were a child? Why?
- Who was your favorite friend? What did you do together? What did you admire about your friend?
- How did you spend your summers? Were they very unlike the rest of the year? In what ways?
- What was your favorite book? Movie?
- Who were your heroes? Were they real or fantasy people? Why did they inspire you?
- What haven't you yet done that you dreamed about doing as a child? What is its link to your desires or unfulfilled dreams today?
- What sort of games did you play? What was your favorite?
- What was your role in the neighborhood where you grew up? In your family?
- Did your image of yourself change when you went to school?
- How did you spend time alone?

Focus on Essence

Another block to uncovering our passion is trying to find the specific form our work will take before we've identified the essence of that work. The essence of something is simply the feeling it produces and the function it performs. That could be something like, "My work feels natural and easy. It puts me in touch with a small group of people whom I serve on a regular basis." When you know the essence of what you want, you realize it can come in many ways—opening your options and alternatives.

Think of the essence of your work as the emotional and psychic rewards it will produce. Long before I knew precisely what products and services I wanted to market, I determined that my business would motivate others to actualize their potential while making me feel satisfied and causing me to keep improving myself. Knowing that, an abundance of possible avenues of action became available, while others were immediately eliminated.

One of the first things my friend Ruth told me when we met was that she hated her career as a nurse and longed to do something that involved art and artists. Since we had met at a bed-and-breakfast hotel in London where we were both staying, we decided to visit the Courtauld Gallery together. Once there, the transformation in my new friend was visible. Being in an artistic atmosphere seemed to awaken her spirit. It was apparent that she saw and felt a great deal more than the average museum-goer.

Ruth returned to Provo, Utah, and we had many discussions about her work. "I am tired of working around blood and burning flesh," she'd declare. "I'd be so much happier if I could do something with art." We continued to brainstorm possibilities, but her initial explorations were not encouraging. With no formal training in art history or the like, her opportunities seemed limited. We kept focused on the essence of what she longed for: to share her love of art with others.

For a while, she planned to move from Utah to New York, a favorite city. Several trips there proved disappointing. As much as she liked being there, it didn't "feel" right as a home. At the same time, Provo didn't seem to be brimming with the sort of work she craved.

Eventually, she quit her nursing job and spent a couple of months working on her serenity. One day she mentioned a small company in her area that made custom picture frames. They employed a number of artisans who produced the frames, which were sold to art collectors, galleries, etc., around the country. Ruth had taken several pieces of art to them for framing and said she could hardly tear herself away—she loved talking to them and seeing their magnificent frames. She left the frame shop wondering how she could be of value to them. We brainstormed more ideas. Maybe she could travel around the country and market their work to galleries. Or exhibit at trade shows. We agreed that somehow she needed to let them know that she wanted to be involved with their work. She gathered her ideas and courage and called on them once more. To her amazement, they said they were planning an expansion and were going to open galleries of their own in several cities, starting with Salt Lake. "We've already talked about hiring you," one of the partners confessed. Her passion had been apparent!

Their first shop has opened and Ruth is happily involved in several capacities. She has ideas galore and sees this as her apprenticeship. Although she now has a long commute, she reports arriving home with plenty of energy—and enthusiasm for returning the next day. By identifying the essence of what she wanted, Ruth accomplished the seemingly impossible! This isn't the end of her goal, it's the beginning. And it started in Provo.

What is the essence of your ideal work? What specific feelings will it produce? What intangible rewards and satisfactions? Write a two- or three-sentence description.

_____

_____

_____

Notice What's Happening

Ray Bradbury tells writers wanting to duplicate his success, "In the moment of knowing a love, intensify it." That's precisely what I was doing as I stepped off my front porch, notebook in hand, on my way to a celebratory breakfast.

After a long, frustrating hiatus from teaching, I had conducted my first seminar in months the night before. It had been even more fun than I'd remembered. As I walked away from the hotel, a little inner voice said, "Meeting rooms are your natural habitat!" Now in the morning sunshine I still felt excited, euphoric even, although I had hardly slept all night.

"How did your seminar go?" a voice called from across the street. It was my neighbor Susan, puttering in her lovely yard, as usual. I rushed to share my happiness with her.

When I finished my detailed account of the seminar, Susan stopped pulling weeds, looked at me and said, "But you know what you want. And that's just my problem. I *don't* know what I want to do. I know I don't want to go back to nursing, but there's nothing else I can do." She went back to her beautiful garden.

"Susan," I ventured, "I think you do know. Every time I come by, you're digging in the dirt. You have the most glorious yard in town. Have you ever thought about starting a gardening business?"

She looked startled. "Who would ever hire me?"

"Anyone who wanted their yard to look as good as yours," I suggested.

Our conversation lasted only a few minutes, but in those moments Gardenscapes was born. By the time spring rolled around, Susan was digging in other people's dirt as well as her own.

Like Susan, your passion may be hiding in plain sight. In order to bring it forth, you need to raise your awareness as you go about your daily activities.

What feels good when you're doing it?
What leaves you exhausted?
What sharpens your senses?
Makes you smile?

Notice your feelings as you are feeling them. Listen, also, to the compliments you receive. What may be obvious to your friends may be obscured from your vision of yourself. When someone points out that you seem relaxed and happy in the midst of some project, file that information away. Since it's very easy, expected even, to develop a routine and stick to it, our responses can become dulled. We stop paying attention.

Passion wakes us up. But first we have to notice.

Movie critic Roger Ebert spends his days working at something most of us do for fun. Long ago he decided to devote his time to doing what he loves most, and advises, "Set up your life so that your personal goals are their own reward. If your life isn't organized that way, it might be well to reorganize it . . . with a higher caliber of goals. What you do instead of your real work *is* your real work."

Expect to be Surprised

Discovering your passion is, of course, an ongoing process. As you grow and change, so do your enthusiasms. And the more things you find to be passionate about, the richer your life will be. You'll have more options, fewer limitations. If you're willing to make the effort to find those things that turn you on, some outrageous ideas may appear. Don't dismiss or ignore them. Often the wildest dreams are the easiest to accomplish. As my passionate daughter keeps reminding me, "What's the point in having mediocre goals?" Passion does not lead to ordinariness!

Several years ago, I made the acquaintance of two young men, George and Jim, who had been trained as architects. When they met, they discovered that they shared a passion for flying kites and decided to open a tiny shop to sell beautiful and unusual kites and a few toys. At first they took turns minding their little store, but they soon outgrew its cramped quarters. They moved to a bigger and better location, increased their inventory, and spent their days meeting others who shared their enthusiasm for kites. Today, a friend informs me, George and Jim are wealthy, but seldom in their store. They now own an even bigger store and a mail-order business supplying kite-flyers around the country with hard-to-find supplies. Their days are spent testing new products—playing with kites and toys. None of this would have happened if they had not paid attention to this unconventional dream.

The poet Goethe said, "As soon as you trust yourself, you will know how to live." Being German, he may not have been thinking about passion, but he certainly identified an important aspect of uncovering it. When you connect with a situation that awakens your passion, you must trust your own feelings, no matter how illogical they may seem at first.

You may also be surprised to discover that your life is already filled with activities that you feel passionate about, or *could* be passionate about with some minor alterations. But whether tiny or large changes are called for, pay attention to the direction in which your passion is urging you to go. See to it that Joseph Campbell's admonition to "follow your bliss" is more than a cliché in your life.

• Can you think of someone you know who is passionate about his or her work? How does that person demonstrate it? If this is a person whose services you have received, how did you feel in his or her presence? Maybe you can recall a waiter who made you the most important person in the world, or a doctor who took time to answer your questions.

• Can you envision what it would be like to live in a world where everyone was passionate about his or her work? What kind of energy would that create? How would it affect the quality of products and services? What would happen to crime? To health? To the economy?

• If you were truly passionate about your work, how would your days be spent? How would it affect your personal relationships?

Passion Leads to Purpose

Nothing is more tragic than encountering a person who believes that his or her life has no meaning, that he or she has no contribution to make. Unfortunately, this commonly occurs in our society when people grow older and are given messages that they are no longer needed. But feeling purposeless afflicts the young as well. At its most extreme, feeling purposeless can lead to depression and despair or even suicide.

A basic need shared by humans is the need to be appreciated and useful. Deep down we all want to know that our lives do make a difference. I believe that finding our passion is a prelude to finding our purpose. We may begin with a small motivation and one day discover that what seemed simple and obvious was more important and far-reaching than we could see at first. For instance, we may think that we're just selling kites and then recognize that we're actually helping others be more playful. Once we get a glimpse of the larger good that we're doing, our passion expands. And that, in turn, propels us to do more and be more.

Try visualizing your passion as a pilot light. Turn up the flame gradually. You have a powerful force at your disposal. What do you see inside that flame? What is feeding it? What can you see all around the flame? What is being revealed in its light? The more determined you are to feed that flame, the more you can accomplish.

Let Love Lead

Here's a simple test to discover whether or not you are working with passion: Are you in a more or less loving mood or attitude when you are working? Does the work improve your relationships? Cause you to whistle or hum? Make you smile? Help you like yourself more?

Jess Lair wrote about Picasso. "You couldn't tell Picasso's work from his play," wrote Lair. "One minute he would be playing with his kids. The next minute he would be playing with his wife. And then he would be drinking wine and then playing with his paintings. It was all just love, love of his wife, love of his family, love of his friends, love of his work. He just floated back and forth between activities without any thought to there being a division or gap."

I believe that would describe all people who have found their passion and live it. And rare as it may be right now, I'm stubborn enough to believe that we should not stop searching until our own lives can be described the same way as Picasso's.

You may be wondering whether it is possible to not find a deep passion and still make a living without a job. Yes, of course you can, just as you can live in a loveless marriage. But why would you want to?

Winning Ways for Finding Your Lost Passion

• A wonderful film which demonstrates how a childhood passion can lead to adult happiness is *Cinema Paradiso*. Although the main theme of this film is friendship, the story of the little Italian boy, Salvatore, who falls in love with the movies as a child and nurtures that love throughout life, is delightful. Rent the video and watch how passion plays an important role in Salvatore's life.

• Many people find meditation a useful technique for tapping into buried dreams. Sitting quietly for several minutes every day, relaxing the body, and clearing the mind, can lead to brave new insights. Meditation has other benefits, such as stress reduction, which can ultimately result in more clarity.

• Give yourself some uninterrupted time. Turn on your answering machine, turn off your television, go to a place where you can be alone and comfortable. Bring along three or more sheets of paper and your favorite pen.

At the top of the first sheet write "Love to Do"; on the second write "Love to Have"; on the third write "Love to Be." Number each sheet from 1 to 100 and list every single thing you can think of that you currently love to do, have, and be. If you've never given much thought to this, you may have a hard time coming up with 300 wonderful things on your first try. Write as much as you can and don't edit out any thoughts, even the ones that seem silly, frivolous, or out of reach. Add to your list every time another pleasurable idea or experience comes along.

How can this help? "Ultimately, an increased ability to feel pleasure will make our inner selves stronger," writes Julius Fast in *The Pleasure Book*. "There is an unconscious reasoning that if we allow ourselves to have pleasure, it means we are worth that pleasure, that we have more value as a person. If you have this outlook, you automatically think more of yourself. You have higher self-esteem, a better outlook on life, and a greater ability to enjoy." That's a lot of benefit from a simple exercise.

• Following is a checklist that encourages you to stretch your imagination a bit. On the list you will find a number of activities, qualities, etc., that you might like to incorporate into your ideal way of making a living.

Read through the checklist and, without thinking too much about it, select every item that appeals to you. Yes, you may find yourself checking items that seem to contradict one another. That's perfectly okay. There are no right or wrong answers to this and no scientific interpretation for the exercise. It's another method of tapping into your reservoir of passion.

____ Lets me work alone
____ Lets me work with a team
____ Is physical
____ Is idea-oriented
____ Allows me to work at home
____ Pays me to travel
____ Is seasonal
____ Is people-driven
____ Is product-driven
____ Allows me to use my expertise
____ Contantly teaches me new things
____ Lets me get a great suntan
____ Is portable
____ Is very part-time
____ Involves several diverse activities
____ Lets me be silly
____ Makes a difference in people's lives
____ Comes from my personal values
____ Is personally satisfying
____ Makes me wealthy
____ Contributes to my mental health
____ Lets me work at my peak times
____ Serves a few happy clients
____ Serves the general population
____ Is different every day
____ Is unlike anything I've done so far
____ Feels like not working
____ Lets me grow personally and financially
____ Makes me famous

____ Draws on my education and skills

____ Involves my family

____ Brings new people into my life

____ Sometimes scares me

____ Seems natural for me

____ Lets me work hard for several months with long periods of time off

____ Surprises my friends

____ Can be done on an island

____ Can be done outdoors

____ Involves partners

____ Enriches lives, including my own

____ Is innovative

____ Takes an existing idea and improves on it

____ Fires my creativity

____ Adds to my self-esteem

____ Gives me a sense of purpose

____ Lets me manufacture a product I've invented

____ Is sales-oriented

____ Lets me discover things I didn't know I could do

____ Makes me excited to get out of bed in the morning

____ Is national in scope

____ Lets me wear a costume

____ Combines many talents and skills I've acquired in a fresh way

____ Leads to financial independence

____ Has global potential

____ Improves the environment

____ Heals others

____ Is uniquely mine

PART II

Doing Your Homework

It is not recognized in the full amplitude of the word that all freedom is essentially self-liberation—that I can only have as much freedom as I procure for myself.

Max Stirner

CHAPTER 4

Uncovering Your Assets

There are few human beings who receive the truth complete
and staggering, by instant illumination. Most of them acquire it
fragment by fragment, on a small scale, by successive developments, like a mosaic.

Anaïs Nin

It's not unusual for human beings to underestimate their own
value. Once we've mastered a skill, we tend to take it for granted
and forget how valuable it might be to other people. Yet all of
the self-bossers mentioned so far got started by taking their
personal assets and mobilizing them. The things they owned
became their tools, their experience and skills became their
product, and their dreams provided the motivation. Their attitude was much like Diane von Furstenberg's. "I don't think
things happen in spite of you," says the designer. "I think you
have to help yourself—at least visualize what you want and
project it—and dream. You can only be what your fantasy wants
you to be."

That begins with taking an inventory of what you already have
learned and acquired—and using your imagination to see new
possibilities. It will never happen if you delay, waiting for perfect
conditions. Instead of listing all the things you lack, get busy
listing all the things you have, are, and can become. Focusing on
your assets, valuing what's already in your life, and turning all of
it to your advantage, are preliminaries to success.

What qualifies as an asset? Assets are not just cars, houses, or stock portfolios. Self-bossers take a broader view than that. What about the way kids respond to you? Or your talent for creating beautiful rooms on a shoestring? Or your ability to resolve conflicts? Or your passion for computer graphics? Anything and everything, tangible and intangible, that can make a contribution is given the importance it deserves. Take a closer look at what you've got to work with right now.

Are You Willing?

When I fly, I arrive at the airport early enough to ask for an exit-row seat. Since these seats can't be preassigned, getting one requires a bit of extra effort. Usually I march up to the counter and announce, "I'd like to have an exit-row aisle seat and I meet all of the criteria." (In other words, I speak English, have no physical disabilities, and can follow orders.)

One reservations clerk challenged my request by asking, "But are you willing?" I assured him I was, but wondered why he had asked. He explained that willingness was critical, since exit-row occupants have an important duty to perform in the event of a crash. If I wasn't willing to help others get off the plane, he said, he'd have to deny my request.

Your willingness to make a living without a job is indispensable to getting started. Here are several questions to clarify your level of willingness. Answer each with a yes or no; "yes, but" won't do.

- Am I willing to go against Conventional Wisdom?
- Am I willing to make lifestyle changes?
- Am I willing to make personal sacrifices?
- Am I willing to do my homework and to learn from other self-bossers?
- Am I willing to commit to a path that offers no guarantees of success?
- Am I willing to fail in order ultimately to succeed?
- Am I willing to trust myself more?
- Am I willing to keep going until I accomplish my goals?
- Am I willing to accept money for having fun?

Obviously, the more yeses you had, the better. If you had several negative responses, that doesn't mean you're disqualified, but it is a sign that you have work to do on making a genuine commitment.

For several years, I've watched a woman I know flirt with self-employment. Her progress has been much less than it could have been. She seems to take two steps forward, one back, never failing, but not succeeding either. A closer look reveals that she is only lukewarm in her willingness to accomplish all she could. If things become difficult or even uncomfortable she beats a hasty retreat, depending on her husband to support her. In fact, she is adamantly unwilling to make even the smallest sacrifice on behalf of her business. While she says she wants a prosperous business, her actions don't support that happening. Consequently, both her personal and business growth are stymied.

You can avoid her experience by recognizing the importance of having a willing attitude and finding reasons and rewards to empower that decision. Knowing your motivation can make a big difference.

What's Your Motivation?

In the summer of 1977, Sheila Lukins and Julee Rosso teamed up and opened a tiny gourmet food shop in Manhattan named The Silver Palate. In the first year, the partners put all the money they earned back into the business. The next two years they drew salaries of only $7,000 each. Within five years, the two had begun to turn their venture into a miniconglomerate that would eventually include a shop in Tokyo, a catering service, a line of brand-name products carried in stores around the country, a mail-order catalog, and three best-selling cookbooks. When they decided to sell their business eight years after they started it, it was valued at $10 million.

Did dreams of fabulous wealth start them on their way? Not according to Lukins and Rosso. In their first cookbook they explain the motivation behind The Silver Palate. "Our lives had become increasingly active and it was getting more difficult to juggle it all. We knew there must be others who were in the same boat who needed help. Our concept was simple: a tiny gem of a shop where the best foodstuffs could be available. Most of all, we wanted it to have a pleasant ambience, to be an enjoyable place for people to discover the joy and excitement of food."

Being motivated means you have a definite and positive desire to do something. The catalyst for that can be many things, including wealth, power, service, creativity, curiosity, and change. Not all motivations, however, are equally sound. Someone said, "The person who starts out with the idea of getting rich, won't succeed; you must have a larger ambition." That pithy observation came from John D. Rockefeller.

So why do *you* want to make a living without a job? If your answer includes a desire to improve yourself or your community or the planet, you've got a head start on winning. If your only goal is to pay your bills, you're missing an important factor and accomplishing that goal will be a struggle. Working for money alone, as our nine-to-five culture has demonstrated, makes for a hollow existence.

The larger ambition that Rockefeller mentioned as the key to achievement happens quite naturally in people of high self-esteem. As you grow as a person, your motivation will grow as well. Keep monitoring yours.

What Assets Do You Have?

During her senior year in college, my daughter called with a sharp accusation. "You've *ruined* me!" Jennie wailed.

"What are you talking about?" I fired back.

"Well, all of my friends are going on job interviews and writing their résumés," she explained. "I can't possibly do that. I can't just go get a job."

Unlike most of her classmates, Jennie went to college to study subjects she found interesting, not to learn how to work for somebody else. Even so, she was facing a familiar dilemma: we may know what we *don't* want long before we know what is right for us.

Identifying the kind of work experiences that you don't want to repeat can be helpful in choosing more satisfying options. Rather than berating yourself for spending years doing work you disliked—and thinking you've wasted all that time—look at the things you've done as useful clues for self-discovery. There is much in life we can't know until we actually dig in and try it. Eliminating less than perfect choices can clear away some of the fog. Now you can turn your attention to fresh ideas and possibilities. Give yourself credit for the lessons you've learned in all your working life. Even the jobs you disliked the most may have given you a valuable skill or insight that can be applied to your next endeavor.

In assessing your assets for becoming joyfully jobless, compile a written inventory of everything that might be a benefit. Your experience, your self-knowledge, your talents, your personality, and the tools and equipment you already own belong on your list. Although you might want to acquire training or high-tech tools in the future, getting started requires only that you mobilize the assets you already have.

To give you an idea of the sorts of things that deserve your consideration, here's a sample inventory compiled by a would-be entrepreneur. You'll notice that it goes far beyond a normal résumé or work history.

- A supportive spouse and kids who keep me laughing
- Friends and contacts in my industry
- An empty basement that would make a quiet office
- My personal computer and telephone
- A car that runs well and is paid for
- Experience gained in three diverse jobs
- My curiosity and desire to learn new things
- My weekly twelve-step group meetings, which give me support
- A generally optimistic attitude
- Access to a good public library
- My fluent Spanish and reading knowledge of Italian
- My pilot's license
- Good personal management
- Good health, which is improving
- Self-confidence

- Goals and dreams that I believe in
- My love of trying new ideas

Now make your own inventory.

_____

_____

_____

_____

_____

_____

_____

_____

_____

Not only is a personal inventory a good starting point, as time passes, you can revise and expand yours as you develop and acquire more assets. Several years ago, I would have listed my love of all things English as an asset. My five visits to England have increased the value of that item immensely. Because of my firsthand experience, I designed a class called "London on a Shoestring" to share the bargains I had discovered. I used that information to write and sell a magazine article. I ran a small catering business specializing in English-style afternoon tea and taught classes on the same subject. My writing file has several article ideas that have come out of my visits. Even a seemingly unimportant asset can grow into something significant if it's nurtured.

How Can You Increase Your Value?

Once you've got an idea about the experience, contacts, skills, and tools that make up your personal list of assets, begin to think about increasing the value of what you have. When you understand how truly precious you are, putting time, energy, and resources into that investment becomes second nature. It's an idea that seems foreign to many tradition-bound folks.

One day I received a call from a stockbroker who began the conversation by asking, "Ms. Winter, how would you like to get a higher yield on your investments?" When I told him that my only investments were my own businesses, he seemed aghast. "You work for yourself?" he said, with an audible shudder. "Isn't that scary?"

"Not at all," I said, "but giving my money to a stranger on the phone is terrifying."

When you are willing to invest in yourself and your ideas, you have put your money and time into the one thing that lasts a lifetime and can never be taken from you. Businessman and author Bob Conklin tells this story: "Twenty years ago, my wife and I evaluated all the ways we had spent and invested money. Stocks, cars, insurance, real estate, furniture, and all other major investments were scrutinized. Do you know what investment outdistanced others by an enormous percentage? Ourselves. Any investment in our growth or self-improvement had paid incredible returns. Books, courses, seminars, conventions —whatever the learning experience—had always returned far greater rewards than any other investment. The best investment in life is in your own self-development. It will pay off the greatest financial and emotional rewards."

Sometimes the hardest investment to make is one of time. Investing in yourself requires a reordering of your priorities so that your time is being spent in ways that truly support your goals. The way you invest your time can be a telling indication of how much you believe in yourself and your dreams.

Patty has talked about becoming a writer for as long as I can remember. She proudly points to years of personal journals she's filled. When she was invited to join a writers' group that had been organized to help the members sell their work, she suddenly became too busy with other projects. Being accountable for completing articles and books wasn't nearly as comfortable as imagining a dazzling writing career. The other members of the group have consistently sold their writing and are building solid careers. They've backed up their dreams with action and encouragement.

If you don't invest in yourself and what you truly want, be prepared, like Patty, to get less than you deserve. "It's no good running a pig farm badly for thirty years while saying 'Really I was meant to be a ballet dancer,'" says Quentin Crisp. "By that time, pigs will be your style."

What Are Your Financial Goals?

Another early step on the road to self-bossing is to determine your financial goals. It's a step that makes many people nervous. "Well, sure, I'd like to make a million bucks," is a familiar knee-jerk response, but it doesn't bear much resemblance to the process I'm talking about here.

It's not surprising that few know how to establish financial aims. Working for somebody else actually discourages us from having much control over the amount of money we receive. Settling for the money that someone offers to pay you limits your power to honestly decide your own goals.

As a self-bosser, you need to think about immediate financial goals as well as long-term desires. How much money do you need to live right now? Where are you spending money? Can you eliminate some of your current expenses? These are critical questions that must be answered before you begin.

Take a few minutes to review your current expenses. What are your monthly needs in each category?

- Rent/mortgage: _____

- Car/transportation: _____

- Living expenses including
  food: _____

telephone: _____

utilities: _____

- Insurance: _____

- Savings: _____

- Credit card payments: _____

- Education: _____

- Entertainment: _____

- Gifts: _____

- Clothes/wardrobe maintenance: _____

- Debt repayment: _____

Once you've determined your minimum monthly needs, you may surprise yourself to see that they're less than you thought. A student once called to tell me she had made an important financial discovery. "When I worked at a job I hated," she confessed, "I spent every weekend shopping, hoping I could buy something that would make me feel better. Now that I'm doing work that I love, it is so satisfying that I need far less money to support myself."

You'll be less intimidated by the lack of a predictable paycheck if you are clear about your priorities. Another student told me she began with a modest goal. She wanted to make enough money to meet her mortgage payment and have her monthly massage. Everything else was negotiable.

Once you know how much money you must earn every month, don't stop there. Set a second goal for the amount you'd like to earn every month. There should be a big gap between your first and second financial goals. Don't be afraid to think lavishly about your future. Keep in mind this tidbit from the Internal Revenue Service: 89 percent of all Americans earning more than $50,000 a year are self-employed.

How Can You Expand Your Options?

Back in college, I took a class called "Marriage and Mating Problems." You can tell from the title that it was a sociology class and, therefore, offered a scientific approach to the subject. I don't remember much about the class except for one statistic we were given which I found startling. The professor assured us that there were 250 suitable mates for each of us, any of whom would make a compatible partner. Being young and romantic, I doubted such scientific nonsense. I was certain that a single soulmate was destined for me and my job was to locate him as soon as possible.

Looking back, I wish I had explored this notion more aggressively. I missed a lot of fun by not trying to locate more of my potential partners. Believing that there's a single career that will make us happy is every bit as limiting as believing in an ideal mate. If we buy that notion (which has been fostered for decades by career counselors), it can lead to procrastination and frustration. "When will it show up?" we ask, before resuming our daydreams. This idea is a self-limiting stall tactic that keeps us from connecting with more possibilities.

Expanding your options demands a different approach. Rather than focusing on the precise form your work will take, concentrate first on discovering the essence of that work. Sanaya Roman and Duane Packer, authors of *Creating Money*, explain it this way: "The essence of something is the function you want it to perform, the purposes you will use it for, or what you think it will give you. Many things other than what you picture might give you the essence of what you want, so be open to letting it come in whatever way, size, shape or form is most appropriate."

This is a liberating concept. When you search for the essence of your work, you can feel as if you have a magic wand in your hand. Limitations disappear, doors open, unforeseen opportunities present themselves. I want the essence of everything I do to include humor, joy, and service. Knowing that I can find these qualities in countless ways and through multiple activities adds to my serenity. If something I've been doing stops being joyful, it's a signal for me to move on.

You can expand your options another way by taking one of your assets and seeing how many different formats you can create to use it. Jan Dean has parlayed her skill for organizing into several diverse ventures. Her first business, The Well-Organized Woman, taught others how to get their lives in order. She went on to teach classes on starting and organizing a home-based business. These evolved into the North Texas Home Business Conference, an annual event she arranged and produced. Jan recently completed an annotated bibliography of gardening books, a project that required her to organize huge amounts of research. While her focus has changed over the years, the common thread in all of her ventures is her natural ability to put things in organized order.

Assessing your assets is both a beginning step and an ongoing one. Annually, or even more often, take time to ask and answer the questions posed here. Your answers will change, of course, and your focus will strengthen. Keeping track of your tangible and intangible capital will prevent you from taking all that you have for granted. It will also show you how far you've come. That can make you very, very rich.

"Great opportunities come to all," said A. F. Dunning, "but many do not know they have met them. The only preparation to take advantage of them is simple fidelity to what each day brings." That starts with valuing every asset you possess.

Winning Ways for Uncovering Your Assets

Businessman and author Bob Conklin once wrote an article called "Find Five" in which he described a formula he had used to build several successful ventures. "If you would launch a new business, sell products, expand a noble purpose, achieve financial independence, found a religion or change an institution, then first, Find Five! Find five people who are dedicated to the same objectives as you."

Before you can do that, you must clarify your objectives. Use the Find Five principle to pull your plans together. Begin by Finding Five in each of these areas:

Things you are good at doing

1.

2.

3.

4.

5.

Positive personality traits you possess

1.

2.

3.

4.

5.

Tools you already own that can help you earn money

1.

2.

3.

4.

5.

Income goals for the next five years

1.

2.

3.

4.

5.

People you trust who support you

1.

2.

3.

4.

5.

Specific ways you are willing to invest in yourself

1.

2.

3.

4.

5.

Decisions you will need to make to get started

1.

2.

3.

4.

5.

Rewards you will give yourself

1.

2.

3.

4.

5.

Self-bossers you admire and can learn from

1.

2.

3.

4.

5.

Obstacles you will eliminate and/or manage

1.

2.

3.

4.

5.

CHAPTER 5

Overcoming the Obstacles

My life has been one long obstacle course with me as the
biggest obstacle.

Jack Paar

I wanted to be an actor," the elderly gentleman told me. I had
just finished conducting a backstage tour at the Guthrie Theater
when he stepped out of the crowd and approached me. The tour
had apparently brought back happy memories which he was
eager to share. I listened for several minutes and then asked,
"What did you do instead?"

His smile vanished and his eyes sought the floor. "I labored,"
he quietly mumbled.

I wanted to put my arms around him and say, "It's not too
late," but I knew he wouldn't believe me. Long ago he had
accepted a life without his dream.

Had I probed, I'm certain he would have explained that acting
wasn't a practical profession, that his family disapproved, or
would have given me whatever reason he had used to numb his
disappointment all these years. He brought to mind Oliver
Wendell Holmes's sad comment, "Alas for those who never sing
and die with all their music in them."

Make no mistake about it. To have a dream is to have obstacles. Yet many dreamers seem to treat impediments as a sign
from God saying, *"No!"* Obstacles may be signs from God, but

perhaps the message is misinterpreted. Tearing down barriers to our goals makes us stronger. Your proudest moments have undoubtedly been when you faced and overcame an obstacle in your path. You were victorious!

Obstacles can empower us, not diminish us, if we can view them in that light. Yet many people never even begin to pursue their goals because they fail to understand that problems and hindrances are a normal part of the process. Others are stopped by imagined obstacles—which can be every bit as powerful as the real thing.

"Why do you have to postpone moving to a warmer climate where you can swim all year until you are so old that you're afraid of the water?" asks psychologist David Viscott. "The worst thing one can do is not to try, to be aware of what one wants and not give in to it, to spend years in silent hurt wondering if something could have materialized—and never knowing." A life sentence of frustration is the inevitable result of avoiding the effort to conquer the obstacles we encounter.

Of course, there will be obstacles on your way to making a living without a job. Plenty of them, in fact. Arming yourself with strong self-esteem and a personal passion for achieving your goal will, happily, knock down some of the obstacles. Keeping your attention focused on your ultimate reward has a way of withering your stubborn opponents.

The difficulty for many newcomers is that the biggest hindrances to becoming joyfully jobless are so subtle and insidious that they may not be recognized and reckoned with. They may bear a strong resemblance to the proverbial wolf in sheep's clothing. You have to penetrate their clever disguises if you are to rout them.

Let's take a look at the most common obstacles faced by all of us who decide to declare our independence. While no single strategy will work in every situation, I'll offer suggestions for dealing with each of these barriers. The sooner you can move past them, the better.

You Get Erroneous Advice from People Whom You Care About

The decline of self-employment has had a profound impact on the consciousness of our society. False information and bad advice abound. Often those people who know the least about self-bossing are its most eager critics.

"How many of you were encouraged to be self-employed when you were growing up?" I ask my students. Two, sometimes three hands will go up. For the most part, we weren't raised in homes where entrepreneurship was understood or valued. Our teachers knew little about self-employment, either. Consequently, we have to fill a huge void in our thinking about working for ourselves.

Imagine how different things would be if you'd grown up in a home where self-bossing was honored. You might have memories like these: "My father and mother spent many of their evenings with Aunt Carrie and Uncle Al, my grandfather and other members of the clan, all of whom shared the interest and excitement of a new venture. Over the dinner table they discussed the events of the day, how one or the other had made a great sale, the weaknesses of the stock. While the store was growing up, so was I." That recollection comes from Stanley Marcus, who went on to become the president of his family's store, Neiman-Marcus. During his tenure, Marcus built the Dallas emporium into an international symbol of style and taste.

Marcus didn't learn just the nuts and bolts of running a business from his family. He learned the philosophy that was the guiding force behind the business, too. In an article in *Fortune* magazine, he explained his family's commitment: "It's beginning sprang from an enthusiasm that has never ceased. My father and his sister channeled every ounce of their considerable selves into four floors of beautiful merchandise. The reason is not that they lacked other interests. It's the other way around. They are exciting business people because they aren't business people at all. Herbert Marcus quotes Plato or Flaubert at you, displays a Canaletto in his dining room, and dreams of owning a Renoir; but his real creative self is released on Neiman-Marcus. It isn't a matter of just being 100% on the job, but rather of being dedicated to some austere and lofty mission."

Should you announce your intentions to make a living without a job, your family may not respond with the kind of enthusiasm you could expect from the Marcus clan. Rather, you might be greeted with something like, "Don't you know that practically all small businesses fail? Remember what happened to Uncle Ed when he got mixed up with that Amway business. He's still got a garage full of soap. You better stick with a real job and forget this nonsense."

Going in a new direction requires that we protect our dreams in their early, fragile stages. While the media might give the impression that our dreams are thwarted by gigantic forces outside ourselves, like the state of the economy, in reality the danger lies much closer at hand. "A man's enemies are the men of his own house," says the Old Testament prophet Micah. It's a warning that John Schroeder lives with every day.

When I first met John he worked as an editor and writer for a large corporation. He also suffered from depression, for which he took medication and received counseling. Quiet, seemingly antisocial, he spent most of his time alone. One day he approached me about a motivational publication I was editing and suggested he'd like to submit some articles. I was dubious, but told him to bring me his writing. Not only was he a terrific writer, he had a surprising sense of humor. On top of that, he was wildly eccentric, and we became fast friends.

Nine months or so after we met, John announced that he was quitting his job. "Have you thought about what you're going to do?" I inquired.

A great deal of thought had gone into his decision, I learned, as he rattled off his plans. "I've got my computer and think I could do desktop publishing," he began. "This company I've been working for uses a lot of freelance writers and since I know the business so well, I'm sure they'd have work for me. Then there's the novel I've started—I want to get that going. You know I love going to garage sales and flea markets. I'm always finding bargains that I resell at my own sales." It was an impressive list of ideas.

Within a few weeks, John's business, The Word Store, was born. In a way, so was John. Almost immediately, his problems with depression disappeared. He stopped taking medication and started looking healthier and happier than I'd ever seen him.

His business has had its share of ups and downs, but his optimism endures. In the five years that he's been self-employed, John has completed a wide range of writing projects, published his own newsletter, built a collection of antique radios, seen his first book published, and received a contract for his second.

Even with his successful track record, there's one difficulty John has not eliminated. My forty-year-old friend endures monthly lectures from his father that usually begin, "Aren't you about ready to get a real job?" Lesser men would have been daunted by these harangues. John offsets the negative advice in a simple way. He calls me to discuss the latest lecture and lets me reassure him that he's made the right decision.

One call was particularly memorable. "I got the lecture again," he reported.

I was becoming accustomed to these calls. "What was his argument this time?" I asked.

John sighed. "Now he thinks I should have health insurance."

"But you have health insurance," I reminded him. "Didn't you tell him that?"

"Yes, but he thinks I should have more."

"Look," I responded, feeling exasperated by this, "you used to have *more* insurance and then you were sick all the time. You've never even used your health insurance since you started your own business because now you're well."

John's experience may be extreme, but it is not unique. I hear variations of his story all the time. Another friend was working around the clock to get her fledgling enterprise up and running. In the midst of this, the man she'd been dating proposed—and demanded an immediate decision.

Far too often, the people who block our goals are those whom we expected to support and encourage us. But change, which can be frightening, may be even more fearful to the ones around you. If you change direction, if you go after your dreams, if you succeed, will you still love *them*? If your life becomes what you want it to be, will theirs look even more drab by comparison? Keep in mind that people who block you are saying more about themselves than they are about you.

If possible, treat their unsolicited advice as you would any other opinion that you don't share. Don't be taken in by it, but don't be defensive, either. Learning all you can about making a living without a job will help you turn a deaf ear to the naysayers—who may even turn out to be your biggest fans someday. Even if that never happens, you can treat this as another opportunity to build character, which it is.

The psychologist Carl Jung said that nothing affects our children as profoundly as the unlived lives of their parents. It's too late to change the conversation around your childhood dinner table, but there's still time to let your own kids grow up with the example of a joyful self-bosser at their table. Sharing your own discoveries about self-employment will empower you and them.

You're Afraid to Try Something You've Never Done

My neighbor Joanne had been making major changes in her life, but when she invited me to see a videotape of her first skydive, I was awed. I felt my stomach grow queasy as I watched her move to the door of the plane. "How did you ever get the courage to do this?" I asked.

"I was scared to death," she admitted, "but I watched a video of other people jumping and I noticed that they all looked so happy."

I'm not an expert on fear, nor am I fearless, but Joanne's experience reminded me of an important lesson in meeting fear head-on. For a long time, I believed that people who had exciting and adventurous lives (the sort I only dreamed of) did so because they were blessed with fearlessness. What a relief it was to learn that people who do great things often do so accompanied by fear. Like Joanne, you don't have to wait for your fear to go away in order to act.

Once when my daughter and I were having an argument about a plan she had, she concluded the conversation by saying, "Mom, I intend to spend my life going in the direction of my dreams, not in the direction of my fears." What Jennie already understands is that every new dream arrives with a new set of fears in hand. Whether it's fear of failure, fear of success, fear of the unknown, or fear of looking silly, to live fully brings daily opportunities to confront this emotion.

Living without a job brings up nearly every fear you can imagine—along with several you probably haven't even thought of yet. If you believe that feeling afraid isn't appropriate for an adult, your fear-management skills will be impaired. You have to face it to deal with it. On the other hand, if you accept fear as a natural response to a new situation, you'll be able to act in spite of its annoying presence. That's what living with courage demands.

In an interview with Cher, Barbara Walters asked her, "Are you ever afraid of anything?" The outrageous entertainer considered the question for a moment and admitted that she was. "I'm afraid," she said, "that I won't live as well as I know how." That's the kind of fear that is a catalyst, not a deterrent. Being determined to live as well as you know how also takes away the power of many fears. It's certainly a shift toward understanding that fear can be a useful emotion.

If the idea of making a living without a job doesn't make you feel a bit fearful, check your pulse. Taking on the unknown is bound to create anxiety. Acknowledge that you are feeling fear. Don't push it away by telling yourself, "I don't know what I was thinking. What a stupid idea that was. It wouldn't work anyway." Too often we confuse fear with bad ideas! It's far healthier to accept that you are feeling fearful about a new plan—and determine that you'll act anyway.

When you feel stuck or paralyzed by fear, you can manage that, too. Try to pinpoint exactly what is making you feel so frightened. Are you afraid to fail? To strike out because you can't do something perfectly? Are you putting too much stock in what others will say? Do you think you might be foolish? Is what's happening life-threatening? If not, stop and give yourself positive reasons for doing what's scary. Write out a list, if necessary, of the rewards that wait for you if you do go ahead. Dangle whatever carrot you need to pull you through this.

Maybe you just haven't prepared yourself as well as you need to or thought your idea through completely. An entrepreneurial friend can be a big help here. Talking it over can bring clarity and serenity.

Make friends with your fears. Let that little twinge in your stomach summon you forward, not stop you dead in your tracks. Remember that life shrinks or expands in proportion to your courage. Fear is your signal that you've opted to grow, to go beyond where you've been. If you never feel fear, you end up with the booby prize.

You Don't Believe You Can Make Money by Having Fun

Until you discover your passion, it will be difficult, impossible even, to make your living without a job. As I've said before, you must be excited, crazy about what you're doing. Having given thoughtful attention to this important subject, you'll have another problem to confront.

We've all been raised on those starving artist stories. Those tales have served to support a well-accepted myth: love and money can't go hand in hand. Believing this becomes, in turn, a powerful self-fulfilling prophecy. How many people do you know who claim that they put up with a boring job so that they can afford to have fun on the weekend doing what they really enjoy?

It can be very hard to accept that having fun can be profitable, too. If you get in touch with your passion, it's inevitable that people will start paying you to have fun. For one thing, you're bound to be very good at what you do if you really love it.

Think about something that you love to do. Can you think of anyone who does that thing and makes money doing it?

Once I was being interviewed by an incredibly obnoxious radio reporter who oozed cynicism. At the mention of doing what you love, he said, "Yeah, sure, I'm crazy about playing tennis. But I've got car payments to make." I was polite enough not to point out that John McEnroe probably drives a nicer car and doesn't make payments.

Warren Beatty was asked to give his personal definition of success. Without pausing, he replied, "Success is when you don't know if you're working or you're playing." Challenge any worn-out assumptions you may have about receiving money. Then make up your mind that it's okay to enjoy your work.

A great motto to adopt comes from *Moneylove* author Jerry

Gillies. "Anything worth having is worth having fun getting," he asserts. You may have to murder your puritan work ethic to bury this obstacle.

Your Ego Is in the Way

One of the most memorable students I've ever had was a handsome young man named Mark. He showed up in my class one night on the verge of tears. After class, he told me about his plight. It seems Mark had worked his way through college running a business blacktopping driveways. During the summer, his business kept him busy and brought in enough money to cover his living expenses and tuition the rest of the year. When he graduated from college, his parents were adamant about Mark's future. He would enter corporate America and work his way up the white-collar ladder. Mark complied, but after two years as a corporate accountant, longed to leave. He wanted to be working outdoors, running his own business. He wanted to blacktop driveways again. His parents were furious. How could their son possibly want to turn in his white collar for a blue one?

It's a familiar story, one born out of a false belief that there is good work and there is bad work. This has led to a class distinction in our attitude about work. Sadly, it keeps us stuck in ways we might not realize.

"The single greatest obstacle the people we studied encountered in attempting to find work they enjoyed," says psychologist Srully Blotnick, "was their own snobbery. They didn't prop a pinky in the air when they drank a martini, but they were monumental snobs nonetheless. For they viewed almost every other kind of work—except the one they were presently doing—as beneath them."

Let me remind you again that there is nothing noble or admirable about doing work that you despise, no matter how prestigious you may think that work is. Any work that makes you happy is good work. Period.

"Most of the shadows of this life," observed Ralph Waldo Emerson, "are caused by our standing in our own sunshine." Challenging your ego may be necessary in order to let the light in again.

You Have Too Much Money or Current Comfort

I have come to expect snickers when I mention that having too much money can be a tremendous obstacle to becoming joyfully jobless. "You've got to be kidding, lady," is written all over my students' faces.

Don't get me wrong. I do not believe that poverty is a virtue. I think money is lovely stuff and I want you to have pots of it . . . pots that you've earned without a job. You do not need a lot of it, however, to *begin*. In fact, if you have a fortune at your disposal, put it away someplace. It's a handicap that you needn't impose on yourself.

Paul Hawken verifies an observation that I made years ago: too much money is worse than too little. "I disagree with the old saw that the major problem afflicting small businesses is a lack of capital," writes Hawken in *Growing a Business*. "The major problem affecting businesses, large and small, is lack of imagination. A ready supply of too much money in start-ups tends to replace creativity." If you are highly capitalized, your natural response at the first sign of a problem may be to throw money at it. Without learning to creatively solve problems, your nest egg—and you— will soon be exhausted.

It's not just large sums of money that become a hurdle. Your current salary, financial responsibilities, and fixed-income mentality may be modest, but you've become dependent on them. "Okay, so my job's a bore and I'm not exactly living in my dream house," goes the reasoning, "but it could be worse."

This argument always brings to my mind those anguishing tales of women who are victims of spousal abuse, who refuse to leave their tormentor. You have to be willing to get out of your familiar misery. Unless you are living the life of your dreams, staying stuck in a situation that is less than you deserve is a hideous form of self-sabotage. Like other forms of dysfunctional behavior, not leaving is accompanied by denial. "At least I know what's expected of me in this company," you sigh, and before you know it another year has passed and all you have to show for it is that you're a year older. Or a year closer to retirement, as the exhausted like to point out.

The only sensible way to deal with this obstacle is to get the facts. Letting go of situations that have outlived their usefulness may be easier after you've armed yourself with the ideas and pragmatic suggestions still to come in this book.

You're Stopped by Not Knowing How

Starting out in a new direction requires that we begin with a new vision. Every new vision, in turn, is accompanied by solving new problems, learning new things. If you accept that as the necessary process involved in achieving goals, you become bold and honest about what those goals are.

Far too often, however, I see people short-circuit their success by prematurely imposing a three-letter word on their dreams. That word is "how," and it's the most powerful dream-basher invented.

Let's say you're driving down the freeway, humming along with the radio, when you get a great idea for making a living without a job. You almost jump in your seat, it's such a good one. Just as fast, a familiar voice in your head speaks up and says, "*How* on earth do you think you could ever do that?" Before you've gone another mile, your inner doubting Thomas has bashed the idea to smithereens.

In order to manage this nasty obstacle, there's a technique you can use whenever your ideas are being challenged by a "*How* are you going to do that?" from yourself or others. Discipline is required here, but after a few practice sessions, you'll find it easier to do. Whenever you hear the "how" question, respond by refocusing your attention on "what." It's a method employed by most successful goal-achievers. Thomas Watson and Joyce Hall knew *what* they wanted to do: help people communicate better. They accomplished that by not giving much thought at first to how they were going to do it. Better communication was their obsession. Eventually, each of them found a way to do that. Watson founded IBM; Hall started the company we now know as Hallmark Cards. If you can keep bringing your attention back to what it is you want to do (for example, I want to live in a log house in Vermont and be joyfully jobless), finding out how you can accomplish that becomes easier. A woman in Connecticut left my class determined to do something she'd dreamed of since the sixth grade—travel to Nepal. As she kept her attention on what she wanted, she realized that she had just what she needed to achieve this dream. She quit her job with an insurance company and put her energy into making jewelry, a longtime hobby. Not only did this give her a new income source, she had a portable business which funded her travels as she went. A subscriber once sent me a sign that read, "Obstacles are what you see when you take your eyes off the goal." Your dreams do not need to be defended by plans about how they will be accomplished—especially not at first. You do, however, have to protect them by focusing on what those dreams are.

I am willing to bet that this is a technique you have already used to banish a dream-basher and manifest a dream. Haven't you wanted something badly, something that seemed out of reach? Because you believed there was no obvious way to get it, you let go of any thoughts about how it could happen, but you didn't stop dreaming about the thing you wanted. You ran the dream over and over in your head. And one day it arrived—and probably in an unexpected way. If you trust yourself enough, you will see that you can repeat this for anything and everything you desire.

As I was setting my goals for 1988, I wrote down several new ventures I planned to start. After daydreaming for a few minutes about the other things I wanted that year, I boldly wrote, "This year I am going to London—and it will be a gift." For years I had longed to go back to my favorite city, but failed to make it happen. I still don't know why I added the part about it being a gift, but there it was. I began doing affirmations about the goal. "I am going to London this year and it will be a gift," I'd repeat it when driving in my car or waiting for the dentist. Once I had this thought firmly in my mind, it led me to begin taking action. While I was musing about this dream one day, I thought, "What if someone asks you to elope? What if he wants to go to London? You'll have to say, 'I'm sorry. I can't go. I don't have a current passport.'" That amused me, but it also motivated me to apply immediately for my passport. When it arrived, I put it on top of my dresser so that it was the first thing I saw when I got up every morning. Believing in your dreams demands that you are prepared to receive them.

I purchased several guidebooks, ordered pamphlets from the British Tourist Authority, and spent free evenings planning my forthcoming journey. Every contest that I saw that offered a trip to London was entered several times. And I kept up the affirmations.

After several months of working on this, no trip was on the horizon. I refused to be dissuaded. When I set up my fall classes, I left the week of my birthday in October open, thinking, "Maybe I'll get this as a birthday present." My birthday came and went. I celebrated it in Minneapolis.

Two and a half weeks after my birthday, I got a call from my friend Jill. We hadn't chatted for a while so we began filling each other in about our recent events. All of a sudden Jill said, "There's something I've been meaning to ask you, but keep forgetting. Do you still want to go to London?"

"Of course," I laughed. "I *always* want to go there."

"Okay," she said. "As a matter of fact I have a ticket that I am not able to use. I'd like to give it to you."

I was momentarily speechless. I looked at the clock and said, "Jill, it's three o'clock on an ordinary Friday afternoon and you've just made one of my biggest goals manifest."

Had I spent the previous ten months agonizing over "how" this trip was going to happen, I'd still be wondering. I'd have lost my faith that such a thing was possible. Instead, I stayed totally focused on the ultimate result and the "how" took care of itself.

When I hear that word getting in my way of any dream, I caution myself that I have encountered a dream-basher and reverse my attention back to the goal. Of course, there comes a time for making practical plans, for implementing how you will accomplish a goal. However, it can't and shouldn't be your first consideration.

Dreams and plans and projects need time to gather strength. That's the purpose of daydreaming. Be careful not to abort your intentions by robbing them of the private mental time they deserve. Or by asking "how."

Winning Ways for Overcoming Obstacles

Review the following list of common obstacles encountered in the early stages of making a living without a job.

- You Get Erroneous Advice from People Whom You Care About
- You're Afraid to Try Something You've Never Done
- You Don't Believe You Can Make Money by Having Fun
- Your Ego Is in the Way
- You Have Too Much Money or Current Comfort
- You're Stopped by Not Knowing How

Recognizing an obstacle is the first step to overcoming it. Which of the above is an obstacle for you? Circle the two biggest barriers you must contend with before you can succeed.

Which of the following approaches might you adopt in dealing with your personal obstacles? Check the ones that appeal to you.

___ If I just ignore it, it's bound to go away.

___ I prefer to weaken obstacles by building bigger success.

___ I'll have to check with my therapist first.

___ Every obstacle can be overcome with determination.

___ I don't have time for this nonsense.

___ Every time I conquer an obstacle, I conquer myself.

___ I hope my friends never find out that my life isn't perfect. They think I do everything easily.

___ Is this some kind of karmic punishment or something?

___ This is not an appropriate subject for an adult.

___ Everything and everyone has a price. I just get out my checkbook and handle it.

___ Oh, so this is the adventure you were talking about.

___ To be honest, I get a lot more attention by not handling my problems.

___ I've tried in the past, but I failed.

___ If you had the obstacles I've got, you'd give up, too.

___ It's a lot easier just to stay put.

___ I'm uncomfortable confronting someone who's in my way.

___ The obstacles look big, but not insurmountable.

Believe it or not, I've seen people use every one of the approaches listed above. A few of them are my own personal pets. The only approach that works, however, is the one that comes from being determined to move beyond what's standing in your way. Hiding from it or ignoring it is ineffective.

A proactive approach will have you handling and managing obstacles like a professional. Here's a strategy you can use to get things rolling:

1. Identify the exact thing, person, attitude that's standing in your way. What is the covert benefit that you're getting by letting it stand in your way?
2. Imagine that this obstacle has been removed. How would your life be different?
3. List three actions you can take to begin removing the barrier.
4. Give yourself a deadline for completing those steps.
5. Assess your progress. Have you eliminated the obstacle or is there more to be done?
6. If the obstacle remains, take three more active steps to remove it. Repeat steps 5 and 6 until you've overcome the obstacle to your satisfaction.

CHAPTER 6

Taking Care of the Boss

The greatest goal in life is not the attainment of fame. The principal thing in this world is to keep one's soul aloft.

Gustave Flaubert

In order to live free and happily," warns Richard Bach, "you must sacrifice boredom. It is not always an easy sacrifice."

In order to live without a job, you must sacrifice not only boredom but stress, time clocks, regular paychecks, strained relationships, rush-hour traffic, annoying coworkers, bosses, repetitive work, imposed vacations, low expectations, office power trips, company rules, and predictability. I know, it's not always an easy sacrifice.

Early one afternoon, I received a panicky phone call from Karla, a fledgling self-bosser. She sounded distraught and I wondered whether she had lost a big client or overdrawn her checking account. "What's the matter?" I asked, expecting the worst.

"I don't have anything to do," she wailed.

"You mean you have no business?" I asked.

"I have plenty of business, but my work is all done and it's only one o'clock!"

I breathed a sigh of relief. "That's terrific," I assured her. "Why don't you go for a walk around the lake?"

"In the middle of the day?" She sounded incredulous.

"Of course," I said. "You don't have to work just to fill up your time anymore. Go to the toy store and buy yourself a present. Read a book. Surprise David with a cake. You can do anything you want."

Managing your freedom can be challenging at first. Almost at once, you see that living without a job is nothing like living with one. Some of the changes that occur will be subtle, while others will be profound. Before long the line between work and play begins to blur. Your life begins to feel as if it's all one piece, not little compartments labeled "Work," "Family," "Friends."

You start looking for less stressful ways of living. You won't participate in old rituals like driving in rush-hour traffic or shopping on crowded weekends. You can bank on Wednesday, if you're feeling frisky. You'll delight in doing things outside the mainstream. You'll realize how much time used to be consumed standing in line, commuting, and sitting in long, drawn-out meetings.

Now that you have time to notice, you'll discover small pleasures that escaped your attention before. Things you never gave a thought to will affirm your decision to succeed. My friend John calls to giggle about not having to drive to work whenever there's a blizzard or ice storm here in Minnesota. We agree that's a lovely benefit of living without a job.

Your vocabulary will begin to change, too. You'll stop using words like "supervisor," "memos," "performance reviews," and "bureaucracy." You'll forget how to spell "résumé." These words will seem obsolete.

Yes, there will be times when you feel unabashedly smug about your new life. It might happen when your doctor announces your blood pressure has gone down or when you're sitting at your daughter's afternoon school play. Or perhaps the big moment will come when you pick up the Sunday paper and see a bargain fare to Paris that's only good for two more weeks—and you have the time and the money to go on the spur of the moment. Better yet, you didn't have to ask for permission. This is like being an adult!

Getting Healthier

Northwestern National Life Insurance recently concluded a two-year study on the effect of stress in the workplace. Their findings were more disgruntling than you may imagine. According to the study, a whopping 72 percent of American workers experience frequent stress-related physical and mental conditions that are directly related to their jobs. Think about it: nearly three-fourths of all employees are getting sick from their jobs and we hardly bat an eye. Some companies, of course, respond to the problem by offering stress management classes to help their workers cope. What about stress elimination? That's a thought that few are willing to consider. Instead, the message seems to be, "Just grit your teeth and bear it. We've got to get this work done!"

Not all of us are willing to sell our health for a paycheck, thank goodness. Our growing attention to physical, emotional, and spiritual wellness has made personal health a priority with many. That awareness has led us to exercise more and to eat differently. With that desire to live a healthier life, leaving a stressful workplace may be part of our personal wellness program.

Taking good care of the boss takes on new meaning when you're in charge. "I've found that most people who have their own little businesses seem to run a little harder, stay a little thinner, drink and smoke less," observes writer Peter Weaver. "In general, most self-bossers tend to take care of themselves. Maybe it's because they realize that they are the most important asset on their company's books. They want to protect their investment. Then, maybe it's because they're happier with life and don't feel the need to overindulge as a means of escape."

My friend Charlie has always loved working out. He'd head straight for the gym in the evening and on weekends. The price he paid for his pumped-up physique was forgoing any other social life. When Charlie lost his job as a sales rep, he started a window-washing business. For the first time in his life, he says, he gets up excited about going to work. But Charlie found another bonus in living without a job. He now has time to work out in the afternoon and see friends in the evening. His life has taken on a balance that it didn't have before.

Being happy with your work is important to your health. Last fall I attended the 100th birthday party of my great-uncle Phil Hauge. This delightful centenarian has spent his life running his own bank. He's done it so well that a few years back *Money* magazine named it one of the best-managed banks in the country. Despite his loss of hearing, Uncle Phil continues to work happily at his bank. He's active, living proof of a finding by *Longevity* magazine that cites self-employment as an important factor in living to be 100. So not only can you expect to be healthier without a job, you might just live a great deal longer, too.

Finding Your Rhythm

I've yet to meet anyone who says, "I'm really at my best from nine to five." While it may be necessary for large companies to structure the day along those lines, when you're in charge of managing your time you'll probably do it quite differently. Your own personal rhythms will determine your schedule. As you map out your personal peaks and valleys, your activities will become appropriate to your energy levels.

Maybe you're a person who wakes up ready to take on the world. By noon you've accomplished more than you used to do in two days working for somebody else. After lunch, your energy level drops, so you might spend time running errands, taking a leisurely walk, or going through the mail. By this time, your kids are home from school, so you spend time catching up on their day. After a relaxing dinner with your family, you get a second wind so you head back to your office until bedtime.

If you're a nocturnal creature, your schedule would be entirely different. Or you may discover that you enjoy long periods of concentrated work followed by equally long periods of leisure. Maybe you thrive on diversity and set up your week so that no two days are quite the same. Finding your rhythm may take a while. You'll need to experiment with different ways of working to see how you feel the most productive, the most balanced. Your personal priorities and goals will replace time clocks and imposed vacations.

Life without a predetermined structure can take some adjustment, of course. You'll be wondering whether you're wasting time, whether you're working on the most important project, whether you deserve a month on the beach. Those concerns will disappear as you become more confident and free. Your need for structure will eventually disappear, too.

Consider what novelist Tom Robbins has to say about that: "The level of structure that people seek," he asserts, "is in direct ratio to the amount of chaos they have inside." Living without a job is going to bring your serenity back. One day you'll wake up and find that your life does not have structure anymore. It has rhythm. Just hum along.

Changing Relationships

All of the changes you make when you no longer have a job will have an impact on your relationships with other people. While most of these changes will be welcome, some of them may cause you to feel sadness. When you first go out on your own, you may miss your former coworkers. You'll vow to get together and, for a time, you will. Eventually you'll find that you have less and less in common. Office politics will not seem an appropriate topic of conversation anymore. Your old friends, alas, may seem petty.

Not to worry. There's a new cast of characters about to enter your life. These folks will be living without a job, too. You'll find yourself in delightful conversations during long evenings spent talking about ideas and dreams. They'll boost your confidence and caution you about their own mistakes. You'll wonder why it took so long to find these energetic and encouraging folks.

If you are married, your relationship with your spouse and children will change, perhaps dramatically. Now that your work makes you smile, makes you feel creative, makes it possible for you to pay attention to them, you'll become their ally, not their enemy.

One of the positive things that happens in families of self-bossers is that they start setting goals together. Getting everyone enrolled in decision-making and goal-setting can add a dimension to your relationships that was unknown. Sacrifices will be made more willingly when everyone is working for a better life. Your kids will have an opportunity to grow up in a well-functioning family where healthy attitudes about work—and each other—are the norm.

Meeting Self-Bossers

My doctor owns her own clinic, my lawyer her own practice. The woman who does my taxes understands small business, because she has one. When I visit Connecticut, Chris Utterback and I have a circuit of bookstores, consignment shops, and antiques shops that we visit, each as unique as its owner. These visits often turn into spontaneous brainstorming sessions.

Finding and patronizing other small businesses is a part of your homework that's both fun and enlightening. As long as you don't plan to open a copycat business next door, most entrepreneurs will welcome you to the fold, offer encouragement, and share their experiences. Become an eager student. On your visits, collect brochures and business cards. Look at ads with a learner's curiosity.

Of course, you'll meet self-bossers in other places besides shops and offices. Seminars, conferences, trade shows, and networking groups offer fertile opportunities for connecting. You will learn more, however, by tracking down self-bossers in their own environment and watching them in action. How do they talk to customers? Answer their telephone? Talk about their merchandise?

Many of these folks are living their dream. That's not bad company to learn from.

Inspiring Yourself

Writer Christopher Morley said, "Read something every day that no one else is reading. Think something no one else is thinking. It is bad for the mind to be always a part of unanimity." Living without a job will, of course, immediately remove you from unanimity. If you are to grow and prosper on this path less taken, allowing yourself to be inspired by books and the lives of other people is essential.

All of us respond to different things at different times in our personal journey. I remember the first time I attempted to read Napoleon Hill's classic, *Think and Grow Rich*. It could have been written in Egyptian. A year later, when I had begun my entrepreneurial apprenticeship, the book sprang to life for me.

"How many a man has dated a new era in his life from the reading of a book," wrote Thoreau. "The book exists for us perchance which will explain our miracles and reveal new ones." There is no more accessible way to inspire the boss than to spend time daily with books that open the window of ideas. While reading for information is valuable, too, it needs to be balanced with reading that stretches and prods and encourages.

A student called from the East Coast to tell me about her brand-new business, which had taken off like a rocket. It was growing so fast, she could hardly catch her breath. There was something missing in her life, she said. "I have no role models. I don't know anyone here in Providence who is joyfully jobless. How can I find someone?"

"Go to your bookstore," I urged. "You'll meet another self-bosser or two before long, simply because you're out there doing interesting things. But you don't have to wait to connect with someone. Start reading about people who inspire you. You'll learn so much, so quickly." I told her about several of my favorites; Helena Rubinstein and Weight Watchers founder Jean Nidetch were early sources of inspiration. Current favorites include Anita Roddick of The Body Shop, Paul Hawken, and poet May Sarton. "You can learn and be inspired by people who are doing completely different things than you're doing," I told her. "Every one of them overcame obstacles, refused to give up on their dream, and has a story to share. For less than twenty dollars, you can hang out with them, sit at their feet, if you like." She agreed to begin there and I knew her business was in good hands. The boss was willing to be inspired.

I'm always surprised to meet people who resist any sort of inspiration. Sometimes their cynicism makes it impossible for any positive thought to penetrate. Don't they know how good it feels, I wonder, to go past limiting thoughts?

Once reading for inspiration becomes a habit, you'll start meeting people who are inspiring, too. Sometimes it's their positive approach, their natural tendency to encourage others that makes them irresistible. At other times, their determination to shape a better life makes them powerfully inspiring. My students frequently perform that function for me, affirming my belief that humans are wondrous creatures.

Let me tell you about one of the inspiring people who crossed my path, someone I never would have planned to know. I picked the letters out of my mailbox one day and noticed one with an unfamiliar return address. Opening it, I noticed that it was impeccably typewritten. It began, "I read about your class in the Open U catalog and I would very much like to take it. I have a problem doing that, however, as I am in prison. Would you consider coming here to teach me or do you have any information I could get from you?" I answered the letter and told the writer, a man named Ed Poindexter, that I had no materials from my class, but that I published a newsletter. I assumed that would be the end of it.

A few days later, another perfectly typed letter arrived, with a check for his subscription enclosed. Jennie was with me and said, "Don't prisoners make about a dollar a day?" I said I didn't know, but thought that was about right. Why was she asking? "Well, Mom, I think your newsletter is terrific, but I don't think I'd work a whole month to buy it."

She had a point, but we didn't realize we were not dealing with an ordinary person. Ed and I began an irregular correspondence. He would write with questions about mail order or some other business idea. Once in a while he would call with other carefully thought-out queries. During one conversation I asked him if he wasn't unusual. I had never, as far as I could recall, heard about building a business from prison—at least not a legitimate one. He seemed surprised by the question and modestly admitted that he was unique. He was also determined. "When I get out of here," he said, "I have to be able to be self-employed."

Despite limited resources, Ed isn't waiting to get things rolling. A couple of years ago, he self-published a book and sold several thousand copies. He's decided to spend his post-prison days deterring kids from a life of crime. Ed is planning seminars and talks that he wants to deliver through public schools. After I sent him a book on becoming a professional speaker, he wrote to say that as he was reading it, he came up with a perfect name for his program. Now he's creating more products to sell and he's recorded an album of rap songs. When I returned from a recent trip, Jennie called and told me to look on page twenty-six of our weekly entertainment paper. Under "New Local Artists" was a listing for Ed Poindexter—The Jammer from the Slammer. Jennie and I let out a cheer.

Ed inspires me often. Every time I talk to someone who is loaded with excuses and reasons for not moving ahead, I think of Ed. He's got the most valid reason of all for not trying, but you'd never know it. I've never heard him complain. What might Ed do, I wonder, if he had the opportunities and resources that you and I have to work with? Now isn't that an inspiring thought?

Getting to know the Ed Poindexters is as much a part of caring for the boss as learning to manage your time and health. The way you spend your days ultimately determines how well you live, as well as the quality of your business. Learning to be the boss is easier when you value and care for the person you've put in charge. Treat yours well.

Winning Ways for Taking Care of the Boss

• For the next several days, pay close attention to your personal rhythms. (If you are working at a conventional job, do this exercise on your days off.) When do you feel the most energetic? Most creative? How does exercise affect your energy levels? What about diet? Sleep? The people you are with? Note peaks and valleys.

• Using this information, how might you organize a working day? What kinds of activities would best suit your different rhythms?

• How would you rate your own time management skills? Have you read a book or taken a seminar to gain mastery in this area? Using time well is basic to successful self-bossing. It is a skill that can be learned, fortunately. How can you make every minute count?

• Initiate a conversation with an entrepreneur. Visit a small business and informally ask questions of the owner about that business. What makes the business special? What makes it attractive to others? What needs improvement? Be a detached observer and see what you learn.

• If you have a family, or live with someone, make a point of starting a dinner-table conversation that includes setting a small, mutually agreed-upon goal. Maybe you could plan a family garage sale or plant a vegetable garden. Spend the meal brainstorming ideas about achieving the goal together. Who will be responsible for which parts of the goal? How will you share the rewards? Celebrate the achievement? Doing this regularly can have positive benefits for everyone concerned.

• Set daily goals for increasing your mental, physical, and spiritual well-being. What action can you take, what can you incorporate into your daily schedule to increase your wellness? Can you set aside time for each of these areas and focus on that for, say, twenty minutes? How about ten minutes?

• Who is the most inspiring person you have ever met? What is the most inspiring book you've read? When do you feel most inspired and alive? How can you expand on that? This month, read one book purely for its inspirational value and quietly contemplate its message.

PART III

Exploring Your Options

An open mind collects more riches than an open purse.

Will Henry

CHAPTER 7

Creating Multiple Profit Centers

Capacities clamor to be used, and cease their clamor only when they are well used.

Abraham Maslow

After a story about my seminars appeared in the Lincoln, Nebraska, newspaper, a young man named Ken Hoppmann called. Was I scheduled to hold any seminars in Lincoln, he wondered. I told him I had no such plans, but suggested he could order an audiotape of the seminar, if he wanted the information.

A few days later, Ken called back with an idea. He belonged to a local association of home-based business owners and thought he might persuade them to sponsor a seminar, if I was interested. I was impressed with his initiative and assured him I'd love to work with his group. Within weeks, the seminars were organized with the backing of the home business group and a community college in Lincoln.

Over the next several months, Ken and I had several conversations to work out the details. When we had first talked, Ken had told me he had a business matching up college students with scholarship funds. Not until our third or fourth chat did he mention he was also a classical pianist with an abiding passion for Mozart. In addition to his scholarship service, Ken also taught at a local college, gave private piano lessons, and was the assistant organist at a church. His enthusiasm for new ideas was completely contagious and I looked forward to talking to him.

Every conversation with Ken turned into an impromptu brainstorming session. He had considered starting a newsletter for Mozart lovers and also wondered how he might put together a tour to Austria to visit places where Mozart lived and worked. "Have you been there before?" I asked. Ken assured me that he had and was going again the following summer—flying on a ticket he had bartered for piano lessons!

Last year, Ken got married and decided to finish his doctoral degree in music. Consequently, his schedule and activities have changed somewhat. He's a full-time student, teaching assistant, and piano teacher with thirty-two students. He's also working on his next big venture, Home Concerts, a booking agency which will arrange concerts in private homes with classical musicians from around the country. Ken got that idea after he was invited to perform at someone's home and found the experience wonderful for both performer and audience.

The last time I talked to him, I asked him about another series of concerts he'd been planning. "Oh, that didn't work out," he said.

"Isn't it terrific to have a lot of ideas?" I responded. "If one doesn't come together you just go on to the next one."

Ken laughed and agreed that that was precisely how he worked. Change, flexibility, and a stockpile of untried ideas keep him from bogging down.

What Ken has discovered—and shares with successful self-bossers everywhere—is the key to making a living without a job. That key is to develop and expand what I call Multiple Profit Centers. Rather than thinking in terms of having a single source of income (as we are trained to do when we see our income tied to a job), the savvy entrepreneur thinks about developing several income sources. With planning—and an openness to additional opportunities as they come along—you can create as many income streams as you desire. In time, you could be managing a great many enterprises, each earning a profit for you. I don't know what the record is for MPCs, but British entrepreneur Richard Branson, the Virgin Airlines founder, oversees more than 150 small enterprises (with help, of course) and keeps inventing new projects all the time.

Multiple Advantages

London Business School professor Charles Handy is another advocate of developing multiple income sources. "Think of it this way," he advises. "You will have a portfolio of work like an architect has, or like your stock portfolio. No prudent investor puts all his savings into one stock, and no sensible business goes after only one customer. Yet that's what you've been doing with your work and talent all these years. . . . Now is your chance to go 'portfolio': to diversify your interests and do some things for money, some because they interest you, some out of love or kindness, and some for the sheer hell of it. And, moreover, it's your chance to flex your portfolio to leave you time for all those other things—for travel, for discovery, for golf, for dining."

Besides the synergy that's created from doing different kinds of work that engage different skills and talents, there's a highly practical side to thinking in terms of building MPCs. You already know that every business, no matter how large or small, goes through cycles. There are times when sales soar; then they taper off, hit a low, and begin to climb again. No business is immune from this phenomenon, but not all of them manage cycles equally well. Those that weather the times when cash flow drops usually do so in one of two ways: they either generate enough income during the peaks to carry them through or they add products or create additional divisions of the business, expanding the number of income-producing sources.

As a one-person operation, keep these two patterns in mind. In your start-up stages, having several projects, each with its own cycle, can be your insurance policy for staying afloat. As one profit center slows down, another will pick up the slack. Keeping your cash flow stabilized this way is easier than you may think.

Plates That Spin

Chase Revel, the founder of *Entrepreneur* magazine, has pointed out that it's easier to earn $1,000 a month from ten little businesses than it is to earn $10,000 a month from one big one.

I think of creating profit centers as being akin to what a juggler does who spins plates on top of sticks. The juggler walks out on the stage with ten sticks and ten plates, but doesn't begin spinning them all at once. Methodically, the juggler positions the first plate on a stick and gets it into motion. Once done, the juggler moves on to the next, then the next, and so forth. Eventually, all ten of the plates are spinning away, each with its own momentum.

Your success can be created in a similar fashion. You can't produce a lineup of profit centers in a single effort. Follow the juggler's example. Take your first idea, get it started, stay with it until it develops its own momentum, then go on to your next idea, and so on. And, yes, some of your plates will fall on the floor and shatter. Do what the juggler does—pick up another plate and start spinning!

Different Styles

While a single passion may spawn several profit centers that revolve around a central theme, many entrepreneurs delight in creating MPCs that are completely unrelated. A variety of designs are possible. Let's look at a couple of ways that it's been done.

A central theme operates throughout Caprilands Herb Farm, a fascinating model of MPCs in action. Since it was purchased by Adelma Simmons and her parents in 1929, the eighteenth-century farmhouse surrounded by fifty acres of fields and woods in Coventry, Connecticut, has been the centerpiece of an evolving enterprise devoted to the cultivation and use of herbs.

It all came about because of Mrs. Simmons's personal passion for all things herbal. "That's how this all began," she says. "Teaching people about herbs is my real interest." Today, sixty-plus years after acquiring Caprilands, she oversees a thriving business that attracts thousands of visitors every year. While Caprilands remains the private home of its founder, her devotion to sharing the magic and mystery of herbs inspired her to open it to the public.

Upon arriving at Caprilands, guests check in at the small shed that serves as a bookshop. If they have come for the lecture and luncheon—a popular daily event—their names are checked off the reservations list. On most days, Mrs. Simmons greets her guests in the bookshop and autographs copies of her books as they are purchased. The shop offers books on gardening, in addition to those written by Mrs. Simmons.

From there it's on to the barn, which contains a gift shop and lecture hall. Visitors are treated to an informal talk by Mrs. Simmons, who gives seasonal advice on herb gardening. At the conclusion of her herbal chat, everyone is ushered off to the farmhouse for lunch. The first floor of this traditional New England saltbox has been converted into dining rooms. (Mrs. Simmons lives on the upper floor.) Fragrant herbs hang from the ceiling and cover the floor, making an appropriate backdrop for the herb-laden meal that's the hallmark of Caprilands.

When the leisurely lunch is over, Mrs. Simmons rejoins her visitors and discusses the food that's just been served. She also points out that the recipes can be found in various books she has written.

Coffee and dessert are served in the greenhouse, giving guests the opportunity to purchase live plants, dried flowers, and wreaths. They are then free to stroll through the impressive herb gardens, shop at the gift and book shops, or take their leave. Should they wish to purchase books or herbal products later, a mail-order catalog is available.

Mrs. Simmons has other profit centers besides the ones seen at Caprilands. Because of her vast knowledge—and the revival of interest in growing and cooking with herbs—she continues to write about the subject. Though her speaking engagements are not as frequent as they once were, she continues to share her fascination with useful plants with everyone she encounters.

Then there's Cher, another woman who understands the MPC concept and has produced an extraordinary number of income streams. As an entertainer, she has built careers as a singer, stage actress, and film star. After years of trying to be taken seriously as an actress, she surprised critics and audiences when she appeared off-Broadway in *Come Back to the Five and Dime, Jimmy Dean, Jimmy Dean.* From there, she proved her acting ability to movie audiences, winning an Academy Award for *Moonstruck.* But performing is only part of the empire Cher has built.

In the past twenty years, she's constructed and renovated fourteen houses, most of them resold for handsome profits. Her passion for personal fitness led her to cowrite a best-selling health book, followed by an exercise video that has also sold well.

Cher has lent her unique voice and face to the promotion of a variety of products including a signature perfume and an artificial sweetener. Recently she's added another successful enterprise via infomercials, selling hair and skin-care products.

Obviously a woman who enjoys a new challenge, Cher keeps coming up with projects spawned by her personal interests and beliefs. As a result, her options keep expanding and her income does, too. In fact, everything Cher does seems to be a natural move for a woman who takes herself seriously and intends to explore all possibilities that come her way.

Both Adelma Simmons and Cher bring to mind E. F. Schumacher's description of the effective entrepreneur. "The structure of the organization," he wrote, "can be symbolized by a person holding a large number of balloons. Each of the balloons has its own buoyancy and life, and the person does not lord it over the balloons, but stands beneath them, yet holding all the strings firmly." While this picture may be more serene than that of a juggler spinning plates, it's equally appropriate. Whether you create two or two dozen profit centers is up to you. Either way, you're certain to discover that you can manage a great deal more than you may have thought. Go ahead and dazzle yourself.

Getting Them Spinning

Students in my seminars seem to be divided evenly into two camps. There are those who say that the concept of Multiple Profit Centers is an affirmation of what they've been secretly thinking. They've longed to try several different things but have held back, remembering that their guidance counselor told them to settle on a single occupation. The other half of my classes is reluctant to consider this idea. "Won't this make me fragmented? Scatter my energy?" they query.

"Take it slow," I advise them. "And stop fretting about how you'll answer the question, 'What do you do?' at your next cocktail party. MPCs are going to make your business fun, as well as profitable."

To get your plates spinning, look at your long-range goals. Getting the big picture in mind and working backward from there, breaking your big goals into little, manageable steps, is the key.

For purposes of illustration, let's use some easy numbers. Suppose you decide that your long-range goal is to create five profit centers each earning $10,000 a year, and you want to accomplish that within the next five years. You have two ideas that you can get started with and another that needs more thought, and you aren't certain what the additional two will be. You think your first two schemes could be started simultaneously.

You've isolated your first step: create two $10,000-a-year income sources. Breaking that down, you'll discover that your monthly goal for each will be just over $800, making the weekly target $200. Psychologically, earning $200 is feasible—even if the larger amount seems difficult. Knowing what your financial goal is makes it easier to determine what action you'll need to take to accomplish it.

For the past several years, I have written and sold quite a few articles to magazines. I was never, however, very consistent about it. If I had time, I'd work on writing and submitting pieces, but it was sporadic. When I had four of my profit centers running smoothly, I decided that the next one I wanted to build was article sales. Since I don't usually start a new project unless I believe that it can ultimately produce a minimum income of $10,000, I took a long look at this idea. It seemed a huge leap from what I had previously earned. When I applied the breakdown formula to it, selling $200 a week of writing seemed quite realistic. Since I had often resold articles to noncompeting markets, I began building this profit center not by creating new material, but by finding new publications to buy old pieces. Seeing some immediate sales was encouraging. I kept expanding this profit center by creating new articles and sending them off to market.

Take another look at the assets and passions you identified earlier. Do any of them suggest profit center potential? "Look at the world as if it's full of customers, not employees," is another tip from the London Business School's Professor Handy. "Ask what you can offer those customers and how you can best package your services. You may be surprised to learn that others look at you as a bundle of underused skills and talents. Someone once said that by the time we die we have discovered only twenty-five percent of our talents. It's an unprovable assertion, but one worth believing—and now is the ideal time to find those missing seventy-five percent." What better way to do that than by creating several MPCs?

Success in creating a profit center depends on two things: being consistent and being persistent. Once you've isolated one or two possibilities, set aside time weekly for planning what action you'll take to start building your profit centers. Any new profit center requires the most attention right at the start. Once you have one or two going, they'll require less of your time. Then you can take your next idea and repeat the process over again. I like to work in ninety-day segments, starting four new profit centers every year while maintaining the ones that are in place. Knowing that not all of my ideas will succeed, this guideline seems to assure me that I'm always managing projects in various stages of growth. After a year or two, a profit center may surpass the financial goal you've established. It's okay to let that happen. Profit centers do have a way of evolving and developing a life of their own, as the following story will show.

Cucumber Sandwiches for Fun and Profit

Sometimes an idea for a profit center will take you by surprise. It may have been coming along for a while before you realize its potential, but when it does make itself known, acting on it is the only sensible thing to do. This happened to me a couple of years ago, and I'm telling it here so that you can see the process of starting a profit center.

"There are few hours in life more agreeable than the hour dedicated to the ceremony known as afternoon tea," wrote expatriate Henry James. Until a few years ago, it was a delight I had missed. Even with my passion for everything English, tea parties were only something I'd read about in books.

Then my friend Jill decided to warm a late-March afternoon with a formal tea. As I recall, the party was more of a dessert potluck than an authentic tea, but I was smitten. At the same time, afternoon tea was becoming trendy again. Numerous books about the rituals and recipes were being published; magazines were raving about entertaining with tea. I began gathering recipes and decided to begin an annual tradition of my own, celebrating St. Barbara's Day with a tea party for my friends.

Afternoon tea probably would have remained just a hobby had it not been for the program director at Open U, who asked if I would teach a class about it. I resisted. Even though I had acquired a fair amount of experience with tea (having graduated to sampling tea in restaurants and hotels that were reviving the ritual), it seemed a bit presumptuous to teach such a class. They persisted, however, and I relented.

I began experimenting with cake and scone recipes, hunted down the best local sources for linens, jams, and clotted cream. The first class was scheduled for late September and I spent days (and several restless nights) in preparation. I can't recall ever being more nervous than I was the day of that first class. But the students were kind and despite less-than-perfect facilities, we had a jolly afternoon. By the second session, I was having a wonderful time cutting up tiny sandwiches, making lemon curd, and polishing all the silver I owned.

I had also become aware that many of my students had first encountered afternoon tea on visits to England, but thought that producing a tea was a mysterious process. Perhaps, I reasoned, there were other Anglophiles who would enjoy having tea served in their homes to entertain their friends, but wouldn't want to do the work themselves. The holidays were coming and I thought afternoon tea might be a lovely and unique way to celebrate with friends. Since I had devised a system for producing a mobile tea, why not expand into catering?

There was not a lot of time to advertise or plan a marketing campaign. I ran a small classified ad in *Minnesota Monthly*, our public radio magazine. I also put together a price list and had a few run off on turquoise paper at my print shop. I began letting people know that I was available.

The day the ad appeared, I began receiving calls. I had several customers in no time. I also made some pricing mistakes. I quickly realized that I had priced my services too low. When I had set my fees, I had envisioned fairly large parties and thought the per-person cost had to be kept low. This was a big mistake. Most of the parties I booked were rather intimate affairs and not as profitable as I had hoped. Nevertheless, I earned several hundred dollars very quickly and saw how I could do much better in the future.

This little service business was a satisfying experience in other ways as well. It tickled me no end to sample tea in a lovely hotel or London tearoom and call it research—tax-deductible research. The real fun, however, was introducing this lovely custom to people who had never before been to tea.

The pleasure of afternoon tea was an exquisite experiment in turning a pastime into a profit center. It was satisfying to know that I had another venture that could easily be expanded should I so choose. And although I'm no longer teaching the class or currently doing any catering, my own passion for afternoon tea hasn't diminished one bit.

Now when I read a Barbara Pym story with its endless cups of tea and sponge cakes, I have a fresh appreciation for the ritual and relaxation that comes with tea in the afternoon. I also have a profit center that is portable and can be revived and re-created indefinitely. Lovely.

Managing Diversity

Even though you may have equal financial goals for each of your profit centers, your investment of time will not be the same for each of them. With experience you'll learn what needs your personal attention, what can run by itself (more or less), and what to discard when it isn't pulling its weight.

Wearing several hats can be energizing and at the same time a source of balance in life. I love the contrast between working alone on writing and working with large groups of people in seminars. Being part of a small team effort from time to time adds another experience. This diversity creates a whole identity that is interesting and enlivening to me. New connections and ideas flow from one project to another, improving the quality of each. Multiple Profit Centers are especially attractive to anyone who has a low threshold of boredom. Moving back and forth between activities can keep your attention high.

Tricia Timmons is a believer in managing diversity, and her array of business cards demonstrates the fun she's having doing several things. I first met Tricia at one of my seminars in Sacramento, a class which she says gave her the idea to put her MPCs in order. Tricia had opened a boarding cattery and was teaching classes called "Fearless Self-Employment for Women." Those classes had led to another profit center: consulting with individual entrepreneurs. She added another profit center to her cat boarding service and began offering pet-sitting when she realized that many pet owners had too many cats to board. Her passion for animals extends to another profit center, called Critter Communication Consulting, designed to help pet owners understand their pets better. In addition, she did marketing for a home remodeling business, but that industry has been at a standstill. She's taken on another project, doing the marketing for the customized boots her husband makes. "I know some people get nervous at the idea of doing several things," Tricia says, "but I point out to the women I teach that this is something they already know how to do. They're already managing different activities in their families and they can apply this just as well to their business."

One of the questions that I am often asked is, "Do I need to have a different business card for every profit center?" My answer is "Absolutely!" These days, I whip out a handful of Tricia Timmons cards, each with a separate profit center listed. The lines between your MPCs may be slim, but giving each its own identity will keep you and your customers and clients clear about what you have to offer.

Plates That Spin by Themselves

Ultimately, you will want to have some profit centers that bring you income with a minimum of time and attention. These plates that spin by themselves take time to get going, but once you've got them spinning you can work on other projects, or go to the beach if you like. Count every income source you have as a profit center. If you already have income from an annuity or a pension that is unaffected by your other earnings, call it one of your MPCs. I have one category labeled "Miscellaneous" to keep track of odds and ends.

It's a good idea to plan long-range projects that require little maintenance. Here are some quick ideas to start you thinking.

• Royalties. Rock stars and best-selling authors aren't the only ones eligible for royalties. Think of royalties as money you earn now for work done at another time. That opens up the window of opportunity quite a bit. If you publish a book or audiotape, invent a product, or sell an idea to another company, your earnings may continue based on future sales . . . while you go on to other projects.

• Rental income. Once you've got this one in place, your biggest task may be collecting the rent. Finding the right tenant makes your job easier, of course.

• Marketing consumable products. If you sell cosmetics, vitamins, or cleaning products . . . and sell good ones . . . you have an ongoing source of income with repeat business. Products that are used need to be replaced. Many successful entrepreneurs concentrate their early efforts on building a customer base and simply service these customers over and over again.

• Mail-order sales. If you study mail-order ads, you'll find that the ones you see month after month never change a comma. It takes time and experimentation to devise a sales-generating ad, but once you've got the one that works, all you have to do is keep it running.

• Selling a business you've built. If your idea is good enough, you may be building more than a current profit center. You could be developing a business that can be sold in the future, bringing you a nice return on your investment. Too many entrepreneurs overlook this possibility once they've lost interest in their enterprise, so they simply phase it out or go out of business. It makes more sense to let somebody else take over—and pay you for the privilege.

Think of MPCs as the building blocks for making a living without a job. Adding, subtracting, and moving them around is the way you grow. Mastering this idea will add to your confidence, as well as your bottom line. Each successful profit center you create will empower you to tackle the next one, and the next. You might become a tycoon this way—or just a miniconglomerate. At the very least, you'll come to believe that the possibilities truly are endless.

Here's a little tip that can speed you on your way to becoming joyfully jobless. If you have a job now, start thinking of it as *one* of your profit centers. It will help you expand your thinking about your own potential and make it easier for you to let go of it when other profit centers prove more fun and profitable. You'll start to view that job in a new light if you treat it as one of several income sources you're developing. It may seem a tiny thing, but it's more empowering than it appears. Check it out for yourself.

Winning Ways for Creating Multiple Profit Centers

Your ability to successfully create MPCs is not only dependent on good ideas. Your attitudes about money play an important part, too. Complete the following sentences and see what you discover about your money consciousness.

My greatest financial achievement was/is _____.

The most fun I ever had earning money was _____.

My favorite way to spend money is _____.

Ultimately, I want to receive money from _____ sources.

To develop a healthy attitude about money, I _____.

The wisest advice my parents gave me about money was _____

_____.

The financial slogan of my family was _____.

My personal financial slogan is _____.

Exploring Your Options

I invest in myself by ————————————————————.

I feel rich when ————————————————————.

I show my generosity by ————————————————————.

CHAPTER 8

Considering the Possibilities

Where your talents and the world's needs cross, there lies your vocation.

Aristotle

Nobody sees the world quite the way writer Tom Robbins does. Wacky, whimsical, and wise, he has given me—and his many adoring fans—plenty of "aha" moments, revealing important truths in his unique way. It's not surprising, then, that he has a fitting observation for becoming joyfully jobless. "Deep down, all of us probably are aware that some kind of mystical evolution is our true task," he writes. "Yet we suppress the notion with considerable force because to admit it is to admit that most of our political gyrations, religious dogmas, social ambitions and financial ploys are not merely counterproductive but trivial. Our mission is to jettison those pointless preoccupations and take on once again the primordial cargo of inexhaustible ecstasy. Or barring that, to turn out a good juicy cheeseburger and strong glass of beer."

Having considered the essence of what you want to do, your personal passions, and the assets you bring to making a living without a job, it's time to consider the form your work will take. It's time to design your own cheeseburger and beer.

You've gathered by now, no doubt, that the concept of making a living without a job doesn't fit ordinary notions about being in business. A more accurate way of looking at it is to think in terms of creating income sources or profit centers. While that may sound like the purpose of all business, there will be a distinct difference.

You could think of it as the difference between having a suit tailored and buying one off the rack. To the untrained eye, they may look alike, but the bespoke suit will fit perfectly. Likewise, your business is going to be custom-tailored to fit you, but first you have to select the fabric.

The most popular ways of working for yourself fall into six broad categories. Within each of these categories there are tens of thousands of opportunities. You may be strongly attracted to only one of these areas or, as is frequently the case, draw from several of them. A single idea sometimes overlaps and blends characteristics of two or three formats.

Each of these ways of making a living has its own advantages; there isn't one that is better than the others. A couple of them are quick-starts; others take more time to get going. They can all be started with little or no investment and expanded once they've earned their keep.

A cautionary note is in order before you begin reading about them. I will give you a general description and a couple of examples in each category. Keep in mind that there are thousands of possibilities with each of them and the examples serve only to clarify, not to limit your choices.

Let's consider what each of these forms entails and the advantages of each. Your ideas are bound to find a good match with one or several of them.

Delivering Personal Service

The first year that I lived in Boulder, Colorado, the onset of the holidays found me in the depths of despair. I hardly knew a soul and was certain there would be no party invitations coming my way.

After several days of fretting about my dismal fate, I got an idea. Why not offer my services to people who were giving parties? I marched to the newspaper office and placed a small classified ad proposing to assist with holiday chores. It wasn't long before I found myself going to parties—and getting paid for it. Unwittingly, I had discovered one of the easiest and quickest ways to create a profit center: the personal service business.

While personal service businesses have existed for a long while, they are growing in popularity in these busy times. As more people find their lives filling up with more than they can handle, they're looking for help, both personally and professionally. You might be just the person to come to the rescue.

Another factor is at work in our world that increases this opportunity even more. Trend-spotter Faith Popcorn first coined the term "cocooning" to describe the growing phenomenon she observed in the eighties. This trend, says Popcorn, has found more and more of us striving to make our homes self-contained living centers from which we are reluctant to emerge. Consequently, products and services which can be brought right to a cocooner's doorstep are particularly attractive.

Personal service advocates have another social factor working on their behalf. That factor is lousy service. "The abandonment of the service ethic in America," notes Paul Hawken, "is the biggest single cause of our thriving small business economy." Service businesses are springing up to offer the same or similar services as those performed by large companies. Frequently, tiny businesses outperform the giants in both speed and quality.

Self-bossers may open a personal service business to market a special skill that they possess. Their customers need them to perform a service that they couldn't do themselves. One of the more outrageous examples of this specialty service is the one offered by Red Adair, the fellow who's an expert at putting out oil-well fires. For years, his business had virtually no competition.

More commonly, personal service businesses offer a service which attracts customers because it saves them time or money. While they may be able to do the service themselves, they choose to let someone else do it for them. My English afternoon tea business fit that description.

You probably possess dozens of skills that could be turned into a profitable service business right now. What about the experience you've acquired working for somebody else? Do you have skills that could be packaged as your own service? A corporate personnel manager did just that when he left his job with a large company to work on his own. Since he enjoyed the kind of work he had been doing, he decided to offer his services to small companies who couldn't afford a full-time personnel department. He now has five clients for whom he works one day a week. Not only does he earn more money this way, the change of scenery is envigorating.

Good ideas for personal service businesses are everywhere. Identifying problems and offering a solution is the basis of the best service companies. I heard an interview on Minnesota Public Radio with a young couple who found a need and created a service business to fill it. Both of them had grown up on dairy farms and dreamed of owning their own operation someday. Knowing that dairy farmers have a hard time getting away from their demanding business, the couple started a cow-sitting service. In their first year, they only had nine days which weren't booked. Their clients enjoyed a much-needed vacation while the couple enjoyed doing work that they loved.

Besides solving problems, successful service businesses also offer to save time for their clients. Karen Kari spent sixteen years as a Wall Street executive before starting her business, It's Done, Inc. The idea came to her as she was commuting back to her home in Greenwich, Connecticut, late one evening and realized that, once again, she would be unable to pick up her dry cleaning because she would arrive home after the cleaners had closed. Reasoning that there must be other time-pressured folks, she decided to offer her services running errands.

Like many entrepreneurial undertakings, It's Done, Inc., has evolved as Kari spotted other opportunities and problems to solve in her community. Today her business concentrates on organizing businesses—from paperwork to filing. "I find I'm using what I learned in my prior life as a Wall Street marketing director managing multiple projects and priorities," she says. "And I have worked for everyone from a poet to corporate executives, so every day is different."

Another way to generate ideas is to look at existing service businesses and see if you could offer a similar service to an overlooked market. On one of my London trips, I read newspaper accounts of a series of rapes that had been committed by a cabdriver attacking his passengers. Naturally, women traveling alone at night were extremely nervous about hiring a cab. A story on the BBC pointed out that there was an alternative available. Ladycabs is a small company that uses only female drivers and caters to women passengers. I thought it was a terrific idea and wondered why more cities didn't have their own version of this venture.

Personal service can be an ideal way to begin—and continue— making a living without a job. One of the easiest and fastest paths to self-employment, this form usually requires little investment, unless you need to purchase special equipment to provide your service. You can begin by making direct contact with potential clients or with a simple flyer or small ad. Many of these businesses flourish through word-of-mouth advertising, with one happy client telling another.

And if you're longing to travel, a personal service business can be wonderfully portable. Once you've put together a successful local business, you can sprout wings and take it with you. Follow the sun or see the world and let your venture be the passport. An accountant with wanderlust did just that. He bought a motor home, quit his job, and took to the road. He would select an area that he wanted to visit. Once there, he made calls on small businesses offering his special service, putting their books in order. Once a project was completed, he'd move on to his next destination and repeat the process.

You may discover, as many personal service owners have, that a good business can push you out of labor and into management. Start out doing a bang-up job and you may have more business than you can possibly handle. At this point, you can expand your business by hiring others to perform the service while you concentrate on management; or you can remain a one-person venture giving impeccable service to a few select clients. Either way, you have options galore. In our high-tech world, providing a well-executed service can be marvelously satisfying . . . and, well, personal.

Packaging Information

"The new source of power is not money in the hands of a few but information in the hands of many," proclaimed John Naisbitt in *Megatrends*. The changes caused by moving from an industrial to an information society have been rapid, forcing individual as well as global shifts. Nowhere is this impact more obvious than in the world of work. Collecting, packaging, and distributing information have become the function of vast and diverse industries. Well-known information packagers include Julia Child, Arthur Frommer, Jane Fonda, and Martha Stewart, who have all ridden this wave to fame and fortune, demonstrating how much we like getting our information from another human being.

If you enjoy doing research, have acquired expertise in some area, know how to do something that could be taught to others, or have good communication skills, an information profit center could be a natural for you. Getting started is a matter of identifying your own area of interest, determining the potential market for your information, and selecting the package you want to put it in. And what an array of packages you have to choose from. Take a look at these popular formats:

• *Writing*. Whether you have a specialty or just good writing ability, putting your ideas on paper can get you going as an information packager. You could write articles for magazines and journals. If your information warrants, it can be compiled in a book that you sell to an established publisher or publish yourself. Personal computers have made it easy for writers to create and self-publish information booklets, which are often sold via mail order. A few years ago, an enterprising woman wrote a "How to Kiss" booklet, which she sold through ads in teen magazines, with stupendous success. Some experts self-publish newsletters, a potentially profitable avenue for selling specialized information.

• *Teaching*. Everyone knows that teaching is a ticket to poverty, right? Would it surprise you to learn that there are experts who earn $10,000—and more—for a single speech? Even though the fees earned by speakers like Henry Kissinger are not offered to ordinary folks, many possibilities exist for building a lovely income teaching classes, seminars, and workshops. Adult education is growing by leaps and bounds, providing a wide range of opportunity. More and more adult ed programs rely on experience-based, rather than credentialed, teaching. Your own life skills could be valuable to others. Kathleen Baxter was in her forties when her therapist challenged her to start dating, something she'd never done. Kathleen had so much fun and success with her new social life that she now teaches a popular course called "Dare to Date," urging others to follow her lead. Problems you've solved, improved methods of doing things, data you've collected can be the basis for teaching and speaking in our information-hungry world.

• *Information products.* Besides print, there are several other formats that are attractive to information buyers. Audiotapes, videotapes, and computer software offer different mediums for sharing information. A hot information product these days is the 900-number telephone service, where callers receive information for a fee which is billed through their telephone company. If your area of expertise includes knowledge of a foreign country, creating and conducting tours could be a delightful way to package your product.

Although information packaging isn't a quick-start enterprise as personal service is, it can be a satisfying long-term way of earning your living. What makes this kind of business so much fun to run is the built-in evolutionary aspect: start with one little idea and additional possibilities keep presenting themselves. This kind of business is also a great teacher, since it compels you to keep learning more about your subject. Obviously, then, you'll want to be certain that any information venture you begin is based on your own enthusiasm and passion for the subject.

Miki Banavige's publicity photo shows her dressed in a tuxedo and top hat holding a magic wand, but Miki isn't an ordinary magician. Her expertise was acquired in her kitchen, not on the stage. Now her time-saving techniques are being marketed through her business, Cooking Is Magic. (Incidentally MAGIC is Miki's acronym for Making Any Groceries Into Cuisine.)

She began gaining visibility for herself by writing a food column for her local newspaper and teaching in community education programs. From there she moved on to doing special demonstrations in supermarkets, specialty kitchen shops, and department stores. Her self-published *Cooking Is Magic* cookbook added another profit center. Miki's ready to move beyond local engagements and share her unique approach on a national scale. Her idea file is bulging with new project plans, such as aligning herself with the manufacturer of the kitchen tools she fancies and helping promote its products.

Like other successful information packagers, Miki has discovered one of the great assets of this kind of business: once you've built your package, your market is geographically unlimited. The shopkeeper down the street may rely on the neighborhood for support, but information packagers know no such restrictions. Take a look at what you already know and see how you can put it to work for you now. Whether you're a world-class mountaineer, financial planner, or party-giver, your audience awaits you.

If marketing and promotion are your areas of expertise, you could get in on this opportunity by packaging someone else's information. The adult education programs that I teach for do just that. They find dozens of independent contractors who have classes and seminars, put them together in a catalog, handle the registrations, and share the profits. Speakers' bureaus, literary agencies, and even public relations firms provide the marketing support needed by information gatherers. Even if you aren't an expert yourself, don't count out this earning method.

Limiting Your Offer

The delightful woman sitting next to me on a flight from Minneapolis to Los Angeles entertained me with stories about her life as a world traveler. She had just returned from a trip to the Arctic Circle, where she'd gone for a summer solstice tour. Ah, I thought, someone created a seasonal business to capitalize on this annual phenomenon.

Holidays, yearly events, and the changing seasons come bearing their own opportunities. A seasonal or holiday venture can be especially attractive if you are (1) crazy about a special time of the year, or (2) like to work frantically for a short period and earn a great deal of money. Limited-time enterprises are perfect if you are also working on projects that take a long time to generate income, because they can fund your non-income days beautifully.

You could divide up your time the way one freelance writer does. He earns about one-third of his income from writing magazine articles, another third from running a handyman service. The rest of his income comes from spending several weeks every summer fighting forest fires. Like many seasonal businesses, this one generates the most money in the least amount of time.

If your disposition is such that you are happiest when you focus all of your attention and energy on a single project at a time, consider your own variation of this writer/handyman/firefighter lifestyle. Rather than interspersing activities, you can devote long periods to a couple of ventures.

Claude Monet was as brilliant a businessman as he was an artist. He created a strong demand for his paintings by offering limited editions to his best customers. Several times a year he would announce a forthcoming series and presell to his regular patrons. That same psychology—buy now because it won't be available later—fuels the seasonal business.

A woman I know was too busy one autumn to make Halloween costumes for her children. When she went to the store to purchase readymade outfits, she was appalled at the selection and quality. There must be other parents who are too busy to sew, she reasoned, but would prefer something other than these ugly mass-produced things. She got busy sewing and the following year opened a small shop in mid-September offering handmade costumes, face paint, pumpkins, and masks. For six weeks every year, she's a shopkeeper. Once the holiday has passed, she begins restocking her inventory for the next season.

Christmas, Valentine's Day, and local holidays are potential gold mines for jobless earners. Although the marketing season may be short, earnings can be great if you are offering something that enhances the season.

If running a seasonal business appeals to you, consider these questions:

- Do I want to spend 100 percent of my time and energy working on a single venture for several months?

123

- Is there a holiday or time of year that I enjoy especially?
- Can I design a venture that will create enough profit to carry me through non-working times?
- Can I budget my time and money to make this work?
- Does my area have a tourist season?
- Do I want to manufacture a product that has a seasonal shelf life?
- Will my personal relationships support my working feverishly for a time?
- How do I want to spend my non-working time?

One of my students told me that his father runs two seasonal businesses, each in a different location. During the summer, he's the proprietor of a general store in Alaska that caters to tourists. He specializes in local crafts and products handmade by the native population. When the cold weather arrives, he locks the store and heads for Belize, where he runs a sort of bed-and-breakfast operation, a resort of guest huts on the beach. Both businesses cater to tourists, but that's where the similarity ends. Like other seasonal business owners, he has created variety and diversity in his work.

Landlording and Leasing

Alicia shares a rambling old house in New England with a husband and two dogs. Much of the year it's an ordinary household, with grandchildren visiting and friends dropping by for cards in the evening. But when autumn rolls around and the tourists begin their annual leaf-peeping invasion, Alicia's home becomes a bustling bed-and-breakfast. By the time the first snowfall appears, normalcy has returned and Alicia is richer by several thousand dollars.

Landlording is, of course, one of the oldest ways to make a living without a job. In earlier days, widows frequently took their only asset and turned it into a profit center. Their homes became boardinghouses, which brought them a respectable income. Although boardinghouses have been replaced by high-rise apartments, there are plenty of opportunities available for would-be landlords—even on a small scale. Assets you already have can be converted to cash fairly easily if you exercise a bit of initiative.

The key to this profit center is to shift your attention to the idea of renting, rather than selling outright. What do you own now that would be valuable to others on a short-term basis? Do you have an extra bedroom that could be rented to a college student? A basement that might become a charming apartment? A collection of old cars that could be leased to a film studio? Would your home make an interesting backdrop for a magazine's photo layout? How about those antiques as a prop for an ad? And what about your face? Could you be just what a casting company needs for the commercial it's filming?

Several months ago, a man I know and his girlfriend built a house together. After two months of cohabitation, the woman moved out, leaving her partner to rattle around in his large, lonely house. "Why don't you look for a roommate?" I asked. He said he'd thought about that, but wasn't sure he wanted to have someone around all the time.

"Look," I said, "you've got to have some criteria here. Why not look for someone who travels a lot?" He thought that might be okay, but didn't know where to locate such a person.

Although I found his lack of imagination exasperating, I calmly pointed out that there was a pool of possible roommates who would qualify a few miles from his house. "If I were looking," I suggested, "I'd run an ad in Northwest Airlines' employee newsletter. There must be all sorts of flight attendants who'd love to come home to a nice new house."

If being a landlord yourself isn't appropriate, how about being one for somebody else? One day I spotted an ad in *The New Yorker* that read: "Farnum and Christ. London flats to American standards." Thinking that a British realtor had set up shop in the United States, I called the 800 number for information. I had expected to hear a crisp English voice answer the phone, but instead was greeted by a woman with a Southern drawl. After requesting the brochure, I asked Anne Farnum how she had gotten her business started. She told me that a friend in London had asked whether she knew anyone who might be interested in renting his apartment there for a while. One thing led to another, and they now handle the rentals for dozens of London flat-owners. All of the properties are normally occupied by their owners, who vacate when Farnum and Christ find a renter. It's an arrangement that works well for everyone. The owner (who might be a film star away on location) earns a tidy sum; the visitor has a cozy place to stay; the agency collects a handsome fee for making the match.

Leasing things other than real estate has great potential, too. Rental businesses aren't just for leasing Rototillers anymore. Everything from ballgowns to sporting goods to photography darkrooms is being leased by imaginative entrepreneurs. For years, Open Air Bicycles has been a fixture at the beach in Santa Barbara, providing bicycles and roller skates to tourists. A couple from Los Angeles owned a photography studio and eventually had accumulated so many props that they opened a second business renting props to other photographers and movie studios. The possibilities go on and on, if you look.

While landlording and leasing can be high-investment businesses, they also offer opportunities for shoestring operators. Take a fresh look at the things around you and you may discover hidden treasure.

Picking Up Your Mail

When I was growing up, getting the mail was a daily ritual conducted between breakfast and school. Since we didn't have home delivery, we stopped at the post office first thing in the morning. Because I was the oldest child, I had the privilege of collecting whatever treasures had arrived.

And treasures there were! As a kid, I was constantly sending away for things with my dimes and quarters taped to cardboard. Through the mail, I began to connect with a bigger world. It's an enthusiasm that has never left me.

An ordinary mailbox takes on an even grander dimension when it becomes a business tool. Having a mail-order business makes going to the post office an adventure. What other way of doing business offers the same possibilities? There are no territorial restrictions, no boundaries on your market. In addition, you can conduct your mail-order business from any place served by the Postal Service. Whether you want to live in the woods in

Maine or in a penthouse in San Francisco, mail order makes it feasible.

Mail order has come a long way in the past few years. It wasn't too long ago that this way of doing business attracted mostly sleaze merchants. Products sold this way were often of dubious quality or arrived in plain brown wrappers. Then along came Roger Horchow, who demonstrated that upscale merchandise can be sold through the mail. Add to that the fact that buying by mail can save time, and it has become the perfect modern marketing method.

Getting started in mail order isn't nearly as complicated as some of the books on the subject would suggest. Basically, you need only three things to get started:

1. a product that lends itself to mail-order marketing
2. the right advertising in the right media
3. a plan for expanding your advertising once you've refined your ads

Finding the right product is, of course, critical. As in any undertaking, think about products that you're crazy about your-self. It might be something that's a new twist on an ordinary item (such as a gourmet cake) or something that's found in your area but not easily available elsewhere.

Or you could look for a product that appeals to a niche market, such as a hobby or craft item that could be marketed to a specialty group. Lots of environmentally friendly products were first sold this way to kindred spirits concerned about the planet.

Your product could also be something you manufacture your-self. Silversmith J. H. Breakell was a struggling Rhode Island artist until a friend urged him to invest his life savings in a small ad in *The New Yorker* magazine offering his silver broccoli pin for sale by mail order. Breakell is struggling no more and ads for his jewelry appear in several upscale publications.

Other mail-order marketers put together a collection of re-lated items in a catalog. The Whole Work catalog, for instance, offers a huge selection of books on alternative careers, self-employment, and personal development. It began modestly in a spare bedroom in Tom and Sue Ellison's home in Colorado, space it has long since outgrown. The Ellisons' catalog makes it easy for their customers to find books they'd never be able to locate in a single bookstore.

I must admit I have a strong predilection for mail-order profit centers. Quite simply, I believe everyone who is determined to be joyfully jobless should have a mail-order business in his or her plans. The secret to success with this method is to be willing to begin modestly and let it grow gradually. If you do, you'll be in fine company. A number of today's mail-order giants, including L. L. Bean and Lillian Vernon, began with a single product.

Start with a modest ad campaign, too. The least expensive and most flexible kind of advertising is, of course, classified ads. Writing a catchy ad takes practice, but reading lots of existing ads can educate you quickly. Know your audience and aim at them. Mail-order pro Tyler Hicks advises, "You will often find it easier to sell 1,000 special wrenches to a list of 50,000 plumbers than it is to sell 1,000 toothbrushes to a list of 50,000 people with real teeth. Sell a mail-order product to a clearly defined audience whenever you can because, in general, your sales costs will be lower and your profit higher."

Besides giving you the freedom to live anywhere you want, mail order has another advantage that makes it ideal. Once you've developed your business, you can keep repeating your ads and expanding your sales, but you don't have to change your product offering. Eventually, a mail-order operation can almost run itself—freeing you to develop other ideas.

With one in every four dollars spent in the United States now going to mail-order businesses, shopping via the mail has become respectable. Cocooners love shopping this way, as do busy people. When you start finding money in your mailbox, you'll love mail order as much as I do.

Marketing a Product or Service

Although marketing encompasses the other five ways of making a living, it also comprises its own category. Many self-bossers stumble onto this earning method by accident. Susan Peterson, the woman mentioned earlier who started the gardening business, is now a full-time potter. One of her earliest pieces of pottery was a fish plate she made as a gift for her husband. When friends begged her to make one for them, she realized that her new passion had profit potential. Today her pottery is sold in galleries around the country, as well as through her own annual sales.

Both products and services offer opportunities for creating a marketing profit center. Donna Buffardi markets both. After careers in nursing and accounting, she now is an aerobics instructor—on the service side—and has started marketing products through her Gifts in Motion business. She told me a story that affirms the great advantage available via this method. Buffardi and her family were returning to Rhode Island after her first buying trip to New York, where she purchased inventory for her new venture. When they stopped at a doughnut shop, she discovered she had only eighty cents in her wallet. Her kids wanted a snack, but she said that it was more important for her to use the money for a cup of coffee. They piled into the doughnut shop, where the clerks and customers admired the watches her kids were wearing. "I've got a lot more in the car," she volunteered and rushed out to bring in her newly acquired inventory. She made several sales on the spot—and her kids got their doughnuts.

Another Rhode Island student, Daniel Kertzner, has been working hard to build a profit center as a storyteller. While he usually sells his services to a client, such as a library or convention, he took his skill to the street during a trip to London. For three and a half hours of storytelling at Covent Garden, Daniel earned £29.60!

When you develop a marketing business, suddenly boundaries and limitations begin to dissolve. You have a new mobility and power that others lack. A young woman I know turned her jewelry-making hobby into a splendid profit center. She had portable displays built, and whenever her inventory was full she'd spend an afternoon in a busy place, like a college campus, with her funky earrings on display. She said it was not at all unusual to earn $100 or more in an afternoon. Her marketing skills came to her rescue when she was on an extended trip abroad. Running short of money during her stay in Egypt didn't faze her a bit. She bought some beads and wire, whipped up a bunch of earrings, and became a street merchant. Because she has learned to be comfortable with marketing, lack of money is never an issue for her.

Even though many self-bossers begin by marketing a product they've created, you aren't limited to things you've manufactured yourself. A lover of Southwestern art travels from her home in the Midwest to Arizona, New Mexico, and Mexico several times a year, returning with paintings, pottery, and ethnic clothes. Some of the items are wholesaled to galleries and small shops; others are sold at craft shows and outdoor markets. As her business grows, so does her knowledge of the culture she's adopted. Consequently, her slide shows about working artists in the Southwest have become popular—and created more customers.

A marketing profit center could lead you to becoming a shopkeeper in a fixed location, or you might prefer the flexibility of a portable shop. Flea markets throughout the country rent space to sellers on a short-term basis, making it possible to set up shop wherever you are. Conventions and trade shows are other great places for on-and-off shopkeeping.

Inventions, ideas, and consulting services broaden this profit center's potential even wider. Even though the thought of marketing is terrifying for many, it needn't be if you commit yourself to marketing only things which you love and believe will enrich, improve, and enhance the lives of your customers. Keep that guideline in mind and you'll be on your way to designing a business limited only by your own imagination.

Your Own Blueprint

With these six formats coupled with your personal interests and dreams, you can move forward to the most exciting part of all—creating a business that suits you perfectly. You'll be designing your own blueprint and building something unlike what anyone else has. Whether you're offering a personal service, selling products through the mail, or opening a guest house for travelers, your profit centers will be a reflection of you.

In this world of franchised operations and look-alike stores, you'll be offering a fresh, unique attitude and perspective. Eventually, you may run profit centers that tap into all six of these formats—or you may happily concentrate on just one. Whatever you decide to do, make sure it fits you perfectly and your success will be inevitable.

Winning Ways for Considering the Possibilities

Here's a quick review of the most popular ways of making a living without a job and the advantages of each.

- Personal service—easy to start; timely; portable; expandable
- Information packaging—draws on past experience; timely; unlimited market
- Seasonal/holiday—large profit potential in short period of time
- Landlord/leasing—turns current assets into profit while retaining ownership; good growth potential
- Mail order—enormous potential; can live anywhere; timely
- Marketing product or service—flexibility and mobility along with potential profitability

Which of these formats has the most appeal for you as a beginning enterprise?

Which could you consider developing over a long period of time?

Pretend that you have $100 to invest in starting a profit center. How might you spend it to get each of these kinds of businesses going?

Why is each of these formats attractive in current society? What makes them timely right now?

PART IV

Turning Passions into Profits

If we listened to our intellect, we'd never have a love affair. We'd never have a friendship. We'd never go into business, because we'd be cynical. You've got to jump off cliffs all the time and build your wings on the way down.

Ray Bradbury

CHAPTER 9

Starting Small, Thinking Big

Every artist was first an amateur.
Ralph Waldo Emerson

Thirty-some years ago, a young housewife in London invested $20 and started her own business from her kitchen table. She was fascinated by old-fashioned textile designs and wanted to duplicate them. At first she did all the silk-screening herself, using antiquated tools.

Before long the business began to grow, and she and her husband decided to pack up their four children and relocate to a rural area. They found a house and an old barn nearby, which they converted into a manufacturing plant. As the business was gathering steam, however, disaster struck. A nearby river overflowed its banks, destroying the factory and all the inventory. They decided it was time for another move. The woman had been longing to return to her native Wales and saw this crisis as an opportunity to do so.

Having experienced a financial setback because of the flood, they were unable to purchase both a house and a new manufacturing facility. They opted for a building to shelter their business and set up their personal household in a tent.

The business was soon up and running again, but in the late

sixties they were confronted by another problem. While they had relied on wholesaling their fabrics to numerous stores, they believed their product was not being marketed as well as it could be. They decided to open their own shop and become the exclusive purveyors of their merchandise.

This arrangement worked so well that the product line soon included clothing, household accessories, and wallpaper. Their trademark style had enormous nostalgia appeal and continued to attract devoted customers.

From this tiny beginning, the couple went on to build an international business. The London housewife who had begun with $20 became known throughout the world. Today Laura Ashley, Ltd., has more than two hundred shops around the world, with annual sales in excess of $250 million.

While much of the advice about starting a business insists that it can't be done without thousands of dollars in capital, there's plenty of evidence to the contrary. Self-bossers who are willing to start with limited resources may, in fact, have a better chance of succeeding. A sound, long-lived business is built slowly—one step at a time. If you are willing for that first step to be a tiny one, you'll be giving yourself the advantage of mastering your business in manageable chunks. Your confidence will grow, your problems will be fewer, your risks reduced.

You'll also be in good company. When I look at the big businesses I admire, I see again and again that they share the common distinction of starting small. If an idea is compelling enough, personal initiative can serve as the catalyst for starting out. "Like most great ideas that people I've known have thought of," says Apple Computer co-founder Steven Jobs, "ours came from something that was right in front of us. We designed this computer because we couldn't afford to buy one."

It will be helpful to your venture if you fall in love with the idea of working for one of the world's smallest businesses. First you may have to challenge another popular myth.

Bigger Is Not Necessarily Better

Many people, particularly in the United States, believe that gigantic size is the true indicator of success. Workers and managers alike have been advised to hitch their wagons to the biggest company that would have them and ride along to success. The business press and corporate flacks parade billion-dollar profits in front of the public and our political representatives so that we act appropriately awed and worshipful. This attitude has promoted what I call Success by Association, a concept that infringes on self-esteem and personal initiative. "Oh, yes, I've been at Megabucks International for twenty years," we announce to strangers at a party. "Great company, wonderful benefits."

"But who are *you*?" your companions may wonder. The only person swallowed by a whale whose name we remember is Jonah.

Only since the collapse of so many supposedly invincible corporate giants have we had the courage to question whether bigger is really better. We're also beginning to wonder whether it was *ever* better.

The British economist E. F. Schumacher never believed that gargantuan business was good for humans. Back in the early seventies, his book *Small Is Beautiful* became the manifesto for counterculture entrepreneurs. Schumacher warned that unlimited growth was not only environmentally irresponsible, but doomed. "I was brought up on the theory of the economics of scale," he wrote. "It is quite true that today there are more large organizations and probably also bigger organizations than ever before in history; but the number of small units is also growing and many of these small units are highly prosperous and provide society with most of the really fruitful new developments. . . . Even today, we are told that gigantic organizations are inescapably necessary; but when we look closely we can notice that as soon as great size has been created there is often a strenuous attempt to attain smallness within bigness." The management fad called Quality Circles, so popular in the past decade, was an example of Schumacher's observation. However, the best-intentioned organization may fail to provide you with the freedom and personal satisfaction that come with going it alone.

Having made the decision to be an independent businessperson, you may be startled to discover that the big-is-better notion still influences you. A self-bosser once confessed to me that he'd been on his own for three years and still heard himself answering the "What do you do?" question by saying, "I have my own business, but I used to be the director of the YMCA." At some level, his own considerable success was not as valid as his prior acceptance as an employee.

The best way to obliterate that limiting attitude is to shift your attention away from the pros and cons of big business and concentrate on the advantages inherent in small business. Adopting a small-is-beautiful approach will lead you to uncover advantages that are numerous and profound.

• *You will learn exactly how your business operates.* Think of yourself as the ultimate authority on your business, which is precisely what you will become if you take time to learn every aspect for yourself. Later, when it's time to delegate to others, you'll know exactly what it is you want them to do. Taking a hands-on approach will, of course, require that you learn new things, explore new options. While it's not uncommon for corporate employees to believe that they don't know what's going on in the business they work for, that will not be true for you. You will know what's happening, and that's an empowering position to assume.

• *You can make mistakes when you're small that won't jeopardize your ultimate success.* When there's less at stake, errors can be seen as learning experiences rather than catastrophes. Don't skip this stage. Nothing that teaches you about your business is unimportant or trivial.

I teach a course called "Establishing Yourself as an Expert." Many of my students arrive in class and announce that their goal is to appear on Oprah Winfrey's or Phil Donahue's show. "Have you done any local appearances?" I ask. "What about cable television?" They often seem insulted that I would suggest anything so uncool. "How do you plan to learn to be a talk show guest if you don't get some practice?" I challenge. "Would you rather make a fool of yourself on a local cable show or a national talk show?"

Performing these little activities takes on a greater importance when you're determined to learn on a small scale so that you can advance to a higher level.

• *You can shift gears more quickly.* In large organizations, change comes slowly, if at all. Your flexibility can be a big advantage, one that gives you a competitive edge. If something isn't working, it's easier for a tiny business to relinquish a method or product and move on to something else. You can make decisions and act on them immediately, without consulting a committee or waiting for authorization. Think of the difference between you and a large corporation as the difference between a jaguar and a dinosaur. Which would you hire if you needed to get something done? Small is not just beautiful—it's speedy, too.

In this changing world, the flexibility that is inherent in your smallness will be a valuable asset—for you as well as your customers and clients. Make it one of your trademarks.

• *You can improve your people skills.* We laugh when we hear television's Basil Fawlty (John Cleese's bed-and-breakfast owner in *Faulty Towers*) announce, "Innkeeping would be a lovely occupation if it wasn't for the bloody guests." In real life, however, self-bossers quickly learn the importance—and joy—of building good relationships with those whom they are in business to serve.

Yet when most people talk about relationships, they think only in terms of personal ones. A small business gives you an opportunity to expand the relationships in your life in a new way. Writer George Seaton made this discovery years ago. He recalls, "It was during the depression and I went to work for a soap company. My job was to go door to door giving away samples. Carrying a thirty-pound case up and down stairs was, to me, degrading and stultifying for a promising author. Worst of all, it left me so tired that I didn't have the energy to write my name.

"One night I was describing my dull fate to a playwright friend of mine and he became ecstatic. The chance of talking to fifty or a hundred new and different people a day was truly exciting to him. From that moment on, my job became a training ground for me as a writer. Each person who came to the door became a character to be remembered—the mannerisms, the peculiarities of speech, the eccentricities of behavior. I couldn't wait to get home and jot down what I had seen and heard."

Your work may bring you in contact with fewer people, but you'll learn—especially when your business is small—the importance and value of each and every one. You'll develop a special appreciation for those who support and encourage you in your early days. The knowledge of human behavior that you acquire when you have time to pay attention will serve you well later on when you have more people to deal with. It's another skill best mastered when your business is small.

• *You can provide the high-touch balance in our high-tech world.* In his blockbuster book *Megatrends*, John Naisbitt wrote at length about the high-tech/high-touch challenge. As our world becomes more impersonal, he predicted, we will look for ways to balance that with personal encounters and interactions. "Technology and our human potential are the two greatest challenges and adventures facing humankind today," says Naisbitt. "The great lesson we must learn from the principle of high tech/high touch is a modern version of the Greek ideal—balance."

This is where small business can shine. Finding ways to add a personal, human touch to your endeavor can provide a needed warmth in an often impersonal world. No matter what product or service you offer, giving your customers the experience of dealing with a person—not a computer or anonymous organization—can be satisfying for them and for you. It's not only making an extra effort that will distinguish you; being accessible and sensitive to your customers is an advantage that is impossible for big companies to duplicate. You can provide a level of service that large companies can only dream about.

A purchasing agent told me he had started buying glue from a young inventor. "I was somewhat reluctant to start doing business with him when he first called on me," said the agent. "His product was less expensive than the one we were using, so I relented and bought a trial amount. It proved to be better in several respects. It dried faster, didn't leave a residue that we couldn't remove, and was odorless. Still, I had always purchased supplies from large distributors, so I hesitated, thinking that this guy might not be able to keep up with our orders. I kind of put Jeff on probation—even though I didn't tell him that. I placed an order and watched to see what kind of service we got. I found out right away that I had gotten rid of a whole bunch of headaches working with him. If there was a problem, he got it resolved quickly. It only took a single call to reach him. With my other suppliers, I often get passed around and have to wait days—or even weeks—to get a problem fixed or a special order. Jeff taught me a lot about small-business owners. He changed my mind completely."

Don't be afraid to admit your smallness, and don't fail to emphasize its advantages. John Schroeder's Word Store prides itself on serving a small number of clients, each receiving personal attention. You can make that a benefit of your enterprise, too, even if you don't plan to stay small forever.

How many advantages can you think of that you can offer your customers or clients *because* you are small? List as many as you can come up with now. Knowing these benefits will make your marketing easier and more effective in the future.

_____

_____

_____

_____

Imagine that your major competition is a *Fortune* 500 company. How would you sell yourself to a prospective client?

_____

_____

_____

_____

Getting the Big Picture

For years I handicapped myself by thinking that if my goal was to build a successful business I had to aspire to creating a large company. Only after I learned to trust myself could I admit that my dreams did not include a glass tower with my name emblazoned on the side. I had no interest whatsoever in reigning over a force of worker bees. Being a one-person, hands-on enterprise was and is the vision that turns me on. What a relief it was to free myself of a paradigm that never suited me!

Earlier in chapter 4, I suggested that you determine a beginning and a long-range financial goal for yourself. You need to use this same thinking in other parts of your enterprise as well. For instance, you might decide that you'll begin by organizing an office in your home. Later on, you might envision your office as a motor home that carries you from place to place. In a way, you need to have dual mental pictures—where you'll start and where you'll go.

One of the seven habits of highly effective people that Stephen Covey talks about in his book of the same name reinforces this: begin with the end in mind. "To begin with the end in mind means to start with a clear understanding of your destination. It means to know where you're going so that you better understand where you are now and so that the steps you take are always in the right direction. How different our lives are when we really know what is deeply important to us, and, keeping that picture in mind, we manage ourselves each day to be and to do what really matters most."

One of the bright spots in my bleak stay in Colorado came when I met photographer Gary Buehler and his business partner and wife, Duncan Larson. Having sold their home in Lincoln, Nebraska, they were beginning a new chapter in their lives, one that included opening their first studio. They hired me to help them launch and promote this venture.

I was curious about their choice of Nederland, Colorado, as a home. "Why did you pick this place?" I asked Gary.

He laughed and said, "I've always dreamed about walking out my back door and catching a trout for breakfast." That wasn't the only vision he had, however. At our first meeting to discuss his photographic career, I asked him what his ultimate goal included. Again, he answered without hesitation. "I want to become so well known for my portraits that people fly in from all over the country to have me take their picture." I learned immediately that his passion was for black-and-white photography, and I saw his impressive portfolio of people and landscapes. Obviously, he was talented, but he was also undisciplined and disorganized. That's where Duncan's talents came in. Her vision was to manage and promote their operation. They made an impressive team, and working with them was a pleasure.

The beginning stages of their business included identifying the most immediate sources of income. We all agreed that Gary's more artistic work required educating people about the merits of black-and-white portraits. They were willing to offer color photographs, an immediate market, while they found ways to interest people in Gary's more elegant pictures. Weddings, family portraits, and graduation photos got their business rolling. It was the grander dream that kept it growing.

Beginning with the end in mind makes everything easier. The smallest task takes on a new importance when you realize that it's a stepping-stone to your dreams. Knowing that what you do today will determine the quality of your life five years from now makes it easy to manage your time and make decisions that will hasten your goals.

The Bible tells us that where there is no vision the people perish. Inherent in every vision is the hope of improvement of some sort. With that picture in mind, getting started takes on an urgency which, in turn, smooths the way in your early days.

You need to maintain a balanced approach in managing the paradox of starting small and thinking big. Television and movie producer Norman Lear points that out brilliantly. "Success is how you collect your minutes," says Lear. "You spend millions of minutes to reach one triumph, one moment, then you spend maybe a thousand minutes enjoying it. If you were unhappy through those millions of minutes, what good are the thousands of minutes of triumph? It doesn't equate." Having a vision does not mean you must postpone your happiness until it's accomplished. You should enjoy the trip, too.

A big breakthrough for me came when I realized that the purpose of a vision isn't to make us happy so much as it is to pull us forward. Having a picture in your mind of where you're headed will challenge you to do things you would never have tried otherwise. Your imagination will be awakened, your energies mobilized. But, ultimately, you will learn to experience both happiness and serenity in the present moment . . . long before your vision has materialized.

More Humble Beginnings

There's something wonderfully romantic about new beginnings. Remember your first house or apartment, the first place you could call your own? It probably was small, shabby even, but it was all yours. The pictures on the walls, the bedspread, the personal touches belonged to you—not your parents. You're going to feel the same way about your first venture. Pride of ownership is a lovely emotion. I'll never forget how I felt about my first business.

It may have been partly beginner's luck, but it took less than a month to get The Successful Woman up and running. Of course, I had spent about nine months mulling over the idea without telling a soul what I was contemplating. When the time came, I was emotionally ready to go.

My plans were simple. I would create and conduct goal-setting, self-esteem, and other personal development seminars for women. In addition, I planned to publish a newsletter, an undertaking which I knew nothing about (and I could find little information to guide me). Fortunately, I lacked much money to invest, so I had to take everything a step at a time and learn to do all sorts of things I'd never done before.

I decided that I needed some sort of logo and letterhead, but couldn't afford to hire a graphic designer. Since I had always loved silhouettes, I got the idea to make my logo the silhouette of a woman with her chin up. I found a profile of a woman in a magazine and carefully cut the outline from black construction paper. It worked! On my first try, I had created a perfect logo. My neighbor ran a tiny printing shop, so he reduced my logo and printed my first business stationery.

Once I had my name and logo, I needed a flyer to promote my newsletter and a brochure to advertise my seminar. I spent days writing both of these, getting ideas from brochures I had collected. I typed them up on my decrepit typewriter and had them printed on brightly colored paper. I mailed newsletter flyers to every woman I knew, all over the country. I realized the value of having a mailing list and began to organize my own. I mailed more flyers to woman-owned businesses that advertised in *Ms.* magazine and others that I read about in the newspaper. That first little mailing brought an impressive response and enough orders to pay for the first newsletter's printing and postage.

Promoting the seminars proved a bit thornier. While I had narrowed my market to women in the workplace, that was a broad category and one that required scouting to reach. I checked with my chamber of commerce and found that it had a directory of local organizations and associations. I began to contact program directors, offering my services as a speaker to their groups, a ploy I hoped would bring me visibility. I did get a number of speaking dates. Every talk that I gave proved helpful, and I always arrived with newsletters and seminar brochures to hand out.

I also did some mailings to large local businesses, but that proved ineffective. At the time, I didn't realize that companies regularly receive numerous promotional mailings—most of which get little attention. Working on building my business through personal contacts proved far more effective; I shifted my attention to making telephone calls to prospective clients and taking advantage of referrals and contacts, forgetting about mass mailings to people who had never heard of me.

Now that I had clarified my ideas, I felt ready to try getting publicity. Perhaps I could interest the local paper in publishing a small article. Although I'd never written a press release, I got out my new letterhead and wrote to the editor of the lifestyle section of the paper, describing The Successful Woman and why I thought it would be of interest to the paper's readers. I sent the letter off to the newspaper and held my breath.

The very next day, I received a call from Ann Beckman, a reporter. She said, "I have your press release here and what you're doing sounds interesting. I'd like to talk to you in more depth about it. When can I come to your office?" My office? I hadn't thought about anyone coming to my home office and didn't think it would enhance my credibility if she saw the card table in my television room that was serving as my executive suite. I thought quickly and asked, "Would it be okay if I came to your office?" She agreed and we set up an appointment.

I had never been interviewed before and had no idea what it would entail. I arrived at the newspaper office nervous but wearing my best dress and trying to appear cool and collected. Ann turned out to be a wonderful interviewer, and we chatted away like old school chums for almost two hours. When we finished the interview, she said they'd like a photograph, so I was marched outside, where a staff photographer took several shots of me squinting into the sun. The story was scheduled for the following week.

I had expected a modest little piece, maybe a filler buried inside the local news. Instead, the story filled the entire front page of the living section—complete with a five-by-seven-inch photo of me being blinded by the sun. My phone began ringing immediately, and my first seminar sold out.

The newspaper publicity also generated a steady stream of speaking invitations. I said yes to anyone who asked. In the first six months of The Successful Woman I appeared on local radio and television shows, talked to adult Sunday-school groups, appeared at every woman's conference in the area, taught in the university extension program, and even showed up as a "celebrity" at a local telethon. While the initial flurry of publicity lasted, I could see a positive result in my business. However, I learned that I had to keep up other promotion efforts as well. I expanded my mailing list, began advertising my newsletter in a small classified ad in *Ms.* magazine, and recruited friends in other cities to help me set up seminars through community colleges near them.

In less than a year, I felt as if I'd earned an M.B.A. My emphasis had been on learning, not earning, but I had managed to realize a modest profit right from the start. I had made my share of mistakes, but considered myself fortunate to be making them while I was still a beginner. My self-confidence kept growing along with The Successful Woman. Even more important, I had gotten my dreams back and finally believed I was doing something that truly mattered.

This one-step-at-a-time approach has continued to be my method for starting new ventures. This willingness to keep business on a small scale to start with has proved over and over again to be a key in creating strong profit centers that continue to grow with time.

First Things First

Setting up shop begins with handling details, large and small. Make up your mind to complete these chores as quickly as possible so that you can move on to more interesting things. Many of these details need to be dealt with only once, and then you're finished with them. Decide which of the following details apply and put them in place as soon as possible.

One of your very first decisions will be to decide where you're going to work. Do you have a bedroom that you can convert? Office space you can rent or share? A motor home that will be a traveling office? Some self-bossers run fine businesses with only a clipboard and appointment book that they carry with them. Virgin Records and Airlines founder Richard Branson has built his billion-dollar empire without ever setting up a formal office or desk. For many years, his headquarters was a houseboat docked on the River Thames, and he continues to eschew any conventional office setting.

If you're going to be creating a product, where will you do so? If your space is limited, you may have to begin working on your dining room table with baskets on wheels to hold your supplies.

Whatever you choose as your office, make it as inviting and personal as possible. Indulge in all those personal touches that many corporations forbid. Burn incense, if you like, to start your day. Play Mozart or Guns N' Roses in the background. Add plants, posters, family pictures—or anything else you fancy. Make your office a fitting backdrop for the great scenes that will be played out against it.

For more than a dozen years, Rhino Records has been the leading independent reissuer of old recordings. The company began in the garage of a couple of friends, Richard Foos and Harold Bronson. Although Rhino has come a long way and now employs more than one hundred people, the founders work hard to keep their counterculture environment alive. In a competitive, high-powered industry, Rhino cultivates its laid-back image. Employees who volunteer sixteen hours a year of community service are rewarded with a week off at Christmas. Not only mothers, but also fathers, get sixteen weeks of unpaid parental leave and two weeks' paid leave. Each employee has a beanbag chair to bring to quarterly staff meetings. Founders Foos and Bronson believe that staying irreverent is necessary to maintaining the corporate environment that suits them best. You, too, can design an atmosphere that is as conservative or zany as you are.

You'll also need to find out your legal obligations, which vary from state to state. In most places, you must file a fictitious business name (also called a d/b/a, for doing business as) if you're going to use a name other than your own for your enterprise. If you fail to do this, you may not be allowed to open a bank account with your business name on it. Depending on where you live, you may need to apply for permits and/or a sales tax license. These things are usually inexpensive to obtain, but take time. You can pay an attorney to file your fictitious business name, for instance, but doing it yourself is simple and will save you money.

In Minnesota, we have a Small Business Assistance Office which publishes *A Guide to Starting a Business in Minnesota*. This annual publication is indispensable for any would-be entrepreneur, as it contains all the nuts-and-bolts information necessary for operating legally. Check to see whether your state has such a publication. It will direct you to the proper offices for getting permits, explain different ways to set up a business, and generally make life easier.

Consider, also, the team of experts you want to assemble to assist you in doing things efficiently. Look for lawyers, accountants, and other advisers who are familiar with small enterprises. Often these professionals run their own small offices and will be more helpful than a larger firm would be. Ask for referrals from other entrepreneurs and use your own intuition about whom you want to work for you. It's to be hoped that you'll keep things simple enough at the outset so that you won't need a great deal of advice, but it's a good idea to locate your personal advisers so that you can call on them quickly if you need to.

Less Is More

You don't need a gold-embossed letterhead to start making a living without a job. (Come to think of it, you may never need gold embossing.) You will, however, need a few tools. Some of the most important ones are things you already have. Your inventory might include a telephone, an automobile or access to public transportation, contacts from the past, perhaps a personal computer, ordinary office supplies. Mobilize all of your existing resources before you spend huge amounts of money to create a high-tech dream office. (That can come later.)

Keep things as simple as possible here, too. You may be able to begin with a neat letterhead, a few hundred business cards, and some office supplies. You don't need fancy mailing labels or printed invoices or all those other tempting goodies that await you in an office-supply store. You can acquire these more expensive tools as you go. The basics are fine at the beginning.

A student called to tell me that she wanted to buy a knitting machine and start making sweaters for children. We talked about the ways she could market her sweaters, how she could distinguish her product, and so forth. Then she said she was considering purchasing a $4,000 knitting machine that could be connected with a personal computer for design transfer. She didn't own the computer yet, either, so accumulating all this equipment was going to represent a substantial investment. I suggested that she might begin a bit more modestly and upgrade her equipment once she'd established her market. "I would think," I surmised, not knowing a lot about knitting machines, "that you could resell your equipment when you got ready to get a more elaborate setup." That triggered an idea. "Maybe I should look for a used machine myself," she proposed. We agreed that that option made a lot more sense than beginning with a larger investment.

Know, too, when it makes sense to lease equipment rather than buy it. Or when it is cost-effective to use available equipment rather than buy your own. Unless you're doing enormous volumes of photocopying, for example, using your neighborhood print shop is probably wiser. Be aware of all of your options and pick the best ones for you, knowing that as your business grows and changes, so will your needs.

This is the time to become masterful in using your imagination more and your pocketbook less. Not only is it good training, you'll realize a profit sooner if you can keep your overhead as low as possible. This isn't, however, an invitation to be a certified cheapskate. Think of thrift as an exercise in creativity.

Body Shop founder Anita Roddick says much of her cosmetics company's success was due to the fact that she had little money to work with when she began. In an industry that spends millions on packaging and advertising, the Body Shop took a different approach, one it continues to use today. Roddick has never advertised, but her unorthodox method of doing business, along with her social activism, garnered countless articles and other publicity. Early on, Roddick had discovered that it was possible to promote a business using attention-getting and imaginative means. Since her first store was off the beaten path, she used to spray a trail of scent from a busier street corner to the door of her shop to attract passersby. That practical, creative thinking remains a trademark of this international organization.

It often seems to me that many new entrepreneurs spend foolishly to compensate for their lack of confidence. It makes more sense to ask yourself frequently, "How can I do more with less?" A friend of mine who once managed a multimillion-dollar budget for a government agency started his own business and learned how to stretch small amounts of money. He laughingly recalls, "I went from spending five million dollars a year to saying, 'Well, we've got fifty dollars to spend this month. What should we do with it?'" He now has much more money to work with every month, but continues to make imaginative choices in his spending.

If you need more help resisting the temptation to spend unnecessarily, reflect on this story from Orville Redenbacher:

> Although I'd been successful in developing my new popping corn, I evidently had no talent for selling it. I traveled to Chicago to seek guidance from the advertising and marketing firm of Gerson, Howe and Johnson. I found myself at a table with two young copywriters, a retailing expert, and Mr. Gerson, the president.
>
> "Talk to us about popcorn," he said. I talked on for about three hours, feeling foolish while they just listened.
>
> "Come back next week," they said, "and we'll have something for you."

The following week I returned, wondering what great marketing scheme they had come up with.

"We think you should call it Orville Redenbacher's Gourmet Popping Corn."

I stared at them dumbfounded. "Golly, no," I gasped. "Redenbacher is such a . . . a funny name." I remembered those kids giggling back in Indiana.

"That's the point. People will love it."

I drove back to Indiana wryly thinking we had paid $13,000 for someone to come up with the same name my mother had come up with when I was born.

Do Your Own Legwork

Doing research can be one of the most delightful aspects of starting out. Then why do so many people ignore it?

Nearly every week, I receive a phone call from someone who says, "I've been thinking about writing some articles, but I don't know what magazines to send them to." Usually I ask if they've checked the listings in *Writer's Market*.

"What's that?" is a common response.

I explain that it's an annual publication listing thousands of magazines that buy freelance articles. "Then there's *Writer's Digest* magazine, which lists newer markets," I add.

I realize that we all have to start somewhere, but too many newcomers fail to take responsibility for doing their homework. Publishers regularly receive—and throw away—letters asking, "How do I get started as a writer?" The same is true for many industries. Although the information you need can be uncovered with a bit of digging, failing to do so will handicap you unnecessarily. How can you begin to tap into the information that specifically applies to you? By showing personal initiative and looking in a place that is a gold mine.

Great businesses start at your library. Spend a day browsing every so often. Look in magazines for ads for businesses similar to the ones you're starting. How do they present themselves? Almost every major city has its own publication, and these can be a superb source of ideas. If your library subscribes to any of these, read the classifieds and other small ads. While you're checking out the periodical section of your library, scan the small-business publications and even alternative magazines like *Mother Earth News* and the *Utne Reader*. Publications that are read by people who are forward-thinking carry many ads for creative enterprises.

While you're there, get to know a reference librarian. These unsung folks are some of the most service-oriented you'll ever meet. I always have the impression that reference librarians would be equally happy had they become detectives; they love to hunt down obscure bits of information. Ask them about directories of publications and associations (which are usually stored at the reference desk and not circulated). You'll find all sorts of magazines, journals, and association newsletters read by your potential customers, publications that are sold only by subscription. Scanning these directories may give you numerous new ideas for ways to reach your market. Reference librarians can save you time by connecting you quickly with information on a topic you're researching. They know what their collection contains and can often direct you to other libraries for information their own may lack. Your library may have a telephone service available as well, so that you can call the reference department directly when you need help.

Doing your legwork also includes uncovering other local resources. Does your community have a Small Business Administration Office? They're an excellent source of inexpensive material on starting different kinds of businesses. (They may not, however, be a good source of financial assistance or even consulting advice, since you will be operating outside their concept of business.) Get yourself a copy of their catalog of publications, yours for a phone call.

Another local resource is to be found at community colleges, university extension programs, and adult education schools. Again, with a few phone calls you can get yourself on the mailing list of these schools, which often offer seminars and short courses that may prove useful.

While you're at it, see whether your local chamber of commerce offers a directory of local organizations. These can help you find groups you may want to join or groups which may be appropriate customers.

Knowing what resources are at your fingertips is a good idea at every stage of your development. Self-education will be a continuing function for you, and once you realize how much information you can easily lay your hands on, you'll gain confidence in your ability to find what you need as you need it.

Scope Out Your Competition

If your plans are to market locally, you'll want to know what businesses in your community are similar to yours. If your market is national or global, you'll also want to see what other companies offer a product or service that resembles yours. Even if your idea seems unique, there may be others who are doing the same thing elsewhere or have a business that has something in common with yours. It makes sense to study what they've done and see what benefits you can offer that they don't.

Being ignorant of the competition can be costly and harmful. If you don't know what you're up against, you'll be less effective in your own efforts. Your customers, too, will assume that you haven't done your homework, and your credibility will suffer if you're uninformed about your competition.

I was surprised when a woman who had started a business marketing audiotaped novels called me. I wasn't startled by her business idea, however. Books on tape have become quite popular, after all, and have many enthusiastic listeners. But I was astounded by this woman's ignorance of her market and competitors. When I suggested that she look in *The New Yorker* to see how her competition advertised, she told me she didn't know that any other mail-order companies were selling audiotaped novels. She had no idea her product was being sold outside of bookstores. Like the would-be writers who haven't done the most elementary research, she hadn't either.

Knowing about the competition isn't an invitation to be a copycat, however. You may find benefits in your product or service that you can stress over your competition's. The fact that competition exists at all is an indication that there is a market for your offering. Whatever you do, don't be intimidated by your competition. In fact, let the competition compete against you!

Setting Your Fees

Setting fees for a product or service can be as thorny for the experienced entrepreneur as it is for the beginner. As your product line develops or your services expand, your pricing will change accordingly. But you've got to start somewhere, and there are simple guidelines you can use to determine a fair price.

First let's consider pricing a service. Before you can know how you'll price your service, more local research is in order. A woman called to say she and a partner were starting a decorative housepainting service, but didn't know what to charge. I suggested she call several local painters, find out their hourly rates, inquire whether they bid jobs without an hourly consideration, and ask what was included in their fees. This is just a matter of making a few telephone calls—posing as a potential customer, not a competitor, of course. If you discover that a wide range of pricing exists in your community; you can aim for the middle to begin with. When I started my catering business, I checked not only caterers' fees, but the prices charged by local restaurants and tearooms for afternoon tea. I added $1.50 per person to the price charged by restaurants to compensate for my travel time and expenses, since I was bringing the tea to my clients. If you're introducing a brand-new service to your community, you may have to make a calculated guess about pricing. Knowing a medium-range hourly fee for personal or professional services can make your calculating less wild. One student of mine wanted to offer her services for cleaning out garages and used as a guide the fee charged by housecleaners. You can always raise or lower your fees when it's warranted.

Your fee-setting is simplified if you're dealing with a client whose budget is predetermined. Then you can accept or reject the price the client is willing to pay. If you plan special events for organizations, for example, you'll be given a budget to work with, and out of that will come your fee. I urge you not to accept an unfair fee out of desperation. If you do, you'll end up resenting your client and have a difficult time performing as well as you're able.

You may be building a profit center that offers a service that you previously performed at a job. In this case, you'll need to figure out an hourly fee. Begin by calculating the hourly salary you last received; multiply that figure by 2.5 or 3 to compensate for overhead. If you earned $12 an hour doing word processing, as a freelancer your fee would be $30 to $36 an hour. Some new self-bossers have a hard time doubling or tripling their previous salary because it seems such a leap. Remember that your client is paying you for the work being done, but doesn't pay for insurance, equipment, etc. Those things were a hidden part of your old salary, and you're entitled to them now.

When you offer a service, be clear about exactly what your fee includes. If you're a graphic designer charging an hourly rate, for instance, does that rate include pickup and delivery, or are those free to the client? What about initial consultation on a project? Is that subject to your hourly rate? Knowing precisely what you will and will not do is important—or you may find yourself coerced into doing extra tasks for free. This is also important when you need to negotiate your fee. You can list for your client in detail what's included. If you're dealing with a reluctant prospect, your negotiating position will be stronger if you can say, "My fee includes this and this and this. What would you like me to leave out?"

Whenever possible, avoid quoting a flat fee in your initial contact with a client. Offer to get back to the client once the project has been outlined and you've made some calculations. Try to discover whether the client has a set budget—this isn't always easy, but it's enormously helpful to know what you're shooting at. Nearly every consultant I know has at least one story about losing a project because his or her fee was too *low*. One woman had submitted a bid for a series of training programs that a company planned to offer its employees. When she learned that the project had gone to someone else, she called the manager in charge to see why the company had eliminated her. "Frankly, my dear," came the snide reply, "we're not accustomed to dealing with cut-rate vendors." Despite the manager's arrogance, the trainer learned a valuable lesson and promptly raised her fees. If you're brave enough to keep yours a bit high, you also have more room to negotiate and still realize a profit.

Finally, remember that the money you receive may be only one of the benefits of accepting a project. A client may be giving you an opportunity to expand your experience or enter a new market. With each project your objectives—and rewards—need to be carefully considered. There are always trade-offs to take into account.

Setting fees for a product is a bit different from charging for a service. You'll have some concrete numbers to work with that suggest that pricing a product is a logical matter. Well, it is and it isn't. Ultimately, the price you'll receive is determined by what people are willing to pay. Nevertheless, there are guidelines to be followed here that will help you calculate what you should charge.

If you're manufacturing the product yourself, you must determine your material costs and production time, as well as other expenses—such as shipping—that you incur. Once you know what your product costs are, you can again use the simple formula of multiplying that figure by 2.5 or 3. There's another variable to consider here. Your product price will be lower if you're wholesaling the product rather than retailing it.

Let's say you decide to make birdhouses. Your material costs are quite low, since you have a source of scrap lumber, making material investment $1.20 per unit. It takes you about thirty minutes to assemble a house and another hour to handpaint flowers, a windowbox, and picket fence on the outside. You want to earn $8 an hour with this venture, so your material and labor costs come to $13.20. If you wholesale your houses to a catalog, which sells them for $26, this would be a reasonable price. However, should you take on the marketing yourself and sell the birdhouses at craft shows, you could multiply your initial costs by 2.5 or 3 and price your little masterpieces at $33 to $39. Not all handmade items can be so easily priced, unfortunately. If you were offering handknit sweaters rather than birdhouses, your production time would be much longer, but an hourly rate would push the price much too high—unless you had uncovered an affluent market which was not influenced much by price.

While you can use these pricing rules as guidelines, the marketplace is not a fixed thing. Having a broad overview of your financial and personal goals will help you determine the fair price you need to charge in order to reach your goals. Know what others are charging, know what you have to offer that they don't, and take it from there. If you miscalculate and charge too much or too little, adjust your prices and move on.

Concentrate on Cash Flow

The soundest way to capitalize your business is by generating a steady flow of sales. If you put your energy into generating cash flow, you'll eliminate a large percentage of the problems faced by self-bossers.

A few years ago, I interviewed Curt Carlson, one of the country's wealthiest entrepreneurs. Carlson made his first fortune selling trading stamps to stores, which, in turn, gave them to customers as a premium for shopping. Carlson told me that he began building his fortune by calling on stores throughout his area convincing them to buy his program. On Saturdays, he and his partner would don coveralls and return to the stores to install advertising banners. He probably hasn't worn coveralls in fifty years, but Carlson is still a strong proponent of marketing first.

The best way to ensure a dependable cash flow is to be consistent in your marketing. Don't wait for a crisis or a slump. Your business, like every other, will go through cycles. Market when things are booming *and* when they're not. It will all even out.

Start a Scrapbook

Yes, right away. In the early days of The Successful Woman, I was cutting out adhesive lettering with manicure scissors and thought to myself, "I should really take a picture of this because someday it will seem funny." Unfortunately, no such picture exists.

Don't dismiss these first stages as too unimportant or insignificant to record. You are building memories here, and they deserve to be saved. Put your first business card and brochure proudly in a scrapbook that will hold these memories. Take pictures of yourself at work every step of the way. It's an affirmation about the value of your new venture.

As you grow, add newspaper clippings and testimonial letters from happy customers. You'll be glad you saved all these treasures.

Thinking Big

Although your early days will be filled with managing the details of your operation, finding resources, and scouting your market, this is also the time to build and keep your vision alive.

You may have seen the commercial run by U.S. West in which the woman says, "I'm the CEO of a major corporation. Well, actually it's a pet shop. But we're going to be big someday." Enjoying these busy first stages *and* holding on to a grander dream are important here. If you have a mental picture of great achievement and persist in making it real, the work you're doing now will take on a satisfaction and importance that are not possible if your only concerns are immediate gratification and results.

James Allen recognized the significance of this years ago and wrote about it in his success classic, *As a Man Thinketh:* "He who cherishes a beautiful vision, a lofty ideal in his heart, will one day realize it. Cherish your visions. Cherish your ideals. Cherish the music that stirs in your heart, the beauty that forms in your mind, the loveliness that drapes your purest thoughts, for out of them will grow all delightful conditions, all heavenly environment; of these, if you but remain true to them, your world will at last be built. The dreamers are the saviors of the world."

As all great achievers know, Lord Chesterfield wasn't just talking about money when he advised, "Take care of the pence, for the pounds will take care of themselves." Taking care of the little details and mastering small-scale success represents the most dependable road to realizing big dreams.

Winning Ways for Starting Small, Thinking Big

• Use the following checklist to guide you in setting up shop.

____ Locate and organize work space.
____ Determine immediate and long-range equipment needs.

____ Acquire immediately essential equipment.

____ Research state requirements for filing a business name and getting sales permits and a tax ID number.

____ Fulfill appropriate state requirements.

____ Order printed materials, including letterhead and business cards.

____ Open a business checking account.

____ Plan initial advertising and research costs.

____ Produce a brochure about the business, if appropriate.

____ Contact the chamber of commerce for a listing of local associations and organizations.

____ Request catalogs from local colleges and adult education programs.

____ Do additional resource research at the library.

____ Organize a file of potential customers and possible publicity avenues.

• Learn about others who have built success from the ground up. It's more common than you may realize. Here are some examples compiled by Harry J. Gray to add to your collection. He writes, "Sometimes to make it big, you first have to make it small. Conrad Hilton started out sweeping floors in a dusty New Mexico hotel. He eventually cleaned up as owner of a famous hotel chain. John Paul Getty started with a $500 oil lease in Oklahoma and became one of America's richest men. David Packard baked the paint onto his first product in a kitchen oven. Forty-five years later, he was running a $4.7 billion company. There are anonymous men and women starting small today whose names will be household words in twenty years. Will one of those names be yours? Get started!"

• Imagine that it's five years from today and you have created a successful business. You've surpassed your financial goals, have plenty of happy customers, and are branching out in new directions. Meditate on the changes you have realized.

What new people are in your life who weren't there before?

How are you spending your leisure time?

What does your work space look like? How is it equipped?

What have you learned how to do that you couldn't before?

What differences are there in your health? Your appearance?

What obstacles have disappeared?

What do you consider your greatest achievement so far?

What about this lifestyle brings you the greatest pleasure?

Who is most surprised by your success?

CHAPTER 10

Getting Ideas

Money follows ideas. Money does not create anything at all,
much less ideas. Money goes where ideas are.

Paul Hawken

Not long ago, the largest shopping center in the United States
opened five miles from my home. The Mall of America, as it is
known, received worldwide publicity and attracted shoppers
from around the globe. One of the most successful promotions
for the mall was launched by a British travel agency that put
together a "Shop 'Til You Drop" package. As a result of the
promotion an anticipated 10,000 Brits will hop planes and fly to
Minneapolis for a weekend of shopping at the mall.

It's an idea that should have been mine! Given my passions for
travel, shopping, and the English, and my proximity to the Mall
of America, it would have been a natural. If I'd been paying
attention, I would have thought of it when the young woman
from London sat down next to me on a flight from New York. She
was excited about all the bargain-shopping she had done while
visiting the United States. "I pay thirty-eight pounds for jeans at
The Gap in London," she said, "and here they were thirty-eight
dollars." Since the dollar was low at the time, her savings had
been substantial. She regaled me with stories of other good buys
she had made, and I recall telling her that I seldom bought
clothes in England because of the price. So, you see, all the bits

and pieces of a good idea were right in front of me—and passed me by.

Ideas are the stock in trade of self-bossers, and it's not uncommon for them to claim they have more ideas than they could ever possibly use. One woman told me her mind was spitting out ideas so rapidly and constantly that it felt like a popcorn popper. When you're making a living without a job, you'll come to cherish your own ideas and thrill to see the ones that come to life. Ideas are, quite simply, the ancestors of success and deserve to be cultivated and valued.

Every day I talk to students who call to discuss their entrepreneurial ideas. I've had the privilege of hearing some wonderfully innovative thoughts that affirm my conviction that we are all inherently imaginative, even though many of us don't yet believe it. One day a woman called to discuss a really good, sound idea. After I assured her that she was on to something, she said, "I'm forty-three years old and I've never had any original ideas in my life until the last six months when I became unemployed. Now I keep getting ideas all the time."

"I have an unsubstantiated theory," I said with a laugh, "that ideas are floating around in the air and they simply can't find their way into corporate cubicles, so they go elsewhere." I was only partly joking. The creative spirit may exist in all of us, but it needs to be incubated in the right environment before it will come out and assert itself. The joyfully jobless tend to live and work in an environment that stimulates creative thinking, but they also use a number of techniques to keep the ideas flowing. I'll share some of those methods later on, but first, let's consider what it means to be creative.

A good definition of creativity is this: combining known information in unusual ways to make something new that is pleasing, useful, or both. Writer Susan Goodman elaborates by saying, "The creative process is a kind of mental gymnastics that somersaults between different modes of thought—knowledge and imagination, logic and intuition. The results can be as earth-shattering as evolutionary theory—or as everyday as a new recipe and the inspired interventions you make to keep your children from killing one another."

Creativity is nourished by:

- A sense of adventure
- Rejection of sexual stereotypes
- Exposure to novel circumstances, as in traveling or new hobbies
- Good health habits, including getting enough sleep and exercise
- Laughter and good spirits
- Challenging yourself by working at the height of your skill and competence

Creativity is doused by:

- Needing to perform on demand
- Being pressured by excessive competition
- Being motivated by extrinsic versus intrinsic rewards
- Conventional "I've always done it that way" thinking

Considering this, one can see why making a living without a job is a creativity-enhancer. Even so, maximizing our creative potential requires diligence coupled with a willingness to keep pushing past barriers. "Creativity is more than just being different," the jazz musician Charles Mingus pointed out. "Anybody can play weird; that's easy. What's hard is to be as simple as Bach. Making the simple complicated is commonplace; making the complicated simple, awesomely simple—that's creativity."

Trusting Yourself

My friend Susan used to have this thought from choreographer Agnes de Mille posted on her refrigerator:

> There is a vitality, a life-force, an energy, a quickening that is translated through you into action, and because there is only one of you in all time, this expression is unique and if you block it, it will never exist through any medium and will be lost . . . the world will not have it.
> It is not your business to determine how good it is, nor how it compares with other expressions . . . it is your

business to keep it yours clearly and directly, to keep the channel open.

That quote served as a constant reminder to Susan to trust and value her own ideas, without passing premature judgment. Like everyone else, you will have ideas which are marvelous, some which are mediocre, others which are ahead of their time, and still others which are worthless. How do you know which are which? The truth is, you may be the worst judge of your own creativity; therefore, it's up to you to keep acting on your ideas and see what happens when you do.

When Marjorie Kinnan Rawlings left her comfortable life and marriage in New York and headed for the backwoods of Florida, she was following a dream. Rawlings longed to make her mark as an author of gothic novels. She purchased a run-down citrus grove in Cross Creek, Florida, which she hoped would support her while she wrote. It was a dream that was not to be. Her editor continually rejected the stories she sent, but he urged her to try another project. "Your letters about your life in Florida are fascinating, Marjorie," he wrote. "Why don't you forget about writing gothics and write about what you know? Write about your own life." Fortunately for readers everywhere, Rawlings took his advice; her novel *The Yearling* was one of the results of that decision.

In order really to trust our own creative selves, we must give up limited ideas about innovation. We've been led to believe that it's a rare gift, bestowed on a chosen few. Those who think they don't possess it must be content to copy and follow.

Psychologist Abraham Maslow grew up with the same limited notion. His personal concept of creativity changed, however, when he saw his mother-in-law, who had no money to buy flowers, gather a bouquet of weeds, with which she decorated the dinner table. Maslow realized that her actions were motivated by a creative desire. We are remiss, he concluded, to think that creativity is present only in the arts. "A first rate soup," he declared, "is more creative than a second rate painting." Sometimes the most creative endeavors consist of doing the ordinary in an extraordinary way.

Another clue to creativity was uncovered several years ago

when a company hired a team of psychologists to interview scientists in its research and development department. The managers were alarmed that more good ideas weren't being generated and thought they might be able to change that if they could understand what was stopping the flow of ideas. After several months of interviews, the psychologists reported their findings. The difference, they found, between the creative and uncreative scientists was simple: those who believed themselves to be creative were; those who didn't were not. In other words, creativity is partly a self-fulfilling prophecy. Your own self-image either unleashes or restrains your personal flow of ideas.

A few affirmations, repeated regularly, can strengthen your self-image as a creative person. Here are a few you can use to prop up that image and expand your trust.

- I am highly creative and love expressing my creativity.
- There are an unlimited number of excellent ideas in my subconscious mind right now.
- I trust my ideas and act on them quickly.
- My creative spirit cannot be limited. It expands and grows brighter
- My ideas are the ancestors of my success. I welcome new and better ideas every day.
- The more ideas I use, the more I get.
- I enjoy creating the life of my dreams.

Remember, too, that trusting your own creativity means nothing unless you're willing to act on the ideas that are yours. If you fail to do so, you may have the frustrating and unpleasant experience of seeing your ideas come to life in the hands of someone else. Dr. Robert Schuller once said that his concept of hell would be if God were to show him all the opportunities he had missed. Not following through on your ideas isn't only a matter of not trusting and valuing yourself, it's wasting your unique and precious gifts. In a way, it's the ultimate act of selfishness, for, as Agnes de Mille points out, not expressing your ideas means the world will not have them—at least it won't have your special way of expressing those ideas.

Stay Curious

As I was busily rearranging the hotel ballroom where my class was to be held, a man arrived, marched to a front seat, sat down, folded his arms over his chest, and said in a demanding voice, "This better be good!" I was quite certain he was about to be disappointed.

At the same class, another man rushed up to me during the break, eyes glowing, and said, "I can't believe what's happening. I wasn't even supposed to be here tonight; I came to take notes for a friend who couldn't make it. Already I've thought of three businesses I could start."

Every class I teach is a variation on this theme. While the information is the same, some leave with nothing and others with more than they expected. The only identifiable difference is that of attitude. But that difference determines who gets ideas and who does not. An apathetic or hostile attitude is the enemy of creative thought. Ideas, like people, flourish when they are welcomed and embraced.

Bernice Fitz-Gibbon was a legendary force who revolutionized retail advertising. She also was responsible for training dozens of beginning copywriters. A passionate student of human nature, Fitz-Gibbon identified a common denominator in her most successful protégés. "I've never known anyone who bounced out of bed in the morning, delighted and astonished by the world in which he found himself, who was not a success. A vibrantly alive curiosity and a perceptive awareness will put you right up there with the best of them. This intense interest in people and things—this sense of wonder—can be acquired."

Fitz-Gibbon echoed the words of Marcel Proust: "The real voyage of discovery," he said, "consists not in seeking new landscapes but in having new eyes." The creative process comes alive in those who learn to see, really see, the world around them. The creative person takes the material at hand and begins to see it in a new way, to make connections and observations that others miss. The creative person looks for inspiration rather than waiting for it magically to appear.

When the great painter Matisse was nearing his eighties, he was asked, "What's your inspiration?"

"I grow artichokes," he replied. "Every morning I go into the garden and watch these plants. I see the play of light and shade on the leaves and I discover new combinations of colors and fantastic patterns. I study them. They inspire me. Then I go back into the studio and paint."

My father was a man of enormous curiosity who often entertained us at the dinner table with odd bits of information he'd uncovered in his daily reading. Later in life, he began taking walks, the length of which was determined by how long it took him to find some discarded treasure. His wanting to know about anything and everything was contagious—and his greatest legacy.

Keeping your curiosity alive requires conscious effort. Blindly following a routine, doing things in the same way at the same time, can dull your sensibilities and dampen your idea-generating equipment. A simple act such as stopping to look at the familiar as if you'd never seen it before can reawaken your creative thoughts. When seeing something new every day becomes habitual, you'll never worry about running out of ideas again.

For practice, study the following situations and see what ideas they suggest to you. Imagine yourself in each scenario. What possibilities for creating a profit center occur to you?

• During your marriage, you give little thought to money, but after your divorce you find yourself thinking about it all the time. You decide that you'll master living well within your reduced means. That leads you to scouting through secondhand stores and discount department stores. Soon you know every bargain in the city. When your friends need to make a purchase, they call you for advice before they go shopping.

• You live in an area that is popular with tourists and is a host to numerous meetings and conventions. Although the scenery is beautiful, the souvenirs being offered are not. The beachfront shops and hotel gift boutiques seem to sell nothing but gaudy T-shirts and tacky coffee mugs and keychains. You know that a local winery makes wonderful wine, local olives are sold to gourmet shops, and several beekeepers sell honey produced in the region.

• Although you've had no experience, when you buy an older home and decide to remodel, you act as the general contractor for the project. Not only do you save thousands of dollars, you learn a great deal through this hands-on experience. After living in the home for two years, you sell it for an astonishing profit.

• You're stopped frequently on the street by strangers asking where you got your unusual but stylish overcoat. Since you purchased it on a trip abroad, you can't tell others how they can easily find one for themselves.

• You decide to start an herb garden and want to learn more about growing and cooking with these useful plants. When you go to the library to find books on the subject, you discover that those available seem to be written for people who already know more about herbs than you do. You're also surprised by the enormous amount of information and don't know where to begin learning the basics.

• You love haunting secondhand shops, flea markets, and thrift stores, where you purchase lampshades, small pieces of furniture, and old linens and shawls. You spend your evenings embellishing these finds, often turning an ugly duckling into a spectacular swan. After a while, your apartment is bursting with your handiwork. Many of these treasures have been given to your friends as gifts—winning an enthusiastic response—but that hasn't made a dent in your collection.

• You purchase a computer, ostensibly for use by your kids. When your spouse asks you to help prepare a report, you produce a document that looks professional and attractive. You discover that doing graphic design on the kids' computer is fun and you seem to have a real knack for it. Your neighbor is starting a small business and asks whether you could design his brochure. Your kids, however, are complaining that they never get to use the PC.

• You notice that many people are working from their homes these days. In fact, you regularly talk to a number of home-based consultants. You're appalled that these business conversations are held against a backdrop of babies crying, siblings fighting, and dogs barking. The home-based entrepreneurs seem oblivious to these domestic sounds and the nonprofessional image they convey.

• You keep hearing on the news and from your friends on the West Coast that Californians are migrating in droves. Leaving failing schools, growing violence, and a weakening economy, these former sun-worshipers are heading for places like Colorado and Iowa. It seems like a sweeping lifestyle change. You realize that growing up with a father in the military has given you years of experience in adjusting to wildly varying environments.

What ideas did you come up with for these situations? None of these examples is hypothetical; every one was an idea that launched a profit center. The bargain-hunting woman organized her findings into a popular directory and appeared on local television programs to share shopping hints and finds. The woman who found that the souvenirs being sold in her area were inelegant started a successful gift basket business offering regional specialties. The man with the great overcoat now operates a successful mail-order company which sells unique clothing from around the world. The woman who couldn't resist thrift-store treasures has opened her own shop to resell items she's refurbished. And the woman who found those at-home background noises inappropriate for a business markets a tape of office sounds which can be played to cover the noises of pets and kids.

You, too, may have an overlooked opportunity right at your fingertips, one which you can turn to a profit.

Sparking Ideas

It's important, especially in your early days, to go for volume where ideas are concerned. As pleasant as it may be to have a "Eureka" moment when an idea seems to come out of nowhere, blind inspiration is not a dependable method for building an inventory of ideas.

Remember, too, that ideas are frequently a solution to a problem or a better way of doing something. A student of mine began marketing a fancy shower cap she had designed. The original idea for it had come in the early days of her marriage, when she wanted to appear as glamorous as possible as she showered with her new husband. She realized that other women might feel the same way, so she whipped up a bunch of her spiffy caps and set up a booth at the neighborhood street fair. When they sold quickly, she knew she was on to a good idea. You can invite ideas to appear more quickly and steadily if you begin by stating clearly the problem you wish to solve. Think of a simple problem that has you puzzled and write it in the space below. You could write it this way: "I need to find a way to store magazine articles that I want to keep." Or you could put it in question form, which often helps stimulate ideas; for example, "How can I keep my three-year-old quiet when the phone rings?" or "Where can I carry money when I go jogging?" Pick something that's been a continuing annoyance and write it down now.

_____

_____

Without rushing to find the perfect solution to the problem, consider the wide variety of ways in which you can fire up your imagination. In the next few weeks, try out several of these idea-stimulators, keeping the problem you have defined in mind. How many new ideas can you find? It's helpful to keep a running list in a small notebook that you carry with you as you go about this search. Ideas can be fleeting, so plan ways to trap them on the spot. Then spend time in several of the following ways.

• Brainstorming, that old reliable idea-producer, is most effective when done in the company of someone you trust and find stimulating. For the past five years, John Schroeder and his writing partner, Shane Groth, have met weekly to share ideas and plan joint projects. Twice a year, they take themselves on a writers' retreat. They pack up their computers and fishing gear and head for a cabin or ice-fishing house. When they return, they may not have any fish, but they're always accompanied by a long list of new ideas for writing projects.

• Self-designed field trips are another great idea-jogger. Spend a morning at a flea market, browse in a junkyard, revisit a museum. Put yourself in contact with new people who have an enthusiasm for something you know nothing about. If your city has ethnic neighborhoods, stroll through the streets and shops.

Sample foods and study clothes and customs. Or go to a bustling business and watch the free-enterprise system in action. Often a change of scenery will beget a change of thought.

• Be more than an ordinary tourist. Travel with your eyes and ears open to new ideas, new ways of doing things. I never visit a city without looking for a business that we don't have at home. The television show *Roseanne* illustrated this idea when Roseanne's truck-driving sister convinced her that they should open a restaurant like the one she had found on her travels through Iowa. Many a fine business has begun with a transplanted idea.

• Find ideas in unusual places. Journalist Robert Weider suggests, "Anyone can look for fashion in a boutique or history in a museum. The creative explorer looks for history in a hardware store and fashion in an airport."

• Find ideas in ordinary places. Some idea-generators can be close at hand. I fancy the Yellow Pages as a fountain of inspiration. Classified ads in magazines and newspapers are also fun to read and sources of good ideas. If you live in the East, check out the classified ads in *Los Angeles* magazine; if you're a San Diegoan, find a copy of *Boston* magazine and see what entrepreneurs are doing on the other side of the country. Expose yourself to ideas from outside your own region and see whether you can adapt them to your community.

• Go to a class with the intention of getting ideas rather than just passively receiving information. Learn to do magic or juggle or study acting. Anything that expands your creative spirit in one arena will automatically expand it in other parts of your life as well. Classes that attract other creative people are worth attending for the opportunity of meeting some interesting new folks.

• Calm yourself. Close your eyes, take a deep breath or two, and relax your body. In this calm state, let your mind roam around and free-associate. While you may not get any new ideas during this exercise, it often opens the door to new thoughts which spontaneously appear afterward. It has the added advantage of blocking out distractions for a short time. Other calming activities are taking a walk, browsing in a bookstore or nursery, or listening to quiet music.

• Do something mindless, like vacuuming the rug. Any creative endeavor can get bogged down when the creator feels blocked.

Psychologists suggest that you can shorten the down time by doing something unrelated to the project that has you stymied. In other words, you can solve the problem by walking away from it for a while. When you shift gears and perform an activity that doesn't require much thought, you allow time for your creative batteries to recharge. When you return to the project that has you perplexed, you'll bring a new energy and perspective.

Tapping the Power of a Master Mind Group

In Napoleon Hill's classic success book, *Think and Grow Rich*, the author discusses the value and power of the Master Mind group. Every town in America has informal and formal groups like these that meet from time to time. In small towns you see clusters of business owners, often the movers and shakers of the community, gathering for breakfast or lunch to discuss local issues and make plans.

Hill's concept of a Master Mind group differs somewhat from the networking organizations that have become so popular. A true Master Mind group is small, and its members have been invited to attend. The focus is sharper and the purpose more defined. It goes beyond meeting for professional companionship or business referrals.

"The Master Mind may be defined as coordination of knowledge and effort, in a spirit of harmony, between two or more people, for the attainment of a definite purpose," writes Hill. "Economic advantages may be created by any person who surrounds himself with the advice, counsel, and personal cooperation of a group who are willing to lend him or her wholehearted aid in a spirit of harmony. This form of cooperative alliance has been the basis of nearly every great fortune."

Forming your own group can be a satisfying addition to your own self-bossing. Your group can serve as an unofficial board of directors, offering advice and support for your plans. In addition, this is an excellent format for brainstorming and generating new ideas for all members of the group. While you may each be making a living without a job in a different way from the others, your shared commitment to the success and prosperity of each member is what's important.

To start a group, solicit members by personal invitations to people you know, announcements at other group meetings, or classified ads in newspapers or professional newsletters. If you wanted a group made up of inventors, for instance, you might attend a local inventors' group and announce your interest, see who wants to join you, and, if necessary, select those people you believe would be most compatible. Keep initial membership small. You want your group to solidify at about five or six members. At first, you may hold a couple of meetings with more people and see which ones weed themselves out. Before you can build a group that is really powerful, you'll need to spend time in an auditioning process. Your first few meetings will be for the purpose of building trust and rapport between members, so don't expect great thoughts to be generated right away. Make it clear that a commitment to the group is important and that no one should be involved who isn't willing to make participation for at least six months a top priority. A Master Mind group will never get off the ground if the members only attend when they don't have a better offer.

Meet monthly and limit meetings to two hours. If members want more frequent contact, weekly or biweekly breakfast or lunch groups could be formed outside the main meeting. Use part of each meeting for a planned program or discussion and the rest for informal exchanges of ideas.

Make certain that all members know how to find one another. You never know when one of you will come across a resource or potential client for another member of the group. Encourage informal exchanges of information, which don't have to wait until the regular meeting time. If you find an article in a newspaper that's appropriate for someone else, pass it on.

From time to time, plan a Success Night to celebrate accomplishments. You might include friends, spouses, or family members in these festivities.

A Master Mind group created with a mutual commitment to everyone's success can become a most valued source of relationships that keep you moving forward. It's a success tool that belongs in your plans.

Tuning into Trends

An Eastern proverb advises, "Ride the horse in the direction the horse is going." That's essential advice for entrepreneurs. In order to know what direction the horse is going in, you must pay attention to the changes happening in our world. Doing so will save you a heap of frustration as well as a bunch of money; it will also provide a source of fresh ideas.

You can become a savvy trend-watcher by paying attention to the news—reading as many magazines and newspapers as possible and keeping abreast of fads. Let's suppose you're teaching cooking classes and want to do something out of the ordinary. You see a poll in *USA Today* which reports that people are marrying later, buying their own homes before they marry, and taking a new interest in learning domestic skills. The survey also notes that single men are becoming homeowners at a faster rate than ever before. Does that suggest any trend-related ideas for your cooking class? How about a series of bachelor classes—for men only? Or quick meals instead of fast food? Maybe you could put together a class on buying essential kitchen equipment or beginning gourmet recipes. What about romantic dinners at home? These men are single or divorced, so they're probably dating. Don't just tune into the facts of the news. Watch and read with the question "How do I fit in?" in mind.

Notice what's happening in the world, changes in society, new problems arising. You may come up with a timely idea—or even see a trend coming before it's visible to others. A few years ago, a new magazine appeared on the newsstands that was an immediate success. *Victoria* magazine tapped into a growing interest in nostalgia and a desire to return, albeit vicariously, to calmer times. Filled with gauzy photographs, recipes for elaborate meals, and clothes and furnishings evoking the past, it broke all records for attracting subscribers. Equally interesting are the number of small businesses that advertise their nostalgia-inducing products in the magazine. Certainly some of these advertisers had been in business for years and suddenly had a new venue for connecting with customers. Others are brand-new businesses created to cash in on this growing trend. In either case, recognizing a renewed interest in the past—and creating a profit center to meet this interest—has proved timely and profitable.

A Simple Test for Your Ideas

The difference between a good idea and a bad one is this: a good idea produces the results you desire. That's easy enough, but how can you know whether you have a good, or even a great, idea? Sitting in your living room contemplating your notion won't tell you. Asking your friends and family for their opinions won't help much, either—even when they're encouraging. Ultimately, ideas need to be tested, taken to the marketplace and tried. They also need nurturing time. An idea that bombs may still become a valid one with some changes or refinement.

For the longest time, I just floundered around with my ideas. I had no guideline for knowing when to quit and when to keep going. Sometimes an idea would succeed through sheer stubbornness; other times I'd be dragging a corpse and not even notice. Then I came across a gem in Phil Laut's little book, *Money Is My Friend*. It's a test I now apply to every project I undertake. You'll find it useful, too, I'm sure.

Laut recommends, "Now that you have an idea of what you can do to make your favorite money-making idea a financial success, ask yourself whether you are willing to stick with it, no matter what it takes, until you receive your first $100 from it. After receiving your first $100, you can decide whether you want to continue or not."

This simple idea is surprisingly profound. It offers a guideline that you can easily implement for each new venture you begin. Once you've earned that $100, you're in a stronger position to assess what you've done. Did it take too long to earn that money? If it took a long time, did you learn enough so that you can speed up the process? Did you grow bored with the idea?

Make it your practice to apply this test and you'll be certain that every idea you get will be given a fair chance to prove itself. If it flunks the $100 test, go on to your next idea.

The $100 Hour

Activating your creative spirit and using it to become more aware of the opportunities that exist make it easier to generate profit center ideas. The trick is to be consistent and disciplined about seeing money-making ideas. The chemist Linus Pauling said, "The best way to have a good idea is to have a lot of ideas." This is certainly true where being joyfully jobless is concerned. You can't just wait for inspiration to arrive.

If there's one technique for successfully making a living without a job that outshines all the others, it's the $100 Hour. It works with such infallible certainty that once you make it a regular part of your plans, it's like a rocket propelling you to your goals.

Since I discovered this idea, I have realized that my own jobless earning would have been smoother and faster had I known about it earlier. Now that I've found it, it remains an essential part of my business. Several years ago, I was working on two large consulting projects and suddenly realized that once they were completed, I had nothing lined up. Because my time was limited, I set aside an hour a day for the purpose of creating new business ideas. Before long, I had a lengthy list of projects and had begun working on several of them. By the time my consulting assignments were completed, there was no income gap. I have eliminated—forever, I believe—the slumps and down times that used to plague me.

You can begin implementing the $100 Hour even if you now have a job or other commitments that clamor for your time. Begin by making a pact with yourself that you will set aside time daily, if possible, or at scheduled intervals for the purpose of finding an idea that will bring you $100. You needn't complete the plan in this hour, but if time permits use your surplus to get your idea rolling. Do research, make calls, or write letters— anything that advances your goal. If you're focusing your energies on a single profit center, then come up with an idea for expanding it in a way that will earn another $100. If you're going to try a number of different ideas in order to figure out what you most want to do, then this time can be spent designing a variety of projects.

This idea sounds obvious and, perhaps, small. A hundred dollars isn't a fortune, after all. But it isn't insignificant, either. Great fortunes and grand achievements have been accomplished by steadfast devotion to creating tiny successes—which ultimately add up to enormous successes. Don't let impatience cause you to dismiss this technique, thinking that your time will be better spent if you work on, say, a $10,000 project. If you devote your time to mastering this concept at the $100 level, you'll find it much easier to leap into higher levels of income. Making this a habit will be the single best thing you can do to guarantee that your ventures will grow.

$100 Idea Starters

To show you how easy this is and to get you thinking along these lines, I've included a list of some $100 ideas. Each of these ideas could be worth far more than $100, and each could be adapted and embellished by anyone—no matter what that person's previous experience. All of them happen to have appeared during one of my $100 Hours.

• *Sell a tip.* Many consumer magazines pay their readers for ideas. If you've found a better way of doing something, send it in. Check the magazines you read and scout for others at your library to locate potential markets. Your idea may be valuable, even if it's something you take for granted. One night I surprised a friend when I whipped out my kitchen scissors to cut up a pizza. The very next week, I read in a popular magazine that scissors make a fine substitute for a pizza cutter. The person who shared that tip got paid $100. I didn't.

• *Be a model.* Talent agents are always looking for "ordinary-looking" people for both print and commercial ads. Your face might be your fortune—even if you look nothing like Cindy Crawford. If you live in an area where movies are filmed, why not sign on as an extra? Some people build steady profit centers doing just that. *Entertainment Tonight* recently did a report about nonactors who work as extras and in commercials. A young man I know sat at a computer in a commercial for a business college. That ad ran all over the country and earned him several thousand dollars. Get signed up with local talent agencies and see what happens.

• *Self-publish a booklet.* Bruce Van Bronkhorst teaches relationship classes and turned some of his material into a terrific little booklet called "101 Plus Romantic Things to Do in the Twin Cities." He doesn't need to sell 100 to earn $100. What information could you gather and sell? If you own a personal computer, you can eliminate typesetting costs. Find a printer who is willing to do small runs so that you don't amass more inventory than you can sell. This one is a natural for mail order or as a product to market along with a class or seminar you teach.

• *Clean out a closet.* There's cash in your trash. Isn't it time for a yard or tag sale? I know several folks who run sales every month, earning at least $100 each time. If you're really loaded with old stuff you want to sell, consider renting a table at a flea market. Clothes, especially high-quality ones that are in good repair, can be taken to a consignment shop, which will do your selling for you and split the profit. You could also organize and promote a neighborhood sale, and collect a small fee from other sellers in exchange for doing the advertising and promoting. Now that recycling is trendy again, used merchandise is politically correct.

• *Sign on as a temporary worker.* All sorts of temporary agencies match workers with work. Many are general, such as Kelly Services, while others specialize in computer operators or medical workers. Some people make a career out of doing temporary work; you may want to use it as an emergency profit center. If office work doesn't appeal to you, call several temporary agencies in your area and see whether any of them have marketing assignments. These often involve public contact—but little actual marketing. An agency in my area specializes in supermarket demonstrations, coordinating demonstrators, food manufacturers, and stores. These kinds of assignments can be great fun if you like people. You may have to put in a lot of hours to earn $100 this way, but it's nice to know you can if you must.

• *Eliminate an expense that doesn't bring you joy.* Every so often, use your $100 Hour to save $100 that you're now spending. It's the same as earning it, in a way. Quit smoking. Or find a credit card company with a lower interest rate than you're now paying.

Find a tax deduction you've overlooked. Cancel the movie channel you never watch. Sometimes our spending becomes automatic and habitual. It's healthy to reevaluate and change our spending habits from time to time.

• *Deliver a valentine.* There are dozens of possibilities if you're a natural romantic. You could specialize in enhancing romance all year long. (If you're good at this, you may not realize that you have a gift!) How about selling a gift basket of erotic massage oils and other romance-enhancing treats? Or catering breakfast in bed? Or setting up mystery evenings in conjunction with a limousine service? I once drove by a boulevard where a table was set with a white linen cloth, a silver candelabrum, crystal, and china. In the middle of a quiet neighborhood, a romantic alfresco evening was in store for some lucky couple. If you love love, this one's for you.

• *Be a broker.* Match up a buyer with a seller and collect your fee. If you're smart about automobiles, you could be a consultant for people shopping for a used car. Or you could develop a referral service for professionals. That's what speakers' agencies do, finding the right professional speaker for various audiences. If you know a lot about art, you could broker the work of artists. Read some classified ads and see whether you might be a matchmaker.

• *Organize a tour.* Is there a geographic area or subject that you know a lot about? Do you live near a historic battlefield or favorite fishing spot? You could create a tour right at home that would appeal to visitors. Several companies in London offer fascinating walking tours covering everything from Shakespeare's London to places where the Beatles hung out. If you long to travel, find a travel agent or company that will work with you to organize a trip abroad. In exchange for marketing the tour, you can receive a free trip. A focused specialty tour offers the best possibilities, so concentrate on planning a trip around your area of expertise. You could produce regular $100 Hours with this one.

• *Take in a paying guest.* You may not want a full-time roommate, but what about an occasional out-of-town visitor? You could specialize in providing homey accommodations for business travelers in town for long-term assignments, or hook up with a local college that hosts visiting professors and conference-goers. If you speak a foreign language, be a paid host to travelers who aren't sure about their English.

• *Barter services.* Some people thrive on exchanging services, building their own underground economy. This moneyless way of doing business can be great fun if you find other traders who enjoy bartering, too. I've known friends who have bartered for everything from laser printers to time in a vacation home.

• *Clean something.* Windows and floors always need cleaning, but you might aim at something larger—like an airplane or boat—and collect your $100 more quickly.

• *Teach a class.* Not long ago I found an old $100 Hour list of mine. One of the ideas was to send a proposal to Open U in Minneapolis for a class called "Making a Living Without a Job." That single idea has brought me tens of thousands of dollars in income . . . and hundreds of hours of pure bliss in the classroom. What are the hobbies you love to do? Where's your expertise? Build a class around what you know and start teaching. This idea can, of course, be repeated endlessly, bringing you many $100 bills.

• *Throw a party.* Planning special events can be fun and profitable. Or offer to cook for your busy friends for the price they'd pay in a restaurant. If you have abilities as a confident host or hostess, this is a wonderful way to indulge your partygoing personality—for pay. Companies, too, often engage the services of professional party planners, so this could become a lucrative profit center, should you decide to expand it.

• *Get a grant.* Thousands of dollars go unclaimed every year. All sorts of private foundations offer grants for a huge range of projects. If you want to do research, work on a product design, or investigate another culture, there may be a grant just waiting. You need to do a lot of legwork and proposal writing for this, but you may qualify for funds. Your reference librarian can point you to the directories of available grants. My archaeologist sister received a grant which allowed her to spend a year doing research for a book. The money came with no guarantee that her book would ever be published—although it has been. She would never have been able to spend the year doing research without the grant. It's worth checking into.

• *Contact former customers.* Remind them that you're available and willing. Generating repeat business can be easier than finding new customers all the time. Don't wait for the phone to ring. Do a mailing. Call and see whether they need your product or service again. Once you have customers to call your own, keeping in touch with them should be a regular event.

• *House- or pet-sit.* House- and pet-sitting are popular ways to earn money. You could have a specialty, such as caring for cats or vacant houses waiting to be sold. One enterprising fellow offered his services through real estate agents. His special service was to house-sit for people who had moved away, but had not yet sold their house. He'd bring in some oriental rugs and a few pieces of nice furniture, making the empty place more attractive. If you live in an area like mine, where many folks go away for the winter, that could be your slant. One woman I know got hired to house-sit for a client's home in the South of France. If you're flexible and love a change of scenery, this could be perfect.

• *Finish things.* How about a follow-through service to complete unfinished projects? If you're handy or do superb needlework, this could be a gold mine. Busy people often start more than they can finish; you could be in great demand.

Every single one of these ideas can be started easily and inexpensively. Better yet, they have the potential to grow into large, luscious profit centers. You might think of them as acorns. Get busy planting.

Protecting Your Ideas

A common concern voiced by my students is the fear of having their good ideas ripped off by someone else. In a free marketplace that is, of course, always a possibility. Some commonsense precautions will lessen the chance of that happening, even if it's not possible to eliminate it completely.

First of all, exercise judgment in discussing your plans with others. While you can't keep your ideas to yourself forever— you'll never make money with them that way—stay mum about your specific plans until you're confident that you're close to acting on them. When you're ready for advice or outside assistance, know as much as you can about the person you're seeking the advice from. Caution is also in order here. You may feel timid about, say, a product you've invented and decide to seek the counsel of an invention-marketing firm. While some of these are reputable, others earn their money from charging you fees, large ones at that, and often perform no service that you couldn't perform for yourself.

There are several legal ways to protect yourself. One of these is copyright, which applies to written materials including books, articles, pamphlets, songs, and computer programs. Copyright protection prevents anyone else from taking your work and slapping his or her own name on it. Any work you do, even advertising copy, should carry the standard copyright protection, which is the word "Copyright," followed by a capital C enclosed in a circle, the year, and your name. For maximum protection, you can register with the Copyright Office, Library of Congress, Washington, D.C. 20559.

Brand names for products and services cannot be copyrighted, but can be protected by using a trademark. Next to the name, the letters TM are printed to warn potential thieves that someone claims ownership of that name. However, registering a trademark is more complicated than registering a copyright, so should you need this form of protection, you'll want to engage the services of an attorney and expect to pay a fee of several hundred dollars. This may be an excellent investment if you have a name that you want to protect.

Finally, your inventions can be safeguarded with a patent. This is the most complex form of protection and is costly in terms of time as well as money. You will definitely need to consult a patent attorney. Once you've developed a prototype of your invention, see a lawyer who can advise you on how to proceed. Not every product needs this type of protection, and you can begin manufacturing a product before your patent is approved, provided you aren't copying someone else's patented product. Although you need to consult an attorney for both trademarks and patents, you can get applications for both from the Commissioner of Patents and Trademarks, Washington, D.C. 20231.

Winning Ways for Getting Ideas

• Some self-bossers carry three-by-five-inch cards with them and jot down ideas as they occur. These cards are then filed and reviewed from time to time.

• Your Living Without a Job notebook could contain a section specifically for ideas. File articles about potential profit centers in this section, too. Keep plenty of blank sheets of paper here so that you can maintain a running log of ideas. If you have a variety of profit centers, have a separate page for each—consulting contacts, writing ideas, upcoming craft fairs, marketing to pet owners, etc.

• You can brainstorm to expand existing ideas as well as generate new ones. Begin by posing a question and let your imagination fly in coming up with answers. Remember that brainstorming is an activity for generating ideas. Edit later. Here's an example.

How can I turn my fluency in Italian into a profit center?

- Contact Giorgio Armani and offer my services translating sales material.
- Sign on with a local translation service.
- Start my own translation service specializing in Italian.
- Add other freelancers to translate other languages.
- Contact the Italian consulate and offer my services as an interpreter.
- Contact the trade and economic development department in my state to see what local businesses trade with Italian firms.
- Organize a tour to Italy.
- Organize a tour from Italy.
- Teach a class on Italian opera and accompany members to the opera, with after-performance discussion.
- Teach a beginning Italian class in an adult education school.
- Start an import business bringing in Italian olive oil.
- Teach a beginning Italian class to corporate executives and their families relocating to Italy.
- Be a companion to a wealthy person traveling to Italy.
- Locate computer firms marketing their products in Italy and offer to translate manuals and programs.

- Rent a house in northern Italy and advertise for American guests.
- Write subtitles for Italian films.

Take one of your ideas and do a practice brainstorming session to see how many items you can generate. Your ability to visualize multiple possibilities will increase the more frequently you flex your creative muscles.

• Begin to implement the $100 Hour daily. The sooner you make this a habit, the sooner you will see income from your ideas. List your idea for each day along with action taken. Keep track of all activities connected with each $100 Hour.

CHAPTER 11

Marketing on a Shoestring

Passion persuades and, by God, I was passionate about what I was selling.

Anita Roddick

As my friend Jill and I left the consignment shop where we'd been browsing, I turned to her and said, "I'm going to appoint myself Marketing Policewoman and start handing out citations."

"Oh," Jill groaned. "Wasn't she annoying?"

The "she" who had bothered both of us was the salesperson, who had spent the entire half hour we were there delivering a monologue on llamas to a friend who had stopped in to chat. This was just another in the series of personal conversations that I've endured in shops.

Less than an hour later, at a trendy optical shop, I had cause to issue another citation. The man working there was downright insulting and became argumentative when I casually mentioned that I wasn't impressed with the Mall of America. Isn't it just common courtesy, I wondered, to let potential customers have their own opinions in matters of taste? This guy didn't think so; he was determined to be "right." His bad manners cost him two customers—and probably several more among our glasses-wearing friends who would hear about him.

Since sales and marketing are critical success factors for businesses large and small, why are they done so poorly? Often, a lack of awareness apparently causes marketers to forget that they're in business to serve others. Just as often, small-business owners treat the salespeople they hire as expendable. Instead of teaching them how to deal with customers, shop owners and entrepreneurs use a sink-or-swim approach and assume that if clerks or salespeople don't work out someone else can take their place. These are, of course, the same entrepreneurs who grumble about the lack of good help!

An even bigger factor is that almost nobody starts a business because he or she loves sales and marketing. Only after the original idea for a business has been hatched do self-bossers realize that they must rely on marketing to make the idea work. At this point, the fear of selling often takes over and becomes a deterrent to many would-be business owners.

Your business, at least at the beginning, will be marketed by you. A full-time salesperson or two will probably not fit into your scheme or budget. If other people are going to know about what you have to offer, it will be up to you to tell them. You'll be the one collecting the money, too. Sales and marketing will be two important functions of your operation, and they deserve your best efforts.

While these two aspects of business are closely related and interdependent, each has an individual role to play as well. You could think of marketing as the first stage of getting your message out. Marketing is the preliminary, behind-the-scenes activity that determines the personality of your business, the strategy you'll use, the audience you'll be directing yourself to. Sales is the implementation of your marketing plan. Sales is the phase in which you interact with your potential customers, answer their questions, share information about your product or service, and make the sale. You won't, of course, always view these as compartmentalized functions; there will be overlap. If your business was theater, marketing would be designing the sets, lighting, and props and rehearsing the actors. Sales would be performing in front of the audience.

What Pleases You?

Forget the outworn notion that selling involves memorizing manipulative phrases and forceful "closes." Instead, think of sales as a matter of common sense with good manners added on. You could learn more about selling from reading an etiquette book than you could from most sales training programs.

Begin your own sales training by paying attention to the ways in which other things are sold. What do you like about a television commercial? Or the way a salesperson treats you? What gets your attention? Do you respond to humor? Do you feel repulsed by exaggerated claims? Instead of tossing out the advertising mail that comes your way, study it. Read ads in magazines, too, along with classified ads in your newspaper. What do the good ones do? Why does one get your attention, but not another? Raise your awareness every time you go into a store, call a business on the phone, or have personal contact with an enterprise. Let's say you have to return a purchase to a store. When you've finished your transaction, give thought to what took place. "I liked the way they quickly credited my account and invited me to come back," and "I felt that they resented my returning the product" are very different responses. The more aware you become of what you do and don't like as a customer, the easier it will be for you to adopt techniques you admire.

One common fear of inexperienced self-bossers is of being perceived as an obnoxious salesperson. You can recall, no doubt, people who fit that description, and you certainly don't want to emulate them. Nevertheless, since models of good and bad salesmanship are easy to find, you can learn a lot about selling by studying the techniques of others.

I was on a flight from Orlando to Los Angeles when I observed (for five long hours) a man who still holds my All-Time Champion Obnoxious Salesperson Award. The moment the seat-belt sign was turned off, he positioned himself outside the lavatory door, where he remained for the entire flight. Every person who came to use the bathroom had to hear his sales pitch for vitamins and food supplements. Some folks humored him, but most were appalled. He was undaunted and didn't seem to notice that his technique didn't make a single sale. (He had probably been taught that every "no" brought him one step closer to a "yes"!) I imagined that he went home and bragged at his next sales meeting about how diligently he had worked on the flight. He was, in a reverse way, a good teacher for me. I learned that although persistence is admirable, pushiness is not.

There's one other thing to be especially aware of in your sales and marketing efforts. Don't handicap yourself by saying or thinking, as so many new self-bossers do, "I'm not a salesperson." When I hear that, I recognize that it's (1) a self-fulfilling prophecy and (2) coming from someone who has a limited concept of the fun and function of selling. It makes a lot more sense to replace that statement with an affirmation such as "I'm an enthusiastic salesperson and selling gets easier the more I do it." Rethink, too, your notion about who and what a salesperson is. Many fine people have mastered the art of selling with grace and charm and put the Golden Rule into action with every customer they meet. Replace the obnoxious salesperson image with an example of a helpful and knowledgeable one. It will make the thought of selling far more attractive.

Start with the Three Questions

Planning your marketing can begin by answering the Three Questions I used in my seminars:

- Who are you?
- What do you do?
- Why are you here?

Devising a clear answer to each of these, one that uses twenty-five words or less, will make it easier for you to communicate what you're doing and easier for your customers to know whether you offer what they want or need. Yet many people who want to make a living without a job find this difficult to do. They call themselves consultants or desktop publishers or graphic designers without realizing that those terms may mean something different to each of us. At its vaguest, you'd hear the Three Questions answered with something like, "Well, I'm a desktop publisher and I do desktop publishing for small businesses and I

heard you might need some done." This is only slightly exaggerated. A clearer description would be, "My desktop publishing
company specializes in brochure and pamphlet design for small
businesses like yours. I offer a one-stop service providing writing, design, and layout."

When Belinda Plutz and Linda Stein decided to open a career
counseling service in New York City, they knew they were
entering an industry that already had many established businesses. They began by doing extensive research on the competition, with an eye to identifying ways they could set themselves
apart. They were convinced that they wanted to provide a service
that was client-oriented and tailored to the individual needs of
each person. This would not be another boilerplate operation.

Each of their marketing tools was designed to convey that
philosophy. For starters, they gave their business a descriptive,
memorable name: Careermentors. They produced an eye-
catching, professional-looking, but user-friendly brochure that
pinpointed two dozen common reasons that people might use
their service. The brochure included a pithy listing of what they
could do.

With experience, they discovered that most of their clients
shopped around before settling on the service they would work
with. Careermentors decided to offer a half-hour free session to
help potential clients get a glimpse of their methods. Providing
this "free sample" has proved a valuable marketing tool for them,
since it gives prospective clients personal contact before they
make a commitment. All of Careermentors' advertising and
marketing is intended to let people know who they are, what
they do, and why they are there.

Once you can succinctly describe your product or service, the
rest of your marketing becomes easier. You can monitor the
effectiveness of your business description with this feedback
exercise: Ask ten or twelve people who know your business
(family, friends, and customers) to tell you what they think your
business does. How accurately can they describe your business?
If their answers are vague or inaccurate, how can they refer
customers to you? Keep refining your business description until
it's crystal clear to everyone you do this exercise with.

Making It Personal

There's no greater marketing tool available than your personal touch. We've all become used to apathetic service and impersonal computer voices as part of our buying experience. Once in a while, a master like Roger Horchow will come along and show us that the human touch can be a part of marketing. Horchow, founder of the mail-order emporium bearing his name, humanizes his catalogs with personal essays, his photograph, and merchandise descriptions that sound as if a friend is telling you about a treasure he's just found.

From the moment you set up shop, be determined to make adding a personal touch your marketing trademark. Attention to details that have your stamp on them will set you apart from the competition and keep you creating a business that is uniquely yours. Whether you're marketing professional services or a hot new window cleaner, make yourself unforgettable in a positive way. Here are five building blocks that belong in your marketing plans.

• *Your personal touch.* A woman I know was marketing training programs to small businesses in the New York City area. She had plenty of competition and was determined to find a way to set herself apart. In her third year of business, she got the bold idea to try an experiment which she named The Cookie Project. Every Sunday night, she'd bake a batch of chocolate-chip cookies and put them into little bags with her business card attached. On Monday morning she'd make sales calls, as she'd always done. At the end of each presentation, she'd thank the potential client and leave a bag of cookies. What do you suppose happened to her business that year? Would you be surprised to know her sales tripled? She credits The Cookie Project with making the difference, since it was the only change she made. She added a personal touch that was natural for her and prospects remembered her—and did business with her.

When you consider ways to add your own touch, look for things that will help you be a visible person, not just a business name. A friend of mine uses her photograph on her business cards and in ads for her real estate business. Often hers is the only ad with a photo, so it immediately stands out from the others.

New clients find they quickly build rapport with her, since they can attach a face to the name. On their initial encounter, they feel as if they already know her.

Other personal touches can be added by having a trademark color, like the pink that is the signature of Mary Kay Cosmetics. Your logo or a slogan could be another memorable detail.

It's easier to create your own brand of flourish if you remember that good business is just another kind of good relationship. Being thoughtful and caring about the people with whom you're in contact will lead you to add touches that are appropriate for you. Sending handwritten notes of thanks, for instance, is a gesture that displays good manners and consideration.

• *Your presence.* "Eighty percent of success is showing up," observed Woody Allen. In marketing your business, your persona can be a powerful factor. Your presence isn't only the way you dress and look, it includes your attitude, listening skills, and respect for the customer. The more opportunities you give yourself to "show up" and talk to people about your product or service, the more your business will expand.

The importance of this was evident during the 1992 presidential campaign. All three candidates were frequent guests on television talk shows and the morning news programs, happily chatting away with Phil Donahue and Katie Couric. For the first time in history, the candidates seemed eager for us to see and evaluate them in an informal setting. It's an example worth following.

Keep in mind that you also make your presence felt in the way you answer your telephone, deal with problems, or follow up with a customer. Be watchful of things that interfere with your ability to connect with people. Simple things like bad breath, using profanity, or having a cluttered, unwashed car can detract from your success.

• *Fall in love with your product.* Coco Chanel said she looked at every design she made and asked herself, "Would I want to wear this dress?" If the answer was "no" she discarded the design. The best marketing advice I know is this: only market things that you're personally crazy about. If you're wild about your product or service, the selling part becomes so much easier—even effortless. The decision to avoid products that you don't care about needs to be consciously made and adhered to. It's an essential aspect of your marketing philosophy.

Cooking expert Miki Banavige and I were browsing in a kitchen shop when she pointed out a potato peeler that she and her husband loved. I found it hard to believe that anyone could get that excited about something so mundane, but decided to get one for myself. The first time I used it, I was instantly enamored. It was unlike any potato peeler I'd ever used before. I kept looking for more things to peel. When I noticed that a department store had them on sale, I decided to purchase several as gifts. The clerk asked why I was buying so many of the same thing. I explained how I loved this tool and raved on about it. Before I had finished, the people behind me in line had rushed to the display and each grabbed one. The saleswoman confessed that she still struggled with a potato peeler she'd gotten twenty years ago at a wedding shower, and vowed to try this new one. I told Miki we should set up a card table on a street corner and sell these potato peelers!

Ironically, when you're in love with your product or service, selling doesn't feel like selling at all. It's a natural result of sharing your genuine enthusiasm. Like a great romantic relationship, the more you get to know your product, the more you should find to love.

• *Target your niche.* Niche marketing has become a trendy concept, and with good reason. Determining whom you want to market to before you begin makes your job easier because your efforts are focused.

How do you determine who qualifies as your personal niche? Paul Hawken suggests that you create a business that is the kind you'd like to do business with yourself. Your best starting point, then, is other people who are like you in some way. Perhaps you share a common profession or location or ethnic origin or hobby. You might discover a niche market among people who collect Edsels, or American computer programmers living abroad.

A friend of mine who has had years of experience—not terribly happy ones, but lots of them—running training programs for large corporations decided to go out on his own. He mentioned that he'd been thinking about his possible target market and decided that he'd focus on large corporations such as he'd been working with all these years. On the surface, that seems a sensible decision; after all, he has that experience to back him up. But I suggested that he might reconsider his decision. "It appears to me," I said, "that you've targeted this market because you believe it would be the most profitable. But are people who are entrenched in corporate management really your favorite people to work with? Why couldn't you aim your programs at other freelance consultants? You've always been fascinated with metaphysical things. Why not work with New Age entrepreneurs? There are thousands of trainers trying to tap the corporate market. Do things differently. Pick a niche that is being ignored, but one that you're comfortable with." He took my advice and is on his way to building a training company that suits him personally and allows him to work with people who share his values.

In identifying your niche, keep in mind that it will be a group with whom you share a bond. Your niche is a group that you are already part of or know a great deal about because you share its problems or interests. A niche isn't "them"— it's "us." Stay focused on serving the market that you know well. Once you have developed one market niche, you may find it's a simple matter to identify another niche and repeat the process.

• *Build from referrals*. Linda Gannon's business, The Magick Garden, mail orders personalized gift baskets. The majority of Gannon's business comes over the phone, with Gannon and the customer planning the contents of the basket. Her business has grown primarily in one way. "As soon as somebody receives a basket," she says, "I'll get a call ordering a basket to be sent to one of their friends." Her product is so special that a built-in domino effect works on her behalf.

You've always heard, no doubt, that word of mouth is the most effective form of advertising. It's certainly one that you'll want working for you, but you may have to help it along. Asking your satisfied customers for referrals can be a valuable part of your marketing plan. After all, it's easier to talk to someone when the door's been opened a bit by a mutual acquaintance. Have a consistent method for asking the customers you've got to suggest new ones. "Do you have any friends or colleagues I should talk to?" is a natural way of expanding your market.

So many small-business owners get into trouble because they

think of marketing as a crisis activity. Only when sales lag do they start making calls, running ads, or planning a new strategy. Far more effective is to make marketing a continuing activity that is a weekly, or even daily, part of your business.

Using the aforementioned strategies will keep you close to your customers as well as detering you from spending money foolishly on expensive marketing methods. Your marketing plans will be most effective if you concentrate on creating ways to use your imagination more and your pocketbook less.

Even if you're unsure about what product or service you'll be marketing, the following questions will point out areas to consider.

• What are three qualities that you possess or could develop that would have a positive impact on your presence as a marketing tool?

_____

_____

_____

• If your business were a color, what color would it be? How could you use a color as your signature? How would that color make a statement about your company?

_____

_____

_____

• Who is the best salesperson you've seen in action? What made that person special? Did you buy from him or her? Did you tell your friends?

_____

_____

_____

Sales Aids for Shoestring Marketing

Flyers, brochures, a snappy demonstration, or any tools that help tell your story add fun and interest to sales efforts. There are numerous possibilities for developing sales aids; let's concentrate on those that are inexpensive to produce and add a personal touch. Some of these are rather mundane, but a bit of panache can turn them into extraordinary assets. Give thoughtful consideration to every sales aid you decide to use.

Brochures, cards, and flyers. You'll start out with a business card and, perhaps, a brochure describing your product or service. These basic tools are easy to produce, with or without the aid of a graphic designer. The main thing to keep in mind in designing these supporting materials is that you want them to look good enough that you'll feel comfortable handing them out.

A question I am frequently asked is, "Do I need a different card for each of my profit centers?" That depends, of course, on how diversified your profit centers are. If your enterprises fall under a single umbrella and are closely related, one card might do fine. In recent times, I've used a business card that lists only my name, address, and telephone. If you're more diversified, by all means have separate cards printed. I've seen some tiny cards that list everything from window washing to brain surgery.

Think of your business card as a traveling billboard. It should help people recall their meeting with you. If your business has a logo, put it on your card. Your photograph might also be appropriate. One of my favorite cards was one I did a couple of years ago. I had my name, address, and so forth printed in very simple type in black ink on white card stock. I added a splash of color across the top with acrylic paint, which made the card dramatic and eye-catching—for a fraction of the cost of color printing.

Once you've got your cards, carry a good supply with you at all times, and don't just hand them out—exchange them. Make certain, too, that the cards you carry don't get dirty or dog-eared.

Brochures and flyers are other sales tools that can help you tell your story and show that you're serious about your business. A good brochure should be simple and easy to read. Don't, however, expect it to do more than it's capable of doing. Brochures are supporting materials—they can create interest, but seldom make sales on their own.

Your brochure should do two things: (1) highlight the main features of your product or service, and (2) make it easy for potential customers to find you. Mailing brochures to a list of strangers may prove disappointing, as well as expensive. A better use for a brochure is as a leave-behind after you've made a verbal presentation or other direct contact. Invest cautiously in your first one and do a modest printing. You're bound to see changes you want to make as you go along, so don't go overboard the first time around.

Mailing lists. Another sales tool that almost any undertaking can use is a customer mailing list. Begin building yours right from the start. Compile a list of people you know, and as your business grows, keep adding to it. Then find ways to communicate regularly with the people on the list. A woman I know who began selling real estate promptly gathered a roster of friends, old school chums, business contacts, and even friends of her parents. She does regular postcard mailings that usually contain a friendly greeting and reminder, with little or no sales message on them. After two years of building her business with mailings, she says that 80 percent of her business can be traced to the referrals generated by this system.

Remind people that you're there and willing to serve them. Remember, too, that people's needs constantly change. Someone who wasn't ready to buy from you the first time may need your product or service six months later. If you don't keep in touch, that person may forget about you or not know how to locate you again.

My favorite ways of staying in touch with a mailing list are through postcards and newsletters. Postcards are, of course, less expensive to produce and mail. They have the added advantage of being quick to read and seem to capture more attention than more complicated forms of advertising. My insurance agent uses frequent postcard mailings with pictures of his staff—often engaged in a sport or interesting activity—to keep his customers posted on changes in the industry, new services, and so forth. Another idea you could adopt is to print cards that are a blown-up version of your business card with room on the back for a personal message. Any time you add a new service, offer a special discount or sale, or just want to say hello, consider sending a postcard.

Then there are customer newsletters. John Schroeder's Word Store sends out a quarterly newsletter called *Word Stories* to clients and prospects. The four-page piece contains news about John's business, an inspirational or informational essay (kind of a free sample of John's writing), and chatty articles related to various projects he's done. It gives John a way to showcase his writing ability and desktop publishing skills while communicating with old customers and potential ones in a personal way.

Every small business I know that has used this form of customer communication is enthusiastic about the results. Shopkeepers report an immediate increase in store traffic; consultants find their phones ringing with new business; service businesses see an increase in repeat clients and referrals.

A good customer newsletter is not just a long commercial for your business. It should contain information that's of interest to your targeted audience. The tone can be chirpy or serious, depending on your personal style. If you own a computer, producing a newsletter is relatively easy; if not, hiring a desktop publisher to do it for you can be an excellent investment.

None other than F. W. Woolworth once admitted, "I am the world's worst salesman; therefore I must make it easy for people to buy." It's advice every shoestring marketer should hold dear. Find ways to make it ridiculously easy for people to do business with you.

From time to time, ask yourself, "If I were new in town and needed my services, how would I find me?" If your answer is, "I'd hope for serendipity to intervene," you're making it too difficult for your market to come to you.

When Karen Kari opened her business, It's Done, Inc., in Greenwich, Connecticut, she wasn't shy about letting the media know. As a result, two local newspapers wrote feature stories about her errand-running service. Karen took it a step further and began writing her own articles for a local women's newspaper. As her business evolved into an organization service, she continued to tap sources of publicity, shifting her emphasis to reflect the changes in her business. Her newspaper column, for instance, began with stories about merchandise offered by local businesses; now she writes on subjects such as getting organized for the holidays. Naturally, she lists her credentials as a professional organizer in each piece.

Don't overlook the possibilities of using free publicity to assist you in marketing. What are you doing that's newsworthy? Let the media know about it. Are you the first in your area to do what you're doing? The youngest? Oldest? Do you have an answer to a problem that's currently getting media attention? Could you offer an expert solution? While newspapers and radio and television stations might show no interest in you if you appear to want a free commercial, proving that you're an interesting item can bring you to the attention of a lot more people.

Body Shop founder Anita Roddick has used free publicity masterfully. Her political activism, feuds with the British government, and trade with Third World companies all have kept the spotlight shining on her. Without spending a penny for conventional advertising, Roddick has used media attention to keep her name and business in the news. Once she realized how good publicity could be for the Body Shop's image, she became skillful at staging newsworthy events—and she always made sure the press was invited. Her flamboyant style and outspoken opinions have brought her millions of dollars' worth of free advertising. Don't overlook the publicity available to you. Be willing to take advantage of it whenever possible. Such attention can add to your visibility, your credibility, and, ultimately, your bottom line.

Making the Sale

British actor Robert Morley once said, "Every child should be placed on a doorstep to sell something. It's the best possible training for life." It's also the moment that strikes fear in the hearts of many.

Much of the fear that comes with asking someone to buy from you can be diffused if you've spent time doing the things discussed in this chapter. Defining your business, knowing who your market will be, and using sales aids that give you a professional appearance will bolster your confidence when it comes time to sell. You're entering the marketplace with thoughtful preparation behind you. Taking the next step will be easier if you keep in mind a few basic concepts about selling.

• *Selling is talking and listening to people.* If you care about the product or service you're selling and know how it can make other's lives better, your enthusiasm opens the way to talk about it with others who you believe could benefit. Super-salespeople, contrary to popular myth, are often great listeners, not glib speakers. Ask questions and quietly listen for answers. If you do, your customers will frequently sell themselves.

On my last birthday, I decided to treat myself to a new compact disc player. A local chain store was running a special, so I rushed in on the final day to make my purchase. When the salesperson found out that I was not planning to buy a $5,000 system, he vaguely waved me in the direction of the smaller units, where I stood perplexed. I knew nothing about CD equipment, and he wasn't about to teach me. I left the store empty-handed.

Later that day, I recalled that my daughter had bought her equipment from another branch of the same store, which had been very helpful. I decided to give it another try and drove there. I had barely located the CD section when a young man approached and offered his assistance. I told him I wanted a small system, but didn't really know what I was doing. He patiently showed me several models and we narrowed the selection to two. "Why don't we listen to them both?" he suggested. He turned one on and when heavy-metal music blasted out, immediately stopped it. "That's probably not the kind of music you'll be listening to," he surmised. "What would you like to hear?" When I told him I was a classical music fan, he scouted around for a Mozart concerto. After the demonstration, I had almost made up my mind, but asked if he had a preference. "Yes," he said, pointing to the one on the left, "I prefer this equipment myself. In fact, that's what I have at home."

I told him I appreciated his help. "You really seem to know a lot about this equipment. Have you worked here long?"

"Only two weeks," he said. Then he added, "But I'm the

co-owner of a business that installs car stereo systems, so I'm familiar with different brands."

Did he make the sale? Absolutely. He cared about his customer.

• *Know the features of your product, but emphasize benefits.* A cardinal rule in selling is stressing what the user can expect to gain by purchasing your offering. Will your customer become more efficient? Handsomer? Healthier? Able to run faster? When I talk about my newsletter, *Winning Ways*, I mention its features, such as book reviews, personal development articles, and business ideas. I know, however, that people don't become subscribers because of those features. They must be shown that they'll benefit in a way that interests them—such as becoming more successful at making a living without a job.

As you present your product or service, be mindful that your prospect really wants you to answer the question, "What will it do for me?" Here again, your listening skills will give you clues about the particular benefits your customer seeks. Once you've determined that you can meet those needs, emphasize the ways in which your product can deliver.

• *Experiment with a variety of selling formats.* Some people are comfortable talking about their business over the phone; others love making a group presentation; still others find it's easiest for them to sell face to face, one customer at a time. As you gain confidence in your product or service, you may find yourself moving easily from one format to another. In the beginning, it makes sense to work in the way that feels most natural. If you freeze at the thought of making cold calls, but don't mind having strangers call you to inquire, your natural selling style would be to run ads or do mailings that encourage prospects to call you for more details.

Many fine small businesses have been built by folks who enjoy exhibiting at trade shows and conventions. Others prefer building a clientele whom they call on regularly, getting to know each customer well. Your personality, as well as your product or service, will determine what method is best suited for your selling. Master the method that feels right for you.

• *Set sales goals.* Your selling will be most effective if you have a goal as well as a plan for accomplishing that goal. If you want to earn $10,000 a year from selling the divine chocolate truffles you make, you'll need to sell enough of them every week to earn $200 profit. Unless you have a single customer who purchases automatically, your weekly assignment will be to place more than $200 of your candy. Your goals will be determined also by the seasonal nature of your selling. Candy sales will obviously be higher during the holidays and around Valentine's Day. Since every business has its own cycles in selling, after a year or so you'll know which times of year are good selling periods for you and which are not. Your goals need to reflect what you know about those cycles. You may, for instance, achieve your $10,000 profit by selling for five months of the year, bringing in a weekly profit of $500.

Few entrepreneurs reach their sales potential, however, with a vague goal to sell a lot. Put a dollar amount or a unit amount or a client amount on those goals and you'll realize them faster.

Selling Ideas

My friend Ruth was telling me about several ideas she had for the art gallery where she now works, but added that she wasn't certain she'd be able to convince the owners to implement those ideas.

I urged her to be patient. Over the years, I've had a great deal of experience selling products and selling ideas. Ideas take far more time to sell. "The problem is, Ruth," I explained, "we forget that we go through a process *before* we accept a new idea. We think about it, consider this and that possibility, refine our thinking, and so forth. That process often goes on for a long time before the idea crystalizes and we think it's a good one. Once that happens, and it's perfectly clear to us, we're miffed when others fail to see immediately what a great idea it is."

You, too, will probably be faced with a similar situation at times. Convincing someone to invest in an intangible requires patience and a willingness to let others go through their own mental processes. You can help move the process along by painting a mental picture for the other person. Can you describe what you envision will result should that person accept your idea? How might his or her feelings change? What doors might open? What problems would be alleviated?

If there's a tangible way to help sell an idea, by all means use it. The Body Shop insists that the purpose of a moisturizer is to replace skin moisture. The company goes on, in contrast to the rest of the cosmetics industry, to insist that fancy packages and high prices do not improve the ability of such products to do their job. One way The Body Shop sells this idea that its natural moisturizer is worth our consideration is by having in-store testers available, along with informative labeling on the bottles. By educating its customers, The Body Shop defies the competition. But Roddick and company also know they must sell the customer on the idea first—and the product sale will follow.

By all means, answer questions, entertain discussion, and realize that you'll need patience when you offer an idea for sale.

Minding Your Manners While Minding the Store

A couple of years ago I received a call from a woman who was starting a magazine and wanted to know if I would be interested in writing articles for her. The conversation was particularly memorable because it was apparent that she was eating as she talked—I had a mental picture of her lounging on her sofa nibbling cheese and crackers. Even so, I agreed to meet with her to discuss her project. When she didn't appear at the restaurant where our appointment was scheduled, I waited—and waited. After forty-five minutes I left. Eventually she called, but it wasn't to apologize. She scolded me for not waiting longer! After these two encounters I knew that this was not someone with whom I wanted to work.

Even though we have no shortage of bad-mannered businesspeople to annoy us, not all of them (I would like to believe) are intentionally rude. More often, bad manners are the result of ignorance and oblivion.

Where do good manners come from? Some people think that manners are important only to the wealthy; etiquette is to be practiced on grand occasions such as weddings and formal dinners. Nothing could be further from the truth, of course. Good manners should be the concern—and practice—of everyone. Correct behavior is much more than knowing the rules and fine points in an etiquette book. What we call common courtesy really stems from two sources: high self-awareness and concern for others.

Rude or indifferent treatment occurs when people have no sense that their behavior has an impact on others. Wrapped up in themselves, they treat customers as an intrusion. The person who gruffly answers the phone may be annoyed that you interrupted him when he was busy planning his next date.

If you are working with passion and genuinely care about the people whom you are serving, good manners and courteous treatment will occur naturally. Self-awareness causes us to monitor what comes out of our mouth. Knowing that what we say and how we say it makes a difference leads us to treat everyone with respect—the essence of good manners. While none of us can avoid the occasional jerk, behaving politely to everyone we meet through our business will ultimately have financial benefits along with the psychological satisfaction that comes from treating others well.

A friend of mine was feeling stressed and decided to have a massage to relieve his tension. He made an appointment with a massage therapist who had been recommended. During the appointment, however, the therapist spent the entire session delivering a sermon along with the massage. Nothing about my friend's body was right. His posture, health habits, and so forth were criticized in detail. He emerged feeling worse than when he went in. He did, however, find a way to eliminate his stress: he wrote a hilarious article about his bad experience, which he called "Rubbed the Wrong Way."

"The thoughtless are rarely wordless," observes Howard K. Newton. When those who are thoughtless are also running a business, their customers may not retaliate by pointing their poor manners out to them. They'll simply take their business elsewhere.

How can you make good manners part of your marketing plan? You can begin by recognizing that business etiquette is not a matter of knowing the protocol for a state dinner but a sensitivity to the feelings and comfort of others. While few etiquette books specifically deal with business manners, you can demonstrate your own courtesy in some simple ways.

Start with the telephone since it will most likely be an important tool for your work. People who are normally smart and sensitive are often oblivious when it comes to telephone manners: dogs bark, babies howl, televisions blare, conversations with family members are conducted simultaneously. When your telephone makes the transition from being a social tool to being the lifeline of your business, it needs to be treated differently. Here are a few things to consider in using this indispensable tool:

• Give your business its own line. If you receive enough calls to warrant it, the extra expense will be worthwhile. When the phone rings you'll know that it's a business call and be prepared to handle it. If you decide to keep a single line, always answer as if it's an important client calling. Your friends may not mind if you are in the habit of picking up the phone and hollering "Yo," but your customers won't be charmed.

• Teach your kids how to answer the phone and how to behave when you're on the phone. Your client will not enjoy hearing you yell at your children to shut up. My daughter knew from an early age that if the phone rang, silence was in order. She also learned how to take messages and be polite (although she forgot some of that during adolescence).

• When you're on the phone, *be* on the phone. Joan Collins startled readers of her autobiography when she confided that during the time Warren Beatty was her lover he would handle business calls while making love to her. I'm not certain I've ever had a conversation where someone was so engaged, but I'm amazed that people often do several other things during a conversation. Would you balance your checkbook while a client was in your office? If you aren't giving your caller your full attention, he'll know—even if he can't see you. If you can't give your attention to a telephone conversation, turn on your answering machine and return the call when you are free.

Expediency is another aspect of good business etiquette. Returning calls, answering your mail, and being on time for appointments are ways you demonstrate your respect for others.

When you are unable to do things in a timely fashion, common courtesy dictates that you let the person who's waiting for an answer or meeting you for lunch know that you're detained. Doing what you say you're going to do, when you say you'll do it, is as good for your soul as it is for your bottom line. Working from integrity demands nothing less. If you can't be trusted to come through on the little things, no one will trust you with the big things.

Corny as it may sound, remembering to say thank you is absolutely essential. One day I was balancing my checkbook and discovered that the bank had failed to deduct a fifty-dollar check from my account. I called to report their error and the man who handled the call never bothered to show any appreciation for my honesty. He told me, "It's taken care of," and hung up. I was fuming and considered closing my account. Simple kindness from him would have produced a positive response instead of an angry customer. During my brief career as an interior decorator, we had a policy of handwriting thank-you notes to everyone we talked to. Customers frequently commented when they came back to buy furniture that our note had surprised and pleased them. Don't underestimate the goodwill that you can create with such a simple act. I keep a stack of museum postcards for that purpose and find it takes almost no time to acknowledge a kindness that's been done to me.

Good manners, quite simply, make our days go more smoothly. Being aware of etiquette also endows us with greater confidence. Even when we commit a faux pas (as we're all bound to do from time to time), being willing to apologize for our blunder makes committing it less awful. Treat others with respect and consideration, be willing to do more than is expected of you, look for ways to show courtesy to others, and you'll acquire a reputation as someone worth doing business with.

It Does Get Easier

If you make marketing and selling top activities, your dream of making a living without a job will come true faster than you may think. Even when selling is uncomfortable and frightening, your determination to master it will be the most positive thing you can do for your business. It will have a positive impact on your character, too. Anyone who has ever pushed through a fear of public speaking, for example, knows how empowering it can be. The same is true of selling.

Give yourself the advantage of selling things you truly care about and believe in—and the rest of your job will simplify itself.

Integrity, service, enthusiasm, and joy are the qualities that will attract people who are eager and happy to do business with you. Concentrate on developing those qualities and you're on your way to breaking sales records. Artist Andy Warhol understood, as few artists ever have, the importance of sales and marketing. He was relentless in his efforts to sell the world on his particular vision of things. Warhol had a healthy respect for the business side of his work. "Business art is the step that comes after Art," he observed. "And good business is the best art of all."

Winning Ways for Marketing on a Shoestring

Which of the following methods will you incorporate into your marketing plans? (As your business grows, refer to this list for further ideas.)

____ Business cards
____ Personal telephone contact
____ Networking
____ Exhibits at conventions, trade shows, air fairs
____ Customer mailings
____ Referrals contacts

____ Niche marketing
____ Brochures
____ Paid advertising
____ Publicity
____ Customer newsletter
____ Direct mailings
____ Wholesaling
____ Product demonstrations

If you could design the perfect customer, what would that person be like? How would he or she treat you? How would you show your appreciation for your customer's business?

_____

_____

_____

What different kinds of marketing environments can you imagine for yourself? Could you sell on a beach? On a cruise ship? At a street fair? At a trade show or convention? In a park?

_____

_____

_____

If you were completely confident about the product or service that you're selling, what difference would that make? Whom would you sell to? What limitations would disappear?

_____

_____

_____

Set a sales goal for the first year for one of your profit centers:

_____

What percentage of increase would you project for your second year? _____ Third year? _____

What is your weekly sales goal, based on your first year's total goal? _____

PART V

Creating World Headquarters

If I were to wish for anything, I should not wish for wealth and power, but for the passionate sense of potential, for the eye which sees the possible. Pleasure disappoints, possibility never.

Søren Kierkegaard

CHAPTER 12

Making the Transition

The important thing is this: to be able at any moment to sacrifice what we are for what we could become.

Charles DuBois

Jane was distraught. Her company had just asked for voluntary resignations. Employees would be given five months' salary if they chose to leave. Should she take the money and run? I asked whether she had given any thought to what she would do if she left. Oh, yes, she had been dreaming of a new life for several years now. She longed to move to a warmer climate and had three excellent profit center ideas. I wondered, What's the question? What I said, though, was, "What a great opportunity!"

She wasn't convinced. "But it's so scary," she wailed.

"What exactly is scary?"

"Giving up twenty-seven thousand dollars a year salary," she replied.

"That's not the scariest part," I said. "What's really frightening is never going after your dream. If you don't act on this, ten years from now you'll still be wondering if you could have made it. You already know that you can get a job for twenty-seven thousand dollars. If you stay where you are, you'll never find out what's possible and you'll be earning thirty-two thousand dollars."

Jane's story is particularly frustrating, it seems to me, because she seemed oblivious to the gift she'd been offered. Like many

211

people, she hasn't learned to tell the difference between a crisis and an opportunity. For her, making the transition from employee to entrepreneur required taking a much smaller leap of faith than most of us are asked to take. Jane stays stuck despite a multitude of supports.

At the other extreme is novelist Tom Robbins's experience. "One day I had gone to the bank, and was hurrying back to my job at the *Seattle Times*," Robbins recalls. "I was walking very fast, with my coattails flapping and my tie swinging over my shoulder. I was a harried young man, on the way up. And in the distance I saw a figure approaching—a man with red hair, bewhiskered. And he was singing, walking up the sidewalk singing. When he got really close to me, he looked me in the face and laughed. It was as if he'd seen through me, and registered all my areas of discontent, and then laughed at it all. The next Monday I called in to work well. I said, 'I've been sick for a long time, but I'm well today so I can't make it in.' I went to New York."

Tom Robbins could make this abrupt move into making a living without a job because he grasped a truth that has eluded Jane: real security is not a regular paycheck. Just knowing that, however, is not enough; you must act on what you know. President Bill Clinton summed it up profoundly when he said, "Security flows from initiative, not from inertia." Making the transition from employee to entrepreneur requires action. It also demands that you know yourself well enough to do it in a way that suits your style.

There are four major transitional paths you might take. Each of them can get you out on your own, but one of them probably makes the most sense for you.

• *Turn adversity into opportunity*. During the recent recession, numerous people who never planned to be jobless have found themselves without work. Some of them have discovered a hidden blessing in their unemployment. For the first time in their adult lives, many of these folks have found themselves in charge of their own schedules—and they enjoy it. They're reviving an interest in an avocation, getting to know their families again, and seeing how good it feels to be out of a stressful workplace. Having tasted these side benefits of a job-free life, they begin to look for options that will make it possible for them to earn a living without giving up their freedom. They may not have spent years dreaming of entrepreneurship, but the idea is appealing now. Had they not lost their jobs, they might never have known what they were missing.

• *Jump in with both feet.* Other people are emotionally equipped for making a change that is dramatic. They may not have been working visibly to make such a change, but months, or even years, of thought and planning have gone into their decision. They've quietly selected which bridges to cross and which to burn. When the time comes, they're ready to give 100 percent of their attention to self-bossing. Depending on the level of risk that is comfortable for them, they may make the change with or without a financial cushion. Frequently, however, people who take a single giant step are supported by their own confidence and belief in their dream.

• *Dabble with a sideline business.* A friend tells of her experience and says, "Not long ago, I was leading a double life. By day, I was a corporate employee—cooperative, efficient, and bored. At night and on weekends, I came to life as an entrepreneur, selling my handmade evening bags to boutiques and at craft shows. It was rugged and often exhausting, but when my job came to an end a year ahead of my plan, I had built a foundation that was strong enough for me to make it on my own." My friend's experience is encouraging, but not all sideline businesses turn out so well. Dabblers tend to keep dabbling. Without a greater commitment, sidelines may stay small and keep their owners from ever making the break. This transitional path *looks* sensible, but it may be a mirage.

• *Design and implement a transitional plan.* The most workable solution for most of us is to plan our transition in a way that fits our goals, circumstances, and personality. Giving yourself a deadline, knowing what needs to be completed before then, and getting busy putting your plan into action are both logical and empowering. Let's consider some of the ways you can put your house in order.

Making a Mental Move

Before changes can occur in the outer conditions of our lives, we must make inner changes in our thinking. If you begin to think like an entrepreneur before you take the big step, your transition will be smoother and easier.

One of the best perspectives you can adopt is to start thinking of your current job as *one* of your profit centers. Once you do this, you'll find your relationship to that job altered. You'll stop thinking of it as the only income source available to you. Instead, you'll treat it as a temporary choice you've made to bring money into your life or to learn from. When you make this switch in your thinking, you'll find that your job no longer has the same hold on you. In fact, this simple shift in attitude may help you relax as you begin to view the job as part of a larger, more exciting plan, a plan you're in the process of designing to create a richer, happier life.

One evening during her student days in Italy, my sister, Nancy, and two friends were on their way to dinner. As they neared the restaurant, two men on a motor scooter came up alongside Nancy and attempted to rob her. Since she had her hand in her coat pocket, they didn't manage to remove her purse from her shoulder, but she was thrown to the ground and injured in the attempt.

Hearing the commotion, the maître d' came rushing out of the restaurant to see what had happened. He ran over to my sister as she lay on the sidewalk, but before he could ask any questions, Nancy looked up at him and said, in Italian, "A table for three, please."

This story is typical of my archaeologist sister, who has always stayed focused on her goals. Before you can move ahead, you must know where it is you intend to go. Keeping this mental picture in mind, seeing yourself as a self-bosser, is necessary advance work.

Build Your Support System

New members of Alcoholics Anonymous are sometimes startled to learn that their sobriety depends on more than simply not drinking. Lifestyle changes are necessary if they are to succeed. One of the most difficult of these changes involves social life. Hanging out with their former drinking buddies is dangerous. They're reminded, "If you don't want to slip, don't go to slippery places."

You, too, need to find people who will serve as models and mentors, people you trust who will support your goals. Your transition plan needs to include a support-building segment.

There was an audible gasp at the Santa Barbara Writers' Conference when Jerry Gilles suggested that would-be writers purchase one hardcover book every week. "Support the industry that you intend to be part of," was his exhortation. The audience didn't seem convinced. Didn't he know they couldn't afford such an outrageous expense? Maybe when they were prosperous authors, but now it was out of the question. Gilles showed them a success principle that is fundamental: if you expect to be supported, you must support others.

This is a simple truth, yet many ignore it. At the end of my seminars, I give people an opportunity to subscribe to my newsletter and purchase audiotapes. Usually, 30 to 50 percent of the audience does so. At that moment, they have not just made a purchase from me. They have enlisted my continuing support. These are the ones who have a strong intention to succeed at making a living without a job, and it's my responsibility to focus on supporting their dreams. It's a beautiful arrangement in which both sides win.

Surround your dreams with support. Read books that take you far. Hang out with people who truly want you to win. Encourage others who are working on their dreams. Take time to call the dreamers and doers in your life. Do things that enhance your self-esteem and physical well-being. Alexandra Stoddard says, "Life is too short for you to be the caretaker of the wrong details." Taking care of the right details will make your transition to entrepreneurship a joy.

As Jess Lair points out, "We should stay away from the people who aren't good for us as much as we can and we should go frequently to those other people who lift us up. When we go to people who lift us up, they give us the most precious thing that there is, which is a deeper self-knowledge. So we don't leave these encounters to chance."

This is your time to build your entrepreneurial consciousness, to see yourself as a self-bosser. Here are a few thoughts to stretch your imagination. Pick one or two of these images, close your eyes, and visualize yourself in the situation.

• You go to your mailbox and instead of a pile of bills you find a stack of orders for the software program you designed.

• A television producer calls to say a local talk show is doing a series on bootstrap operations and would like to have you as a guest.

• You receive a standing ovation after giving a talk to a self-bossers' group called "How I Went from Failure to Success."

• A friend calls to tell you about a special airfare to Hawaii and suggests you drop everything and go with him.

• Your banker calls and says the bank has noticed a huge balance in your checking account and would like to discuss your putting some of the cash into an investment fund.

• You get a letter from an ex-boss congratulating you on your business success.

• Your teenager knocks on your office door and offers to help you get out the mailing you're working on—for free.

• You go in for your annual checkup and your doctor asks what you've done to lower your weight, blood pressure, and cholesterol.

• You call an entrepreneurial friend and ask if she can take on your business overload.

• After figuring your business deductions, your accountant tells you that you owe almost nothing in taxes.

Apprentice Yourself

In earlier times, many professions and arts were passed along through formal apprenticeships. Someone who had mastered woodcarving or blacksmithing would agree to teach one or more students, usually in exchange for labor of some sort. Once the student was deemed skillful by the master, he or she was sent out to practice alone. Eventually the student became the teacher, passing along skills and knowledge to another novice. Valuable experience was perpetuated.

While formal apprenticeship programs aren't as common today, creating your own is a possibility. Perhaps your current job is a form of apprenticeship, teaching you things that you can use as a self-bosser. If, on the other hand, you want to do something very different from what you have been doing, aligning yourself with someone in that field can be a terrific education. If you long to run your own bookstore, for instance, go to work for a bit for an experienced bookseller. Learn about ordering, marketing, and customer relations. You may discover that an occupation you've fantasized about isn't as satisfying as you anticipated. Your apprenticeship can be another aspect of clarifying your goals.

Practical Considerations

Actress Liv Ullmann once made a poignant confession. "I had a life with options," Ullmann said, "but frequently lived as if I had none. The sad result of my not having exercised my choices is that my memory of myself is not of the woman I believe I am."

Exercising all of your options, but not being limited by them, is another important aspect of your personal escape plan. Your situation will be unique, of course, but a quick review of your employee benefits can help you make wiser decisions.

Take into consideration your current benefits as an employee. Can you see them as a form of support for your dreams rather than as a chain to your employer? A friend of mine who decided in midlife to enter the ministry worked for a company that paid a percentage of educational costs for its employees. Sandy took advantage of that benefit as a stepping-stone to her goal. If you have responsibilities that need to be fulfilled before you go out on your own, perhaps your benefits can contribute to making it happen.

What about pensions and profit-sharing? If you've accrued these things, you'll have to decide what you want to do with them. Can you leave them where they are for future use, or does it make more sense to convert them to a liquid form? Know what trade-offs you'll have to make with each separate benefit. If you have unused vacation or sick time, must you use it or can you convert it to cash?

For most people, health insurance is the biggest dilemma. Your job has probably been your major health insurance provider, and you may never have given it much thought. How long can you stay on the group plan after you leave? Might you be better off switching to another carrier right away? Investigate the alternatives. You may be surprised at the number of appropriate health plans available to you. Besides doing independent research on various insurance companies, check on plans offered through fraternal or professional organizations. Churches, even some hobby associations, have insurance plans for their members.

Let me remind you, too, to stop thinking about being jobless as being benefitless—a common error. As a self-bosser, you can decide each and every benefit that you wish to give yourself, including retirement plans, health coverage, and all the vacation time you desire. When you're self-employed, benefits are like any other goal—you determine what they will be and plan a way to create them. Anything you deem important to your serenity and well-being belongs in your benefit plan. Even if you can't provide all the benefits right away, adding them as you grow is your prerogative.

Another part of your escape plan that can be completed in advance involves finishing up the details of organizing your business. If your plan includes a home office, clear out the space you'll be using and get it furnished. Open your business checking account; get your printing done. Handle these things as quickly as possible. You've got more interesting ways to spend your time.

Working with a Deadline

We all know people who talk about what they'll do "someday." Ah, yes, when the time is right, of course, they will leave the rat race and sail around the world. To avoid falling into that trap, I keep a reminder on my desk from D. H. Lawrence: "Life is something to be spent, not to be saved." There's no such thing as a Perfect Time to do the important things in life, such as get married, take your dream trip, or set up shop. Even so, giving yourself a deadline for completing your stay as an employee will give you focus and motivation.

Your deadline can be set using various criteria. Many self-bossers began by setting a goal using the calendar, figuring in the time needed to manage the preliminary details. Others use a financial guideline. Some people start a sideline business while they have a job, predetermining the point at which they'll make the move. Sally Laird, a student of mine who dreamed of being a tour guide, worked as an independent contractor for a large corporation while exploring opportunities for escorting tours. Once she had established her travel profit center, she filled in her days at home by returning to her temporary office work. When her travels were beginning to pay off, she gave herself a deadline for severing her ties with the corporation.

Financial guidelines could be something like, "When my business brings in half as much money as my current salary," or "When I have three profit centers clearly planned," or "When I have my credit card debts paid off." These kinds of deadlines only work, of course, if you are diligent about moving toward them once you've decided what they are.

Be Selfish with Your Time

We all know about Parkinson's Law, which says that work expands to fill the available time. If you're currently employed and starting a business part-time, you might believe there's never enough time or energy to do it all. In the long run, you'll accomplish more if you have daily goals for your business. Build the habit of doing something every day that contributes to moving you from employee to entrepreneur, and be ruthless about how your time is spent. Especially at the beginning, you must jealously guard your time and be certain that you aren't spending it in ways that are counterproductive.

Doing this may bring accusations of selfishness. A student in one of my classes came up to me during the break and said, "I've always been told that if I do what I want I'm just being selfish."

"In what way?" I asked.

"Well, you know, I've been wanting to write a book, but people tell me that's selfish."

"How can that be an act of selfishness?" I countered. "What *is* selfish is to keep information to yourself when it could be valuable to others. Not writing your book is the real selfish thing."

I have met plenty of genuinely selfish people, and often their behavior was born of hostility. Selfish people hoard their possessions and even their affection, thinking they must protect the little they've got. That isn't the kind of selfishness I'm advocating. Spending your time in ways that are satisfying to you isn't the same as hoarding scraps of it. To use your time magnificently, you may have to learn to say "no." The Cub Scouts will be here next year, even if you don't volunteer your time. I promise.

Another Option

Many ventures are necessarily begun in secrecy. If you have the rare good fortune to work for an enlightened boss who truly has your best interests at heart, you may have a valuable ally. Many of my students have made their transitions by quitting their jobs but keeping their employers as clients. This idea seems less outrageous as more companies discover the value of using freelance talent and independent contractors to complete specific projects. If you're in a situation where this might be a possibility, explore altering your relationship in this way. It's not always feasible, I know, but when it does work it can be a boost to a new venture. You may be able to perform some of the work you're now doing on a per-project basis or on fewer days of the week in exchange for your freedom. This will liberate your time to develop other profitable projects while doing some of your work in an environment that is familiar and comfortable. Don't rule it out as an option.

Out, Not Up

Your transition from employee to entrepreneur can be hastened and smoothed with advance planning and determination. Tie up loose ends, manage the details, and aim for a deadline. Even if your leave is delayed, knowing that you're doing all you can to create a new and better life will lend necessary emotional support. Action, consistent action, is the proven success ingredient.

Here's a wonderful image to keep in mind. "I find the great thing in this world," wrote Oliver Wendell Holmes, "is not so much where we stand, as in what direction we are moving: To reach the port of heaven, we must sail sometimes with the wind and sometimes against it—but we must sail, and not drift, nor lie at anchor."

Winning Ways for Making the Transition

Complete the following statements.

The details I need to manage before I leave my job are

_____

_____.

Until then, I work toward my goal every day by

_____

_____.

My deadline for becoming joyfully jobless is

_____

_____.

A time-waster that I can eliminate right now is

_____

_____.

I continue to expand my entrepreneurial consciousness by

_____

_____.

The benefits my business will provide me include

_____

_____.

CHAPTER 13

Enjoying Your Spaghetti Days

It's smart to defer gratification. Indeed, deferring gratification is
a good definition of being civilized. Take less at first in order to
get much more later.

Bernice Fitz-Gibbon

Susie Thompkins, a cofounder of the clothing corporation
Esprit, wistfully recalls the early days of her business, when she
and her partner shared tuna sandwiches and scrounged for
change on the floor of their car to find enough money to pay
bridge tolls. Like many of us, Thompkins looks back on those
beginning moments and remembers the excitement and romance that went with them. These Spaghetti Days, as I like to call
them, are often a time of heightened creativity when every tiny
victory is cause for celebration. No wonder entrepreneurs love to
reminisce. This is the period when we discover our ability to rise
to challenges, to substitute imagination for money, to affirm our
commitment to our goals.

Whether you make drastic changes or alter your life only a bit,
your Spaghetti Days will be the first chapter of a new story you're
writing about your life, your declaration of personal independence. The pace at which you work, your choice of profit centers,
your personal vision, will all play a part. In a society that has

trained us to expect instant gratification, dealing with uncertainty for a while or learning to live on less money demands that you approach things with a patience and persistence you may not have needed in the past.

Your first months, or even years, of being jobless will require adjustments of all kinds. You'll be exposed to new people and you'll be learning new skills. You'll be drawing a new map, one that will take you places you've never been before. If you treat all of this as an adventure—which it certainly is—you, too, will be able to look back fondly when you tell the story of your early days of making a living without a job. There are trade-offs, for sure, but many of the sacrifices you'll make are only temporary. Your attitude about the personal adjustments you must make, more than any other factor, will determine whether your Spaghetti Days are a time of deprivation or personal growth. And while it's *not* true that everyone who goes out on his or her own encounters reduced finances, a shift in thoughts about money, in priorities, in values, frequently does occur.

Years ago, when I felt as if I was the only person around making sacrifices on behalf of a dream, I came across a quote from the English writer Doris Lessing which put things back into perspective for me. "It seems to me like this," Lessing said, "it's not terrible—I mean it may be terrible, but it's not damaging, it's not poisoning to do without something one really wants. . . . What's terrible is to pretend that the second-rate is first-rate. To pretend that you don't need love when you do; or you like your work when you know quite well you're capable of better."

This is your opportunity significantly to raise the quality of your life—and to discover how little money has to do with that.

Less Can Be More

After she was widowed early in life, my Aunt Marge was left with a farm to manage and two small daughters to raise. Her sunny disposition brought her through many difficult times, and I loved spending time in her house. Marge did things differently than anyone I knew. She was the only working mother I'd met who left her kids alone. Even better, her idea of dinner might be a big bowl of popcorn. As a kid, I thought this was the most delicious freedom possible! I also remember the periods when money was in short supply. While an ordinary parent might have fretted silently about money, Marge had a different tactic. She'd call her daughters in and declare that they were going on an Austerity Program. These belt-tightening periods always had a time limit and involved everyone. They'd discuss ways to lower their spending and ways to "make do." Should I suggest to my cousin Karen that we go to a movie during one of these times, she'd shake her head and say, "Not right now. We're on Austerity." That was the signal for us to cook up an alternative outing that didn't require money. None of them seemed to feel deprived during these times, because they believed they had options. There was always a feeling of abundance in that household which made it a wonderful place to be.

"Who is rich?" asks the Talmud. "He who rejoices in what he has." *Moneylove* author Jerry Gillies echoes this definition: "Prosperity is living easily and happily in the real world, whether you have money or not." Metaphysical teachers have always pointed out that prosperity is a state of mind, one that has nothing to do with a specific amount of money or number of possessions. Adopting a less-is-more attitude has nothing to do, either, with being impoverished. It is, rather, a healthy emotional state that comes from knowing your personal definition of wealth—and actively creating a life that reflects your definition.

Which of the following items would be included in your definition of wealth? Which would your parents include?

My idea of wealth includes:

____ A savings account	____ Designer clothes
____ Happy children	____ Small indulgences
____ Physical health	____ A college education
____ A luxury automobile	____ Inner peace
____ Time for myself	____ A regular paycheck
____ A large home	____ Emotional health
____ A hot tub	____ A funky automobile
____ An art collection	____ Time for my family
____ Adventurous travel	____ The envy of others
____ Employees	____ A stock portfolio
____ Philanthropy	____ First-class travel

____ Servants   ____ Personal freedom
____ Employers   ____ Good relationships
____ Time to volunteer   ____ Self-reliance

The important thing to remember about wealth is that we each have our own idea about what it takes to make us feel wealthy. Writer Natalie Goldberg says, "I feel very rich when I have time to write and very poor when I get a regular paycheck and no time to work at my real work." What are the times when you feel rich? How can you spend more time feeling that way?

Thinking that money is the only form of wealth is an adolescent's perspective. Robert G. Allen, author of several books on investing, has a maturer, healthier thought: "Wealth is knowledge, confidence, attitude. It has nothing to do with the accumulation of money. You can take away my cash, my credit, my statements at the bank—everything the world considers wealth. But I'll always have the only thing that really counts: my own resources."

Finding the Best

Squeezing every bit of pleasure out of each situation, each opportunity that comes your way, seems to be easier during your Spaghetti Days. Sometimes it happens out of necessity. You don't have the funds to do things expensively, so you learn to improvise and find ways to spend less while getting the highest possible quality. A woman in a seminar I once attended got up and said, "My attitude has always been to look at whatever I had and ask myself how I could have the most fun with it. If it was ten dollars or a thousand dollars, that's been my approach—and it's always worked."

Several years ago, Stanley Marcus, of Neiman-Marcus fame, wrote a book called *Quest for the Best*, in which he told eloquently of his life scouring the world for goods worthy of his store's customers. "I learned to differentiate, not between good and bad but between better and best, and to pursue the best," says Marcus. "The difference in cost to achieve the best may be negligible, but overcoming the inertia of the status quo and the willingness of most people to settle for less than perfection always takes greater effort."

If you're determined to do the very best with what you have—and to keep finding the best and making it your own—you'll be far more patient and far less willing to settle for the mediocre. Raising the quality of your life is a function of your imagination, not your bank balance.

Ask yourself questions like these, and you can raise the quality of your days immediately:

> What is the best use of my time right now?
> Who are the best people to spend time with right now?
> What is the best book I could read right now?
> What's the most scrumptious meal I could eat right now?
> What's the best way to promote my business right now?

Focus on doing, having, and being the best in the present moment. It's the secret to mastering the art of living well.

Heightening Appreciation

There's another hidden treasure to be uncovered during our Spaghetti Days, one that would be a shame to miss. That unexpected gift is the opportunity you have to develop genuine appreciation for the miracles and everyday pleasures that life has to offer. Often it's an appreciation that we fail to notice during times of financial ease.

In *A Movable Feast*, Ernest Hemingway wrote about his early years in Paris, when he was not yet a published writer. "You got very hungry when you did not eat enough in Paris because all the bakery shops had such good things in the window. When you had given up journalism and were writing nothing that anyone in America would buy, the best place to go was the Luxembourg gardens where you saw and smelled nothing to eat. There you could always go into the Luxembourg museum and the paintings were sharpened and clearer and more beautiful if you were belly-hungry, hollow-hungry. I learned to understand Cézanne much better and to see truly how he made landscapes when I was hungry."

You don't have to be a starving artist to develop an attitude of gratitude, but if you've never learned to appreciate the small pleasures life has to offer, chances are you'll never receive the bigger ones. What we focus on expands, and, therefore, the greater the number of things you appreciate, the more opportunities you'll be given. Think about a time when you were in love and kept finding more wonderful qualities in the object of your affection. Conversely, a person who annoys you will produce more and more irritating situations.

There are a number of cities where I prefer not to teach anymore, even though class enrollments remain high. I'm not certain why prevailing attitudes vary so much from place to place, but they do. In some cities people seem jaded; they may be alive, but they're not living. In other cities, I find an open and enthusiastic attitude. Local cultures obviously determine whether or not it's acceptable to show appreciation. No matter how much information I provide, an apathetic person can never be transformed into a joyfully jobless one. We build enthusiasm in our small moments, not our grander ones.

The day after I put up my Christmas tree, my friend Jill came for dinner. She walked into the living room and went directly to the tree, where she oohed and aahed over my creation, just as I'd known she would. Jill has made a daily ritual of appreciating the people and things in her world. When she received a gift of Godiva chocolates, she decided to use it as her Advent calendar, savoring one truffle a day. She says her new Audi is the first car that's ever given her great pleasure, but her appreciation extends to people more often than it does to things. A great movie, a writing workshop taught by Natalie Goldberg, and the kindness of a stranger have all been recounted in delighted detail. More than once I've found a message from Jill on my answering machine that said, "It's wonderful to have you as a friend." Genuine appreciation isn't just good manners, although it is that, too. People like Jill connect with life's abundance and, as a result, live in an abundant world. Why settle for less?

You Don't Have to Wait to Live Rich

Linda McCartney, wife of the former Beatle, is another person who appreciates small wonders. Although her husband is one of the richest pop stars in history, with a personal fortune estimated around $500 million, the self-determined McCartneys chose to raise their four children in a two-bedroom cottage. Eccentric millionaires? Not according to Linda. "My outlook is that little things are the trip," she told a *Vanity Fair* interviewer. "I'm very happy with very little. Maybe that's why I have so much."

Incorporating special pleasures into your daily schedule is a habit worth cultivating. Here are a few personal favorites that you can use as idea-starters. Not one of them costs much money, but taking time to do them will make you feel like a million bucks. Yes, you can do these even *after* you have pots of money.

Visit a Japanese garden, a place designed for serenity.

Burn incense in your office before starting your day's work.

Gather your favorite cartoons in a scrapbook so that you always know where to go when you need a laugh.

Be generous in sending thank-you notes.

Eat vanilla ice cream for breakfast.

Read aloud a story with another adult.

Celebrate your first (or fifth) year in business with a party.

Fall asleep in a hammock.

Kidnap an overworked friend and take him or her to a movie matinee.

Put all of your favorite music on a tape to play in the car.

Invent your own holiday complete with made-up traditions and celebrate it annually.

Get travel brochures of your dream vacation and make a collage to hang in your office.

Invite your friends to a slumber party and stay up all night.

Write a fan letter to your favorite magazine, your favorite author, your favorite entertainer.

Send a card of congratulations to yourself.

Start a collection and add to it on your travels.

Have afternoon tea complete with scones, jam, and cream.

Give time to a cause you believe in.

Do a photo essay with your friends as the subjects.

Replace your ratty bathrobe with an elegant kimono from a thrift store.

Change something in your personal environment every day.

Splurge on something elegant, such as a crystal paperweight, for your desk.

Send flowers to someone who'd never expect them.

Shine your shoes or have them shined.

Start a piggy bank for a special purchase.

Treat someone you admire to lunch.

Have your business card or brochure printed on a new color of paper or in a colored ink.

Wear a button declaring your stand on an issue or cause.

Grow something you can eat.

Creating Your Own World Headquarters

The message on my answering machine assures callers that they have reached the World Headquarters of Winning Ways and Barbara Winter. I'd never thought of my home as the international origin of my business until I saw an ad several years ago showing a little house with a white picket fence. The caption read, "To the neighbors, it's 310 Oak Street. To the Clarks, it's world headquarters." Since I live, work, and schedule my life from the place I call home, I promptly had a brass plaque engraved for my door reading, "Winning Ways World Headquarters." If your house, apartment, motor home, or houseboat is going to serve as your World Headquarters, it's up to you to make certain that it serves you well.

In the past few years, our homes have taken on a new importance. Trend-spotter Faith Popcorn has coined the term "cocooning" to describe this emerging lifestyle. We are, she assures us, nesting with our VCRs, hot tubs, and microwaves. Like our counterparts in the sixties who rediscovered natural living, we are enthusiastically embracing hearth and home, filling our cocoons with "country" furnishings, fresh vegetables that we may have grown ourselves, and exercise equipment. Homebuilders are often designing homes to include an office. Self-contained living centers seem to be our goal.

Nesting can be wonderfully nurturing—or the beginning of a disaster. The sixteenth-century essayist Montaigne put it well when he advised, "If you're going to withdraw into yourself, first prepare yourself a welcome." His advice stands up even today if you're going to snuggle into your cocoon and run a solo business.

In the first place, the prospect of working solo can be terrifying. There is camaraderie, after all, even in the most toxic companies. At first, you won't notice that you're alone. You'll be too busy organizing the details of your new life. Once the ink is dry on your business cards, the paper clips are in their holder, and the files are organized, you may notice that it's quiet, frighteningly quiet. There's no gossiping around the water cooler, no buddies to chat with at lunch, no coworkers telling you the latest joke. Sometimes it feels as if everyone else is out playing baseball while you're inside practicing the piano.

When this happens to you, and I promise that it will, relax. It's part of the Living Without a Job lesson plan. You need to discover what part being alone plays in your overall scheme. These times will be important for generating new ideas, getting organized, catching up on the mail. Later on, when your business keeps you busier, you'll welcome these quiet times as part of your personal ecological balance.

Conversely, there can be endless distractions when you work alone. Not a day passes when I don't think about Jessamyn West's confession: "When I'm writing a book, I never get out of bed because if I get out of bed I always see something that needs dusting." Add to that the phone calls and chatty friends and you might have a situation that sends you rushing off to fill out a job application.

Happily, distractions can be handled easily and immediately. If your work is done in a separate room or space designated as an office, keeping regular hours may be all the discipline you need to avoid internal distractions. Let your friends know that you're serious about your business and tell them when you'll be free to talk. An answering machine or voice-mail service can monitor your phone, freeing you to get on with other projects. One writer took to wearing a special hat to signal her family that she was not to be disturbed. If you live with others, you can devise your own version of a Do Not Disturb sign.

The Creative Cocoon

The danger, to yourself or your venture, in consolidating your personal and professional life under a single roof is that it can hamper your creativity. One antidote to this is to make your personal environment the kind of place that's a kitchen for your mind. Too many homes are filled with tools, gadgets, and appliances, but lack the materials needed to spark ideas and imagination. Furthermore, few families have learned to encourage the creative spirits of their members or to involve everyone in meaningful goal-setting. So that we do not grow dull and become mere spectators of life, we have to think about making our personal cocoon the most exciting place on the block. Here are some ideas for doing just that:

• Stimulate conversation with the help of writer and publisher Bill Zimmerman's books *Make Beliefs* and *A Book of Answers*, which are loaded with questions both silly and serious. You'll learn things about the people you live with—and yourself—that will add a new dimension to your relationships.

• Keep materials close at hand to fuel creative sparks. Fill up a shelf or a drawer with all kinds of art supplies; find a box and put interesting souvenirs and scraps into it for doing collage. One rainy evening a friend called and asked, "Would you think I was crazy if I invited you to come over for popcorn and watercolor painting?" We ended up doing childlike paintings for all of our friends, who cherished our amateur results. The same friend and I welcomed the new year by making collages together of our goals for the coming year.

• Launch a group project. Few families have learned to set and achieve goals as a team. Concoct a project that gets everyone involved, one that helps every member make a unique contribution. I met a teenage boy whose family had decided to live in Australia for two years. Each member of the family was responsible for earning his or her own passage abroad and for various aspects of the move. Get family members involved in your business, too. Let them share in the work and the rewards.

• Schedule regular field trips. Everyone can be involved in idea-gathering. Visit museums, trek to the library, browse through model homes together. Look, listen, and talk about what you've discovered. One of my most memorable trips to London was the one which I shared with my daughter, Jennifer, who was then twenty years old and had just backpacked alone through Europe. Her perspectives and interests led me to many sights and sounds I would not have found on my own. Your kids, especially, can make you aware of trends, ideas, and connections that would otherwise elude you.

• Invite people to share your cocoon. Make this your year to meet interesting new people and bring them into your world. Nothing is more enriching than the company of others who can add their vision and passion to yours. Making a living without a job should, by its nature, cause your world to expand. Collect positive people and indulge often.

While these guidelines for creating World Headquarters may seem simple, you must take action to produce the most exciting environment on earth. This is an investment that brings an exceptional return if you're willing to make it happen.

Managing an Up-and-Down Cash Flow

Carola Barn, a native of Greenwich, England, used to pass a junk store every day when she walked her children to nursery school. After dropping off her children, she'd stop and buy something almost daily. Eventually she turned her acquisitive streak into a business of her own. Today she owns two shops that sell fabrics, dresses, and anything else that catches her fancy. While she loves the changing aspect of her business, she says she's never gotten used to living with a fluctuating cash flow. It's an experience shared by many who are self-employed.

After years of living on predictable sums of money, having a variable cash flow can be challenging and sometimes unnerving. With time, you'll grow philosophical about it, knowing that money comes and goes and that your primary job is to be as wise as possible in handling the money you receive. Your general level of prosperity-consciousness will make a great difference, of course. If you believe that you live in an abundant world, you'll react quite differently than those who are convinced that earth is a place of scarcity.

The secret to dealing with an up-and-down cash flow is to get yourself to the point of such contentment with what you are doing that you no longer have an emotional response to money. It requires discipline and experience to get to this stage. After a while, you'll learn to stay focused on building aspects of your business without being distracted by temporary delays in earning. Your experience, too, will show you that there are cycles to what you're doing, and you'll find you're more relaxed about them. Nevertheless, a calm approach will accelerate your prosperity, and learning to handle the ups and downs with class is not difficult.

Here are some simple money tips I've gleaned from other self-bossers who have breezed through their Spaghetti Days with style and grace.

• *Get smart about money*. Even though we talk about and think about money a great deal, it's surprising how little guidance we really receive in financial matters. Our beliefs and attitudes about prosperity may bear a frightening resemblance to those held by our parents, whose financial circumstances and knowledge may be unlike our own. Unless you were brought up by people who had a healthy, happy attitude about money, you might want to challenge your early lessons on the subject. There are many financial teachers around from whom you can learn about wise money management. Since these advisers seldom seem to agree, find one you like and ignore the others. You don't have to get a degree in economics to be money-smart.

• *Don't spend yourself poor*. If feast follows famine, you may be tempted to pay off all your old bills, leaving yourself impoverished all over again. Your mental health will be stronger if you hang on to some of the money you earn and begin to see it accumulate a bit. Just knowing you have a tiny nest egg stashed away can be empowering, and that, in turn, makes it easier to create more income.

• *Regard debt as an investment in your future, not a sign of irresponsibility*. Some years ago, I met a delightful young woman who had gone into farming with her husband. She was obviously enchanted with their business and told me the secret to enjoying it was learning to live with debt. I wondered whether she was sincere, since I had been taught that debt was to be avoided at all costs. That was before I had my own vision. Now I see debt as part of the process of building something wonderful. Debt is neither good nor bad, but rather, sometimes necessary. Keep yours manageable, but don't avoid it if it advances your dreams.

• *Keep a running list of emergency moneymakers.* When things get tight, don't wait for something to happen. Get busy and make it happen. Can you unload boxes? Run a switchboard? Let a temporary work agency find you interim work and help you through a cash crunch. The aforementioned Carola Barn installed an extra bathroom in her home in case she needed to take in lodgers to create cash flow. Being mindful of all your options will add to your confidence in your ability to manage down times.

• *Remember that partial payments are better than no payments.* If you can't meet your obligations—even to the telephone company or utilities—send what you can with an explanatory note. Since bill collectors aren't the most compassionate souls, if you must deal with them, try not to be defensive—or overly optimistic. This, too, shall pass, but until it does, don't go into hiding.

• *Cultivate a creative and flexible attitude about money.* Look for new ways of doing things; consider changing your spending habits; avoid financial ruts. Catherine Ponder advises that if you're in a period of austerity and beans and wieners are on the menu, get out your best china and dine by candlelight. The more fun you can have with what you've got, the less money will run your life.

• *Acknowledge the abundance that you receive in unorthodox ways.* Author Sondra Ray reminds us, "The basic law of the mind is the law of increase. If you concentrate on your surplus, your surplus will get bigger." So don't overlook the additional prosperity you receive when a friend takes you to lunch, the airline sends you a frequent flyer ticket, or you win a night at the movies from your local radio station. All of these things add to your income just as money does. An attitude of gratitude is the secret weapon of the truly wealthy—and it's equally available to you if you start noticing the good coming your way.

• *Be consistent in working with the $100 Hour idea.* If you make this a habit, part of your business routine, your cash flow will even out more quickly and permanently. Knowing that you're taking action daily in the direction of your goals makes your slower times an annoyance, not a cause for panic.

Your Spaghetti Days offer you a glorious opportunity to clear out the clutter, reassess your priorities, and start from scratch, if that's what you want. The lessons you'll learn in practical creativity will serve you well long after these times have passed. Someday you, too, will be telling the story of your courage and imagination in creating something wonderful out of very little.

This is also your time to build faith. Patrick Overton's poem on the subject is one you may want to keep in mind, especially in your early days.

Faith

When you walk to the edge of all the light you have
and take that first step into the darkness of the unknown
you must believe one of two things will happen:

There will be something solid for you to stand upon,
or, you will be taught how to fly

Winning Ways for Enjoying Your Spaghetti Days

Put your brains to work and imagine yourself in the following situations. How could you accomplish these goals *without* spending money?

• You love the symphony, but a season ticket costs several hundred dollars. How can you hear these wonderful concerts for free?

• Several years ago, you visited Greece and long to return. How can you get back without spending a drachma?

• An important trade show is coming up that would be a terrific showcase for your business. The exhibit fee is $500. How can you participate?

• The first anniversary of your self-bossing is coming up and

you want to throw a party to celebrate with your family and several clients. How can you do it without breaking the bank?
• It's time to upgrade your computer. What options can you create to do this?

Here are some ways self-bossers beat the work-alone blues.

• Create a Living Without a Job group. Meeting regularly with a small number of enterprising people provides creative stimulation—and keeps you accountable.
• Know your own rhythms. Plan your working time to take advantage of high energy. Don't push when energy is low.
• Break up your day. Run errands, make phone calls, get away in the middle of your work. You'll return renewed and refreshed.
• Use background music. Needlework designer Kaffe Fassett spends long hours alone in his London studio creating glorious sweaters and needlepoint designs. His favorite companion is the BBC's classical music station. I feel the same way about Minnesota Public Radio.
• Leave some time unstructured. Being spontaneous is as important as being efficient.
• Plan a collaboration. While you may not want a long-term partnership, working on a project with another person can be fun and rewarding.
• Attend seminars. While all self-bossers know that they are in charge of their own education and growth, there are fringe benefits in participating in programs designed for entrepreneurs. You never know whom you'll meet.
• Give yourself a change of scenery. If you live in the city, take a walk in the country—and vice versa. A temporary move to a strange environment can recharge your batteries.
• Reward yourself. There's a good reason why big companies have contests and awards. It's equally important when you're on your own to plan ways to pat yourself on the back. When you're in charge, the prize can be absolutely perfect!

CHAPTER 14

Taking a Dream, Making It Real

If you were born without wings do nothing to prevent their growing.

Coco Chanel

The Japanese have a custom that they employ when making a wish or setting a goal. For each new goal, a daruma doll is acquired. This doll, really a large wooden head, comes with no eyes. When a goal is set, the first eye is painted on. The second eye is added after the goal has been reached. Along the way, the daruma doll stands as a constant reminder of what its owner is working to achieve.

If your dreams are to come true, they must be more than goals written on paper. Persistence and diligent action backed by a positive belief that you will succeed are vital parts of your plan. "Until one is committed there is hesitancy, the chance to draw back, always ineffectiveness," goes the much-quoted observation of W. H. Murray. "Concerning all acts of initiative and creation, there is one elementary truth, the ignorance of which kills countless ideas and splendid plans: that the moment one definitely commits oneself, then providence moves too.

"All sorts of things occur to help one that would never otherwise have occurred. A whole stream of events issues from the decision, raising in one's favor all manner of unforeseen incidents and meetings and material assistance, which no one could have dreamt would come their way."

Seasoned self-bossers have their own stories about serendipitous and miraculous events that helped them on their way to realizing their dreams. Chance meetings, windfalls, and spectacular solutions seem to be ordinary happenings in the lives of committed dreamers. The notion of making a living without a job can become a reality only if you take it beyond the realm of wishful thinking.

Earlier in this book, I wrote about my good friend John. Now it's time for him to speak for himself. John composed this piece just as he was going out on his own. I suspect he wrote it to encourage himself, but it captures the essence of what it takes to make a living without a job. Like me, you may find yourself coming back to it when you want a lift.

> During the 1973 baseball season, the New York Mets were in rough shape, struggling to stay in the middle of the team standings. It was midseason when a Mets pitcher shouted, "You gotta believe," when the team was behind in the ninth inning. The team became "believers" and won that game.
>
> The cry "You gotta believe" caught on with the fans during the rest of the season. Whenever the Mets were behind, their supporters in the stands convinced the team that they could still win the game. "You gotta believe! You gotta believe!" they would chant. That season the Mets made it to the World Series.
>
> I, too, have made the decision to believe. I resigned as director of communications at a large company to become a freelance writer and independent businessman. After almost ten years of writing a monthly magazine, I'm changing course in my writing career, leaving corporate job security behind and taking the biggest risk of my life.
>
> "You gotta believe!" is more than a positive affirmation in my case. It is the decision to have faith in God and my own unique abilities and talents. It is a commitment to achieve success through hard work, creativity, imagination, and using my writing skills to their best advantage. It is a step

toward fulfilling a dream of being an independent writer/ author working at home. And it is an opportunity to challenge myself to live a more balanced lifestyle while accomplishing a wider variety of projects.

One of those projects is to complete and market a book I am writing about a female swindler whose victim saved 280 pages of correspondence between 1930 and 1935. These rare letters tell a fascinating story of betrayed friendship, poverty, and strength. I know this book will be published and profitable. "You gotta believe" you'll be hearing about it.

"You gotta believe" that going it alone won't be easy. I'm already finding that out. As soon as I resigned, my roommate moved out and I had to scramble to fill the vacancy. I'll certainly miss the companionship of the people I now work with. I am also starting to share the frustrations of the self-employed—and I haven't even made a cold call yet.

My firm, The Word Store, will be the second business operated by a Schroeder in the past 100 years. In 1880, my great-grandparents operated Schroeder's Furniture and Funerals in St. Paul. So I am certain I was destined to be an entrepreneur!

George Burns once said, "Fall in love with what you're going to do for a living. It's very important. To be able to get out of bed and do what you love for the rest of the day is beyond words. It's just great. It'll keep you around for a long time."

That quote has been on my office wall for several years. It was the catalyst to do the work I love day after day in an independent environment. His remark also illustrates how writing can change the lives of people. And how one person (like you) can make a difference in the lives of others. We all have a tremendous opportunity before us.

Believe it.

John D. Schroeder

A Never-Fail Formula for Success

Whenever I meet a self-bosser for the first time I ask that person what prompted him or her to go out on his or her own. One of the most unexpected answers I've heard came from Becky Ellis. She told me that after years of working for the Massachusetts Horticultural Society she decided to open her own garden accessories shop in her hometown, Marblehead, Massachusetts. "I wanted a business," Ellis told me, "where I could have my dogs with me as I worked." Her two adored pets now spend their days happily helping her run The Garden Collection. Although this was the first time anyone told me that having pets around was part of her business concept, I realized that many self-bossers do their work with animal companions at their side. It may not be a big benefit, but it certainly adds a lovely touch to working on your own.

Motivation often comes from such ordinary and unassuming thoughts. A little thing like having your pets with you or turning something commonplace into something extraordinary can be the start of a grander dream. I remember the chilly November day when I called my friend Chris Utterback for one of our regular chats. "I just burned myself on my hot-glue gun," she told me.

"Are you making a wreath?" I asked.

"Oh, no," she said. "I got this idea for decorating my Christmas gifts." She sounded excited. "I wrapped my packages in brown paper, tied them with paper ribbon, and now I'm glueing on cones and seed pods I collected in my woods. I think I'll spray them with glitter spray when they're done."

When my packages arrived from Chris, they were the most admired under our tree. She had taken ordinary materials and transformed them into dazzling creations. She could have stopped with the appreciation of her friends and family, but, being entrepreneurial, Chris realized that she had designed something that others would want to know about. She called the editor of *The Herb Companion* and suggested that she write an article about her wrappings. It was eagerly accepted. The following year, Chris retooled her idea and wrote an article for another national magazine.

Tom Robbins said, "If you take any activity, any art, any discipline, any skill, take it and push it as far as it will go, push it beyond where it has ever been before, push it to the wildest edge of edges, then you force it into the realm of magic." Becky Ellis and Chris Utterback have certainly done that, taking tiny seed-ideas and nurturing them into something magical.

They know, as do all successful self-bossers, that there's a simple four-word formula that, repeatedly implemented, produces success. You can use this formula, too, to make your living without a job. Memorize and follow this never-fail recipe:

Get started. Don't quit.

Add Positive Energy

A report on the nightly news stated that violent crime had gone down in the Boston area by a whopping 60 percent in 1992. Much of the credit for this went to Gang Peace, an organization started by a former drug dealer to channel the energy of kids in a positive direction. Recognizing that gangs and drug dealers are actually well-managed enterprises, Gang Peace teaches kids to use the entrepreneurial skills they've acquired on the street—but use them to create legitimate businesses of their own.

A line from the book *The Secret Garden* goes, "Where you plant a rose, a thistle cannot grow." Where you take positive action, you eradicate the power of that which is negative. It's a concept used by a jail counselor in San Francisco who was searching for a way to make incarceration a transforming experience. When she first came up with her idea, cynical prison officers were certain she'd taken leave of her senses. Their attitude was, "Lady, you're dealing with tough criminals. This isn't going to make any difference." She persisted, however, and the results have been so spectacular that former detractors are now her biggest advocates.

What leading-edge technology did she employ to create noticeable change in the inmates? She started a garden. Prisoners now spend their days planting and picking. For most of them, it's the first time in their lives they've been involved in producing something positive. Visible changes begin to take place soon after prisoners start working in the garden. They become more peaceful, more sociable, more interested in the welfare of others. Since the vegetables grown in this garden are donated to local soup kitchens, many prisoners are now feeding people who were once their victims.

The lessons in living that gardening has to offer are not lost on these inmates. "I come out here," says one inmate, "and see the weeds. My job is to pull them out and leave the vegetables. It keeps reminding me to weed out all the bad stuff in my life, too."

The prison garden has been so successful that it has taken a step beyond the prison walls. A vacant lot in San Francisco has been turned into another thriving garden, this one run by prisoners after they've left jail. The produce from this plot is sold to fine restaurants in the Bay Area, providing a profitable enterprise for the ex-inmates.

If people whose lives are in such turmoil and trouble can make such strides by using positive action, what might you achieve if you followed their lead? Your dreams will respond to loving care, too. You can't be of two minds about this, however. You'll never see results if you challenge every idea with a "yes, but" response. Just as you can't dig up seeds you've planted to see whether they're growing, your dreams have to be watered and fertilized and nurtured and protected with faith before you see visible evidence.

Keep Cultivating

For a long time, I've suspected that there's some sort of mystical link between growing a garden and growing a business. Like many self-bossers, I am also a passionate gardener. In the summer, my bleak apartment balcony is transformed into a container garden that is the envy of my neighbors. Cosmos, snapdragons, daisies, salvia, clematis, herbs, miniature roses, and magnificent hibiscus overflow their pots, bringing hours of joy to me and other admirers. After four years of gardening in less than perfect conditions, I've grown wiser about what to plant and how to nurture the things I grow. Gardening teaches patience and reminds me that seeds I've planted in other ways need time to sprout and flourish. Gardening is a fine teacher, and I apply many lessons to my business that I've learned in my garden.

In May Sarton's book *Plant Dreaming Deep*, she tells of moving to a small town in New Hampshire, where she found the perfect balance for her days by dividing her time between writing in the morning and gardening in the afternoon. "Making a garden is not a gentle hobby for the elderly," writes Sarton, "to be picked up and laid down like a game of solitaire. It is a grand passion. It seizes a person whole, and once it has done so he will have to accept that his life is going to be radically changed." Reread what Sarton has to say and substitute "making a living without a job" for "making a garden." What she writes about gardening holds true for self-bossing.

"How much hope, expectation, and sheer hard work goes into the smallest success!" continues Sarton. "There is no being sure of anything except that whatever has been created will change in time, and sometimes quite erratically. And, like parents whose children suddenly shoot up beyond them, I am always taken by surprise."

No wonder good gardeners make good entrepreneurs. After all, they know success will come if they just keep planting!

Growing the Magick Garden

There's an evolutionary quality about becoming joyfully jobless. Being flexible and incorporating new and different ideas as you go is a natural part of that evolution. One such business that has undergone considerable change is Linda Gannon's Magick Garden. I asked Gannon to share the story of that process and she obliged with an account of the history of her business. This is how Gannon did it:

It all began in 1977. I had been teaching severely retarded children for three and a half years and decided it was time to begin my family. I got pregnant and left teaching shortly after, determined to stay home with my baby. We had just purchased a sixty-three-acre farm and moved from the city. Because the land came complete with a quaint little house, we were established in our perfect place to raise a family.

I planted a big garden—vegetables, flowers, and herbs (my new interest). I began to read more about flowers and herbs and the next year planted lots of them. I was eating herbs, drying them for potpourri, and making little dried bouquets and wreaths. By my third year, I was completely engrossed in gardening. I now had a second daughter and a huge garden.

I also had a friend who was home with her new baby and garden. She was doing the same things I was and we loved sharing our projects and ideas. Both of us were decorating our homes, as well as the homes of our friends, with our creations. People loved the things we made.

We decided to see if we had something people would buy. We worked feverishly for six months making wreaths, arrangements, tussie-mussies, potpourris, stationery, sachets, pillows, and dolls out of herbs and flowers. We rented a community building for a day and invited everyone we knew to our first herbal sale. We had asked about 300 people, but over 500 came and we made over $7,000. We were thrilled! We were in business!

Six months later, after we had cleaned and decorated a tiny guest house on my farm, we opened The Little Farm Workshoppe. The two of us kept it full of handmade herbal treasures. After the first year, I ran it and filled it alone. I was expanding my garden, reading more books, taking classes, and teaching classes. I added herbal weddings to my repertoire.

For the next ten years, my little business flourished. I expanded to mail order and published an herbal newsletter. I continued to do weddings, teach, and exhibit. I now had three daughters. I wanted to do it all and for a while I did, but I was quickly burning out. I was often up until 2 or 3 A.M. doing wreaths and arrangements. I fell asleep while writing my newsletter. It was too much. In 1987, I stopped doing weddings. I cut down the hours in my shop, which became "Open by Request." This gave me time to work during the day. Oh, yes, and I had another baby.

I was still reading about herbs and about this time I discovered the books of Scott Cunningham, who wrote about the lore and magic of herbs. I instantly became fascinated with the magical, ritual use of the useful plants. I began to incorporate magic into my work—magical oils, brews, amulets, sachets, wands. I started putting glitter on everything, adding confetti everywhere. Glitz and magic were my new trademarks! I had renewed energy and enthusiasm for my business. I changed the name of my newsletter to *The Magick*

Garden and I became the Faerie Queen of my Magical Herbal Shoppe. I started dressing in a Faerie Queen costume. The theme of my business was whimsy and fun.

A year later, my husband decided it was time to develop the farmland on which we lived and my little shop had to come down to make way for the new road. I moved my business into my basement and concentrated on mail order. I found that I didn't like the work of trying to package up the dainty, fragile herbal arrangements and wreaths. More time went into packaging than creating.

I did, however, like mail order and decided to change my product line somewhat. I ventured into doing gift baskets, baskets and boxes packed with small herbal wreaths as well as other herbal treasures like lotions, oils, sachets, magic wands, incense, soaps, spices, and bath herbs. I included books and tapes in some baskets. Not only was this much easier to produce, the idea was an instant hit. Each and every basket was made up for the individual and the occasion.

The Magick Garden has taken another turn. I spent the past year studying perfumery and have begun selling my own line of potpourri.

Like so many self-bossers, Linda Gannon's business changes and grows as the proprietor changes and grows. In a very real way, The Magick Garden is a mirror reflecting the talent and passion of a woman's self-discovery. Her customers have watched The Magick Garden keep getting better and better.

It Starts with a Dream

Having decided to go down this living-without-a-job path, what can you expect to happen? Neither I nor anyone else can predict absolutely what your experience will be. One certainty, however, is that you'll be part of a powerful trend that's going to change forever the way we think about work. It's the movement that Robert Schwartz, founder of the Tarrytown School for Entrepreneurs, envisioned when he said, "Pretty soon everybody will have to be an entrepreneur._It is simply the next stage of the human journey to be much more independent." On this journey there will be no shortage of new opportunities to grow and learn and prosper. Like John Schroeder, you'll learn to believe in your own dreams; like Linda Gannon, your lesson will be to welcome and embrace change as you nurture your dream into reality.

No matter how great or how small your past success in life, the important thing is not where you've been but where you're going. After all, your past is not your potential. Your age, education, experience, and skills matter far less than your willingness to acknowledge your personal dreams—and commit yourself to making them come true.

In 1927 thirty-two-year-old R. Buckminster Fuller stood on the edge of Lake Michigan reviewing his past and thinking of ending his life. A daughter had died at the age of four; he had five failed factories and was facing bankruptcy.

He decided that, before he killed himself, he would enter into a personal dialogue. And he asked himself, "Do I know best or does God know best whether I may be of value to the universe?"

The very fact of his existence, Fuller concluded, meant that his life had some purpose, some value. He turned away from Lake Michigan and his plans for suicide and spent the next fifty-six years exploring, inventing, and experimenting. So far-reaching were his discoveries that he was called a "twentieth-century da Vinci."

In his later years Fuller was respected for his personal philosophy as much as for his scientific inventions. He was a man who dedicated himself to being a human guinea pig, pursuing the highest goals for the greatest number of people in the world, with the aim of assisting the planet in its own evolution. He believed—and demonstrated—that anyone so engaged would be abundantly supported. Except for a few brief instances, Fuller never held a job.

Your own special contribution to building a better world will only happen if you, like Fuller, dedicate yourself to exploring the unknown in order to benefit others. The point is, you must embrace—not suppress—your grandest dreams. Writer Richard Bach might have been writing about making a living without a job when he said, "You are never given a wish without also being given the power to make it true. You may have to work for it, however." That may sound like a tall order, but being joyfully jobless demands nothing less.

Grow Wings

Going through a scrapbook I began after moving to Minneapolis, I came across the caption, "We put down roots and sprouted wings." The inspiration for that is an adage that says, "The best gifts you can give your children are roots and wings." I happen to believe those are also the best gifts we can give ourselves.

Roots, of course, are all those things in life that give us what psychologist Abraham Maslow called "a sense of belonging." It's more than just those people, things, and experiences that are familiar. Roots come from within, from discovering who you are and what you want to do—and then doing it with gusto. For me, roots include my self-esteem, personal relationships, skills, living in a nurturing environment, and even my ability to ignore naysayers. Above all, roots are grounded in spiritual awareness and faith. Roots give us the strength and security to share ourselves with others.

Wings, on the other hand, are all those things that keep us moving and growing, going beyond where we've been and what we've done. Our dreams, our visions, our willingness to risk, our need for adventure and improvement all urge us to become airborne. Wings prompt us to discover the meaning and purpose of life.

Several years ago, I decided that Roots and Wings would be the theme for my life. Every goal I set is established with the intention of enhancing those two aspects. I've learned that keeping a balance between the two can be tricky; it may, in fact, take me a lifetime to master. As we put down roots and sprout wings, we begin to make a difference in the lives around us. We become spiritually worldly, bringing love and joy and passion to the space we inhabit.

Eleanor Roosevelt once said, "The future belongs to those who believe in the beauty of their dreams." Your future *can* be joyfully jobless, if that's your dream. Unlike me, you don't have to go down that path alone. All of us who are living that dream are here to cheer you on. Your entire life has been getting you ready for this moment. Use everything you've got to create a future that is your dream.

Making a living without a job is one dream that deserves to be shared. Welcome to the party!

A Winner's Bookshelf and Resource Guide

How many a man has dated a new era in his life from the reading of a book? The book exists for us perchance which will explain our miracles and reveal new ones.

Henry David Thoreau

If there's one passion shared by successful self-bossers, it's a devotion to lifelong learning. Books, of course, play an important role in that process, and passing along suggestions of favorite titles seems to come naturally.

The books included here have been chosen from thousands of possibilities. Every one of them is in my own library, and those I've selected are the ones I keep coming back to year after year. Several of my favorites are, unfortunately, no longer in print, but I've included them because they're so special. Perhaps you can locate them in a library, at a used-book store, or through a book-search firm.

Before my daughter was born, I purchased a copy of a children's book called *How Babies Are Made*. I knew the day would come when she'd say, "Where did I come from?" and I didn't want to have to tell her, "Wait until we can go to the library and find a book that will tell you!"

I feel the same way about the importance of building a personal reference library. You may not need a particular book today, but when you do want it, having it at your fingertips is important.

Most of the books on my list should have a place of honor in your office or home. Except for the ones on specific profit centers, you'll find advice that you can borrow and apply no matter what you're doing.

E. M. Forster said, "I suggest that the only books that influence us are those for which we are ready, and which have gone a little farther down our particular path than we have yet gone ourselves." The authors listed here have pulled me forward and in so doing have become my valued friends and mentors. It is with great pleasure that I invite you to discover them, too.

For Personal Growth . . .

Wishcraft: How to Get What You Really Want by Barbara Sher and Annie Gottlieb is a favorite of successful goal-setters. Her system will help you clarify your focus and stay on track. New York: Ballantine Books, 1986.

The Seven Habits of Highly Effective People by Stephen R. Covey is a best-seller that deserves its large following. Covey discusses the personal characteristics necessary for achievement and shows how to cultivate them. New York: Simon & Schuster, 1989.

Getting Rich Your Own Way by Srully Blotnick is based on the author's twenty-year study of more than 1,000 people. His conclusions about who gets rich and why are both inspiring and informing. New York: Playboy Paperbacks, 1982.

How I Found Freedom in an Unfree World by Harry Browne is a provocative manifesto for achieving personal freedom. His ideas are unorthodox, but very persuasive. Read this one for courage. New York: Avon Books, 1982.

Do What You Love, the Money Will Follow: Discovering Your Right Livelihood by Marsha Sinetar guides you to uncovering personal passion and purpose. Excellent exercises for clarifying direction. New York: Dell, 1989.

Feel the Fear and Do It Anyway by Susan Jeffers sets forth techniques for taking action in the presence of fear. New York: Fawcett, 1988.

How to Get Control of Your Time and Your Life by Alan Lakein remains a popular favorite of time managers. This twenty-year-old book is indispensable. New York: NAL/Dutton, 1989.

Getting Organized: The Easy Way to Put Your Life in Order by Stephanie Winston will help you develop a system for keeping your life and business running smoothly. New York: Warner Books, 1991.

Creative Visualization by Shakti Gawain will teach you how to use visualization techniques to manifest the life of your dreams. New York: Bantam, 1983.

Illusions by Richard Bach is a lovely story with an unforgettable message. This one is a modern parable with important teachings on life and living. New York: Dell, 1979.

How to Raise Your Self-Esteem by Nathaniel Branden focuses on learning self-acceptance, leaving guilt behind, and living responsibly. New York: Bantam, 1988.

How to Be Happier Day by Day by Alan Epstein. This "year of mindful actions" is a collection of 366 creative ideas for living more happily. Great ideas eloquently explained. New York: Viking, 1993.

For Thinking Prosperously . . .

Think and Grow Rich by Napoleon Hill is the book many self-made millionaires credit with pointing them in the right direction. Hill spent twenty-five years interviewing the wealthy, and this classic compiles his findings. New York: Fawcett, 1987.

The Dynamic Laws of Prosperity by Catherine Ponder is as empowering today as it was when it appeared thirty years ago. The author, a Unity minister, includes excellent affirmations and numerous real-life examples. Englewood Cliffs, NJ: Prentice-Hall, 1962.

Moneylove by Jerry Gillies points out the link between self-esteem and prosperity. A great handbook for building both. New York: Warner Books, 1988.

Creating Money: Keys to Abundance by Sanaya Roman and Duane Packer tops my list of favorites on developing healthy attitudes toward money. The ideas, exercises, and affirmations make it a perfect tool for anyone who wants to give up the money struggle. This is a book to keep close at hand and consult often. Tiburon, Calif.: H. J. Kramer, 1988.

For Entrepreneurial Inspiration . . .

All in a Day's Work by Eve Arnold is a glorious collection of photographs from around the world showing people engaged in their daily work. Little text accompanies these pictures, which speak for themselves. New York: Bantam, 1989.

The Popcorn Report: Faith Popcorn on the Future of Your Company, Your World, Your Life by Faith Popcorn discusses the most important trends in today's society and offers ideas about being on-trend with your goals and work. It's a terrific book for stimulating ideas. New York: Doubleday, 1991.

Body and Soul: Profits with Principles—The Amazing Success Story of Anita Roddick and The Body Shop by Anita Roddick is the author's personal account of the growth of her international business, The Body Shop. The activist author argues convincingly that the role of an entrepreneur is to be a socially responsible leader. This book is a call to arms. New York: Crown, 1991.

Minding the Store by Stanley Marcus shows you the philosophy that turned Neiman-Marcus into an international icon of excellence. It's a fascinating autobiography of a family with a mission greater than just selling merchandise. Boston: Little, Brown & Co., 1974.

Growing a Business by Paul Hawken is my hands-down favorite book on creating a business that reflects personal values. Lots of nuts-and-bolts information interspersed with stories of entrepreneurial success. New York: Simon & Schuster, 1988.

A Year in Provence by Peter Mayle is the entertaining story of a former London adman who finds happiness and writing success by following his heart to the South of France. New York: Alfred A. Knopf, 1990.

For the Nuts and Bolts . . .

Homemade Money by Barbara Brabec is one of the earliest and most complete resources for anyone setting up shop at home.

That Brabec has done her homework is evident in the volume of practical information she compiles. She'll walk you through the early stages and get your marketing on track. Look for the fourth edition. Crozet, Va.: Betterway, 1992.

Running a One-Person Business by Claude Whitmyer, Salli Rasberry, and Michael Phillips is designed to assist those who truly believe that small is beautiful. The authors cover a lot of ground, including time management, bookkeeping, and choosing office equipment. They also discuss getting emotional support. Berkeley: Ten Speed Press, 1988.

Small-Time Operator: How to Start Your Own Small Business, Keep Your Books, Pay Your Taxes and Stay Out of Trouble by Bernard Kamoroff almost makes accounting sound like fun. This CPA turned self-publisher will demystify bookkeeping, taxes, and legal considerations. Laytonville, Calif.: Bell Springs Publishing, 1990.

A Woman's Guide to Starting Her Own Business by Claudia Jessup and Genie Chipps covers the basics and includes case studies of female entrepreneurs. New York: Henry Holt & Company, 1991.

The Entrepreneur's Road Map to Business Success by Lyle Maul and Dianne Mayfield will guide you from the idea-stage through management. Alexandria, Va.: Saxtons River Publications, 1992.

For Marketing . . .

The One Minute Sales Person by Spencer Johnson and Larry Wilson teaches effective sales techniques that will help you gain confidence. New York: Avon, 1986.

Selling the Dream: How to Promote Your Product, Company, or Ideas—and Make a Difference—Using Everyday Evangelism by Guy Kawasaki is entertaining and educational. The author is determined to convert salespeople into evangelists and offers plenty of how-tos. New York: HarperBusiness, 1992.

Guerrilla Marketing: How to Make Big Profits from Your Small Business by Jay Conrad Levinson presents the practical ideas of this former adman turned self-bosser on grabbing attention and marketing creatively. New York: Houghton Mifflin, 1985.

Marketing Without Advertising by Michael Phillips and Salli Rasberry shows small-business owners more effective ways of getting their message out without conventional advertising. Berkeley: Nolo Press, 1989.

1001 Ways to Market Your Books by John Kremer has great ideas you can borrow to market books or other products. This one is a gold mine for the energetic promoter. Fairfield, Iowa: Ad-Lib Publications, 1989.

For Developing Creativity . . .

A Whack on the Side of the Head by Roger von Oech is full of exercises and thoughts on becoming more innovative. Highly readable. New York: Warner Books, 1990.

Learning by Heart: Teachings to Free the Creative Spirit by Corita Kent and Jan Steward shares the ideas and projects of a masterful teacher and artist who believed that we each possess a creative spirit that must be nurtured. New York: Bantam, 1992.

Writing Down the Bones: Freeing the Writer Within by Natalie Goldberg is a favorite of every writer I know. Nonwriters, too, will find stimulation and encouragement here. Boston: Shambhala, 1986.

Creativity in Business by Michael Ray and Rochelle Myers is based on a popular course taught by the authors at Stanford University. Many entrepreneurs share their experiences of putting creative thought to work. New York: Doubleday, 1989.

For Specific Profit Centers . . .

How to Be an Importer and Pay for Your World Travel by Mary Green and Stanley Gillmar takes you around the world on an entrepreneurial fling. Expert advice for would-be importers. Berkeley: Ten Speed Press, 1979.

Money in Your Mailbox: How to Start and Operate a Mail-Order Business by L. Perry Wilbur is aimed at the shoestring mail-order operator. Excellent ideas on starting small, testing your product, and building at your own pace. Reston: Reston Publishing, 1979.

Housewise, A Smart Woman's Guide to Buying and Renovating Real Estate for Profit by Suzanne Brangham offers practical information on home renovation as a business. Her step-by-step approach is easy to follow. New York: Harper & Row, 1987.

The Self-Publishing Manual: How to Write, Print and Sell Your Own Book by Dan Poynter belongs in the library of every information packager. The author, a successful self-publisher, covers everything you need to know to produce and market your own books. Santa Barbara: Parachuting Publications, 1979.

Writing for the Corporate Market: How to Make Big Money Freelancing for Business by George Sorenson shows how to build a lucrative freelance writing business by cultivating corporate clients. Lots of practical advice. Denver: Mid-List, 1990.

So You Want to Be an Innkeeper: The Complete Guide to Operating a Successful Bed and Breakfast Inn by Mary E. Davies, Hardy, Bell, and Brown covers the basics of hosting paying guests. San Francisco: Chronicle Books, 1990.

The Teaching Marketplace: Make Money with Freelance Teaching, Corporate Trainings, and on the Lecture Circuit by Bart Brodsky and Janet Geis helps you consider the options for teaching on your own or in conjunction with a community program. Berkeley: Community Resource Institute Press, 1991.

The Consultant's Kit: Establishing and Operating Your Successful Consulting Business by Dr. Jeffrey L. Lant will put your experience and expertise to work as an independent consultant. An in-depth handbook that covers everything from finding clients to writing proposals. Boston: JLA Publications, 1991.

Many other how-to books are available from the Whole Work Catalog. Send $1 to Whole Work Catalog, P.O. Box 297, Boulder, CO 80306.

The Small Business Administration has a wide variety of free and inexpensive publications. Contact your nearest SBA office for a catalog of offerings.

Associations

Professional associations exist in nearly every industry and often serve as clearinghouses for information. Many publish journals or newsletters, hold conferences, and have state or local chapters. Several organizations offer membership to anyone who is self-employed, no matter in what business. Others focus on a single profession. Association membership can also be a source of group insurance, travel benefits, and other savings. Don't overlook the possibilities of joining a local inventors' club, desktop publishers' guild, craft council, or professional society.

Here's a sampling of national groups.

American Bed & Breakfast Association
1407 Huguenot Road
Midlothian, VA 23113

Association for Systems Management
24587 Bagley Road
Cleveland, OH 44138

Direct Marketing Association
6 East 43rd Street
New York, NY 10017

Editorial Freelancers Association
P.O. Box 2050
Madison Square Station
New York, NY 10159

Freelance Editors Association
P.O. Box 835
Cambridge, MA 02238

Greeting Card Association
1200 G Street N.W.
Washington, D.C. 20005

Information Industry Association
4720 Montgomery Lane, Suite 904
Bethesda, MD 20014

International Women's Writing Guild
P.O. Box 810
Gracie Station
New York, NY 10028

Meeting Planners International
3719 Roosevelt Boulevard
Middletown, OH 45042

National Association for the Self-Employed
P.O. Box 612067
DFW Airport, TX 75261

National Association of Women Business Owners
645 N. Michigan Avenue
Chicago, IL 60611

National Federation of Independent Business
600 Maryland Avenue S.W., Suite 700
Washington, D.C. 20024

Professional Association of Innkeepers, International
P.O. Box 90710
Santa Barbara, CA 93190

Professional Photographers of America
1090 Executive Way
Des Plaines, IL 60018

Publications

Bootstrappin' Entrepreneur
(quarterly newsletter)
8726 S. Sepulveda Blvd., Suite B261
Los Angeles, CA 90045-4082
$30/year

Home Office Computing
(monthly magazine)
730 Broadway
New York, NY 10003-9511

In Business
(bi-monthly magazine for "green" entrepreneurs)
419 State Avenue
Emmaus, PA 18049

Rolling Ventures
(newsletter for motorhome-owning entrepreneurs)
P.O. Box 2190, #1404
Henderson, NV 89008-2190
$18/year

Self-Employment Survival Letter
(bi-monthly newsletter from Barbara Brabec)
P.O. Box 2137
Naperville, IL 60567
$29/year

Winning Ways
(Barbara J. Winter's newsletter for people living and
   working with passion)
P.O. Box 390412
Minneapolis, MN 55439-0412
$25/6 annual issues

ABOUT THE AUTHOR

Barbara J. Winter is the founder of Winning Ways, a Minneapolis-based training and publishing firm that creates resources for self-bossers. Her writing has appeared in dozens of magazines as well as in her own bimonthly newsletter. A devoted Anglophile, Barbara travels nationally and internationally speaking to audiences about being joyfully jobless.